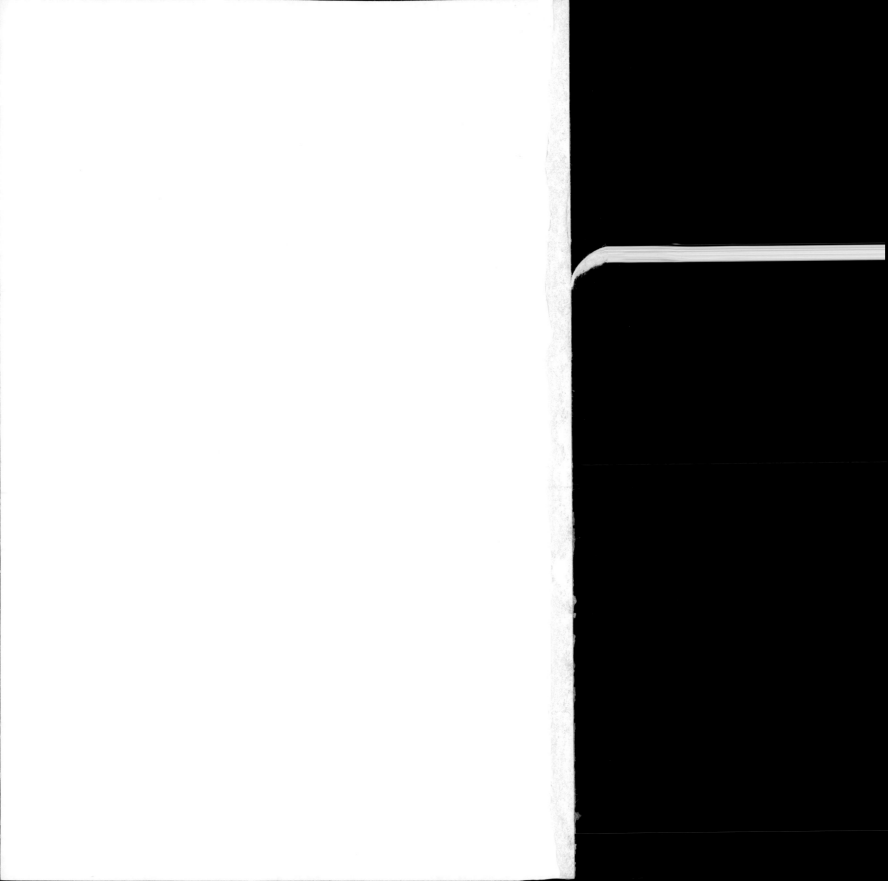

CONTENTS

· · · · · · · · ·

CONTENTS

ACKNOWLEDGMENTS

· · · · · · · · ·

I'm struggling to come up with right words of gratitude for everyone who has been part of this project and my life. I never thought the story of my life and adventures would be book-worthy, but I love being wrong.

Most importantly, I would like to thank my family. My mother and grandmother have been inspirations in fortitude and perseverance, as well as patience and love.

I wouldn't have been able to get beyond page one without the love and support of my wife. She took care of my son, the home front, and gave me the strength to complete this challenge.

I am grateful for the folks at St. Martin's for believing in our project. Our editor, Marc Resnick, was a huge help, and I appreciated how he made the whole process unintimidating and positive.

Thank you, Adam Chromy, for breathing fire into our project and giving it life.

This book could not have happened without the tenacity and vision of Don Rearden. Don worked his way through my stories, then refined and tailored them into a smooth, flowing, and exciting book. Don took extra steps above and beyond what anyone could have expected. Thanks to Annette for supporting and cheering for us both, and thank you, Don, for your sacrifices and sleepless nights.

Speaking of sleepless nights, I would like to thank the entire brotherhood of pararescuemen and their crews. Their selfless dedication has saved thousands of lives around the world. Right now, there is probably a rescue mission going on somewhere. The path of the PJ is not easy. I had many great PJs guide and inspire me along the way. I lived an intense but brief life as a PJ, and I was surrounded by dudes who had been operating for decades. Those men have incredible rescue stories I hope get heard. If you see these guys on the street, buy them a time-appropriate drink and ask for a story. Even a boring PJ has cool stories. I'm proof.

The lifestyle of a PJ is rewarding, adventurous, and dangerous. PJs are masters of risk mitigation, but sometimes the unforeseeable shows up and disasters happen. Many PJs perish each year on duty. Many more are permanently injured. These men are evidence of the creed all PJs swear to, which ends with "That others may live."

The process of capturing my life on paper has been therapeutic. Some of the events I experienced have had lasting results, both physically and mentally. When Don approached me about doing this project, it was a choice I took seriously. I wanted to make sure I honored the people in my life and inspired readers to stay positive and hang on through tough times. Remember this: when life is throwing some INDOC-style hate at you, stay cool, and *never quit!*

Hooyah!

—JIMMY SETTLE

NEVER
QUIT

Prologue

WATER WORK

"I'm already sweating my balls off!" I yelled to Roger. "Are you? What are you wearing under there?"

"Everything!" he hollered back at me.

With my index fingers, I pushed the puffy foam plugs deep into my ear canals until the sound of the chopper spinning up became a muted background roar. I tugged at the rubber noose around my throat, trying to give myself a little more breathing room against the dry suit's choking neck gasket.

I had to dig deep to find a reason to be excited about this training operation as the HH-60G Pave Hawk's rotors picked up speed. My concerns weren't really a premonition, just the nagging reality that the evening's duty would be one thing: cold. January. Minus twenty. In Alaska. The imminent danger of freezing to death in the Arctic waters of this training exercise wasn't the issue at all. Danger isn't in the job description of Alaska pararescuemen, or PJs, as we're known. Danger *is* the job description. For PJs, danger is a dinner bell, and our day-to-day training reflects the situations of extreme danger and chaos we face during rescues at home or in battle abroad. Many pararescue operators have been killed during training, but that level of training is necessary to prepare for the worst-case scenarios inherent in the job. When the world goes sideways, you want the men coming to rescue you to be cool—but not necessarily the type of cool my partner Roger Sparks and I were about to face.

The familiar pressure of takeoff pushed me back into the cold vibrating floor of the helo. Anchorage dropped away beneath us, and the glow of the city, covered in a heavy blanket of January snow, disappeared.

Cold. Nighttime. Water work.

No one willingly jumps into an ice-choked ocean in Alaska at night when the ambient temperature is pushing twenty below. At least, not anyone in his right mind. Yet, there we were. Two choppers hurtling out into the black night sky toward nothing but possible trouble.

If we were operators from the Florida team, nighttime water work would be no problem, maybe fun. Those men do their water work in stylish beach trunks and surf shirts. But for the PJs of the 212th a routine water jump could potentially mean life or death. Alaskan water, even in the middle of summer, is no joke, and this is a fact I've known since birth. Alaska's frigid waters have not been kind to my family.

In general, water work was never my favorite pastime. It really wasn't. I didn't mind training for rescues in our bone-chilling waters in the summertime, or even the occasional daylight splash drill in the winter. But water rescue, even at night, is something I was expected to do. The willingness to scuba dive, parachute, or swim at all hours of the day was my job as a PJ. Anywhere off of Alaska's forty-nine thousand miles of coastline, or in our three million lakes or twelve thousand rivers, was fair game and represented a possible rescue location.

It's not as if I could say, "Oh, sorry, chaps. I don't do water rescues at night." When command says you're doing night work, then that is it. You saddle up.

The situation Roger and I were flying into was designed to be nighttime tactical water work. We weren't training for a civilian rescue of the sort we normally saw in the waters around Alaska. We had our gray tactical suits on. No reflective material anywhere. This was all covert stuff. Something you'd see in a thriller. Everything black. Dark IR strobes, only visible with infrared scopes. Not so much as a light flashing on the chopper.

We raced low over Cook Inlet, the only illumination coming from the glow of Anchorage as it slipped away behind us, reflecting off the hulking white pans of ice that flowed in the ripping tidal currents.

Two minutes out, they signaled to us that we were a few clicks from the drop zone. Roger and I began our routine checks of each other and ourselves. Doing water work in Alaska, you must wear the dry suits, because wet suits won't do the trick. The water is just too cold. We wore specially made survival dry suits—and they are a real pain in the ass to climb into. The suits have two heavy rubberized zippers and painfully tight rubber gaskets at the wrists and neck. The smell of the rubber gaskets always reminded me of bicycle inner tubes. Imagine tying a rubber noose around your neck and then having the strongest person you know wrenching on the business end, and you've got an idea of the strangling effect. To ease the constant choking sensation, we rigged up neck rings. This simple little device closes in around the neck so the thick, death-gripping gasket rolls down off your Adam's apple and windpipe. This provided a little respite and kept us from being purple-faced and choking to death the whole time en route.

Almost to the insertion point, Roger and I slipped off our neck rings. Then, even with everything perfect, these state-of-the-art suits still leak.

Roger gave me the zipper sign, then the neck ring sign, and I nodded back a *Yup, you're good.* Checks like this between partners could be the difference between life or extreme discomfort and death. When geared up for operations, you simply can't see your entire body because you have too much equipment in the way. You rely on your buddy to double-check zippers, rings, buckles, harnesses, and straps. In my career I managed to avoid a few slipups because I noticed a handful of guys who failed to do the buddy check. The mistakes were always kind of funny, so long as no one died. Our unit had been pretty lucky. If anyone had an operator error, the result was generally minor. Normally, when things go bad, you've got your wingman there to help. During water work training, our safeties were our teammates, and we almost always had a safety boat in the water.

But on this night, as we were about make our plunge, no safety boat waited below. Just one monstrous inlet draining into the Pacific Ocean. Two helicopters in complete tactical blackout mode. No lights. The only security for me was the fact that we had some of the most incredible rescuemen in the world on that second bird. And then there was my partner. Roger Sparks. One of the finest pararescuemen to have dropped from the Alaskan sky. A seasoned marine force recon and a veteran of all sorts of missions, trainings, and rescues.

I wasn't naive. It wasn't as if I thought nothing could go wrong. But with Roger by my side, the odds were in my favor if something did.

The event was supposed to be a straightforward exercise, but I suppose they all are. We were to do a "low and slow," where the helicopter is between ten and twenty feet above the water, flying five and ten knots, not very fast. Roger and I would slide open the doors. Jump out. *Splash.* Nothing to it. Then the helicopter would fly a little dogleg and come back. Drop the cable to us. We would hoist up, get in the aircraft, jump back out one more time, and then climb up into the chopper, the last time using a rope ladder.

Although I wasn't such a huge fan of water work at night, I always liked jumping out of the helicopter. This is the cool part of the job, like in the military recruitment commercials, when you see the battle-ready warriors, feet together, come flying out of the chopper, *splash*! It's like that. A huge rush of adrenaline. I relish those moments of free fall most, but that exciting half second in the door isn't bad either, where I'm looking out and thinking, *Whoa baby! This is my job! They are paying me for this!*

Even on this night, as I prepared to jump into the turbulent and frigid waters of Cook Inlet, I was excited and looking forward to the jump. Those ridiculous cold-water concerns that had floated through my mind minutes earlier, as I lifted off from my hometown?

Gone. Gone, baby. Gone.

You accept a degree of faith every time you step to the door of the aircraft you are about to jump out of.

I hovered at the chopper's doors, ever so careful. I wore fins and eased right to the brink. In my mind I ran through the whole process to the jump, attentive so I wouldn't hurt myself or lose all my gear upon impact. Screwing up would put Roger, myself, and everyone at risk.

I've got my right hand smashing my mask to my face, with a death grip on my snorkel, and my left hand gripping the gear on my waist. Jumping from a chopper is, by definition, fun. First, the sensation of free fall hits as your stomach rises in your chest and your heart pounds. Your mind processes the images of the water racing at increasing speed toward you until impact.

For a half second the impact hurts, a sting through your entire being, and then the pain is gone and everything is silent and weightless. One moment you're in the helicopter and the world is all chaos and noise—even with your earplugs—then you're falling, and *boom*, you're under water for a half second and all is quiet and peaceful. You break through the surface, and that helicopter is still there, and suddenly you can't hear a damn thing above the roaring prop wash. The wind pushes you with hurricane force. Even on land, the intensity is brutal. Those giant blades throw sand and rocks and debris everywhere.

This time, when I hit the water, the first thing I noticed was the cold. My face began to burn, like someone had sprayed my cheeks with liquid nitrogen. My body was relatively protected within my survival suit, but my mouth, lips, cheeks, and chin were completely exposed to this burning water, like someone had wet my face and slammed it against a giant flagpole in the middle of winter. I wore a dive mask, a heavy neoprene hoodie, the whole shebang, but none of that gear mattered. That horrible sting of cold sucked the wind right out of me, even though the only thing exposed was my face. Luckily I had a snorkel, but my lips around the rubber mouthpiece instantly froze. The moment I broke the surface, the outside of my mask iced up. I couldn't see shit. I tried to lift the bottom of my mask up to make sense of the world around me.

I needed to locate two things:

1. Roger.
2. The helicopter and the hoist cable.

The powerful rotor wash from the thumping blades lifted the seawater and blasted what felt like thousands of ice needles into my face. Now the burn of cold was combined with the needling and the blinding pain it brought. I had to keep dunking my face into the water to seek protection from this barrage of little flying spikes, and after doing this a couple times I got seawater on the inside of my mask, so now it was double iced, a thick layer of frosted crystal covering the inside and out. I couldn't see a damn thing.

The chopper left us for moment. I could hear only the splashing of the ocean around me. I reached up into my hoodie to pull my earplugs out. I wanted to be able to hear Roger and be ready when the chopper came back.

It took us a minute or two to find each other. At this point, everything was still routine training. Both of us were adjusting to the shock of the icy water, steadying our breathing, and floating, waiting and watching for something blacker than the night sky to appear above us and drop the hoist. When the deafening silhouette appeared, we could only wait and watch for the hoist as best we could as the damn little ice needles kicked up again. We struggled in a cold blizzard of pain that whipped us from all sides. In order to see, I peeled off my iced-over mask. That freezing-cold water, flying a hundred miles an hour, pelted my face and eyes.

I squinted toward the sky and yelled over the *thunk thunk* of the helicopter, "I don't see it! I don't see it, Roger!"

"There it is!" he yelled.

Then I saw the hoist. A thick silver metal cable, the diameter of a pencil, with a big heavy double hook—one side for humans, the other for cargo. I stretched an arm toward our lifeline. The cable dangled just a few feet from my head. Then, as quick as it appeared, the damn thing zipped off horizontally and away from us. Out of reach. In that moment, I lunged toward where it sat in the water.

"No!" Roger yelled.

The urgency in his voice reminded me about one of the important rules about water work. You don't swim for the hoist. Especially if you are rescuing someone with the Stokes litter or are too gear-laden to swim with any speed. The swimmers in the water let the experts in the bird above do their job. They are the best in the business, some of the most skilled helicopter pilots on the planet. They will get the hoist to you. Swim for the line and you're taking unnecessary risks. Things can go wrong.

The crew above kept trying to get the hoist to Roger and me. But something wasn't quite right. Each time the line appeared close enough for one of us to grab, it rocketed away again. We didn't understand what the hell was happening. We had executed this same operation hundreds of times, often in far more precarious situations than tonight. After a few attempts, I felt as if as if we were a part of some sort of not-so-funny joke.

Let me be clear about this: there is no one that loves a good joke or prank more than I. I definitely deserved to have a joke like this played on me, but with the cold setting into our bodies and the circumstances of the situation growing more and more dire with each moment in the frigid water, I was having a hard time trying to find any humor in our predicament.

After one too many times of the hoist landing just out of reach, Roger yelled to me, "Go for it, Jimmy!"

And I did. I dove for that hook with all I had. With the combination of adrenaline and years of water training, I should have swum like an Olympian. But now, with all my gear, and the heaviness of the deep cold gripping my body, and my clumsy numb limbs, I could only flail like a little kid. That blazing swim speed was probably reduced to a knot at best, and the attempt to reach the hoist only a few feet away required maximum effort. I ignored the scream of pain from my frozen body and lunged with a giant kick, clawing with the frozen clubs that were my hands.

Just a few feet from my outstretched glove, the hoist shot off again.

I couldn't. Grab. It.

They kept trying, for nearly twenty minutes, to get the hoist to us, to no avail. And then the black sky above us lit up. The chopper lights blazed over us. Through the ice blasting my face, I watched as the helicopter, tail down, suddenly scooted backwards—actually flew backwards—and anyone knows that is not how a bird that size is supposed to fly. As quickly as that happened, the aircraft hovering above us corrected itself and—*whoosh!*—the Pave Hawk flew off. Gone.

The thump of the HH-60 grew faint, replaced by silence and a soft tinkle, like someone was gently shaking a chandelier. The ice crystals tinkled against each other in the water around us. For a moment, neither of us said a word. We didn't know what had gone wrong, but whatever it was, it wasn't good. We were already freezing, and now we'd been left behind.

Roger turned to me and said, "Well, now what, Jimmy?"

———

Hero.

The last thing I ever wanted to be called in life was a hero. In my line of work, this word *hero* is special, a term solely reserved for those men and women who have made the ultimate sacrifice, giving their life in the line of duty. "Hero" is a designation for a soldier killed in combat. Our credo, "That others may live," reveals the heart of every mission, operation, and training endured by those called to become PJs. PJs are willing to place all desires and comforts, up to and including one's own life, aside to ensure the survival of others, military or civilian. But don't call one of us a hero, at least not until we've got the Stars and Stripes draped over our casket.

1
. . . .

It's Going to Be You, Jimmy

Roger and the boys greeted us planeside as we disembarked from
the C-17 into the dusty world of Bagram Air Base, thirty miles
north of the Afghanistan city of Kabul. A taut angular mountain
of a man, at six foot eight, Roger stood out far above the rest of the
team. We collected our gear and traded a barrage of loving insults.
We were all far from home and in the middle of a war zone.

My good friend Chris Robertson came over to me and gave me
a giant bear hug, saying, "Welcome to Afghanistan, Jimmy!" Chris,
Roger, and the other PJs stood waiting for us outside the chain-link
fence, just off the tarmac where we disembarked from the jet that
had delivered us from Germany.

Chris and the other PJs had finished their deployment, and most
would be back home in Alaska, eating a Moose's Tooth pizza and
sipping on a cold Pipeline Stout, before I'd even adjusted to the
altitude and time zone of Bagram.

That fall, our unit had been split for deployment. We'd left our
home base in Anchorage to participate in a joint military mission
in the mountainous region of eastern Afghanistan. My PJ team

phased in over many weeks, and I was in the second phase of guys. Two more groups would follow. The team members who went before us had put our gear together at the Bagram PJ section and worked out all the kinks to get us fully operational. My teammates and I were replacing Chris's crew for our own stint. They all were returning healthy, happy, and with mustaches. They had seen some action, but none of our PJs were injured or killed. The mission up until that point had been fairly routine: save the lives of soldiers and special operators requiring assistance in the rugged Afghanistan mountains.

It would be a few months of deployment, then we would return to saving civilian lives in the Alaskan wilderness.

I felt encouraged when I saw how great the brothers who had been deployed looked. They had been operating on the front lines for several months at this point, and these guys were salty. We were the fresh meat. The warm welcome felt like the opening moments of old friends gathering before a bachelor party. Once we got through the reception center, our buddies grabbed all our gear and loaded it on the team bus. We were off to get our on-base driver's licenses and secure area passes. The basic IDs they handed us were straight from the 1980s, with a photo and paper laminated together. We would need this to drive vehicles and to get into the area of the base where our special section was located.

We were joking and making faces for our license photos. Chris asked how the trip from Alaska had been.

"Tell them about last night," one of the guys said, elbowing me.

"He's great in bed," I joked, getting a quick slug for my always smart-ass responses.

"I am!" he said. "Last night in Germany."

They leaned in, men who had been at war, away from their wives and girlfriends, suspecting a story of debauchery.

I began rattling off the tale. That was one of my jobs in the unit— unofficial entertainment—and practically my rank. Senior Airman

Jimmy Settle of the Alaska 212th, storyteller, joker, and prank-ster. The way I saw it, the team that laughed together, stayed to-gether.

I relayed the story of our overnight delay in Frankfurt.

We had hopped a taxi, rumbled down the cobblestone roads, and stopped at the pub closest to base. Inside, we just happened to bump into one of my buddies from another PJ team. He also was transi-tioning over to a unit, in southern Afghanistan. Since we just hap-pened to run into each other, this was more than reason to celebrate the one night of reprieve before heading downrange.

I'm enjoying the good German beer, the big timber construction of the establishment, and appreciating the different look and smell from Alaska. We're doing our thing, pounding beers and telling stories, when we meet a few fellow American service members, and after a few more drinks, I hear this one cat sitting next us try-ing to pick up a girl.

He said, "I'm an air force SERE specialist."

PJ and SERE career fields tend to be interwoven. In the spirit of a good-natured ambassadorship, I tapped him on the shoulder. "Did you say you are in the air force? Did you say 'spear specialist'? Is that what you air force guys call missiles? Spears? The air force is so weird."

He leaned into me. Clearly not picking up on my sarcasm, and said, "A SERE is spelled Capital S. Capital E. Capital R. Capital E. And that stands for 'survival, evasion, resistance, and escape,' officer."

So this guy was calling himself one of the elite trainers, a man with the knowledge of some incredibly complex and highly classi-fied tactics. SERE specialists are adept at interrogation and infor-mation gathering, and as such they don't go around offering up so much as the time of day, let alone their particular career field. But this clown? He didn't look or act the part. We had all been around our share of actual SERE specialists. They, like most operators, don't feel the need to advertise their presence.

I felt compelled to call his bluff.

"You're no SERE specialist," I replied, and added, "only special."

And his response? "Well fine," he said. "Let's do this."

I nodded and pushed back from the bar. "Well then," I said, "why don't we do this SERE style?"

By that, I meant slap boxing, like they do in interrogation resistance training. This is a stressor technique that employs an open-palm slap to the face, with the hand starting on the shoulder.

We took turns, one at a time, faster and faster. Slap. Slap. Slap.

I'm laughing the whole time, which only pissed him off more, and the next thing I know we're all being thrown out.

The slapping continued on the cobblestones. I'm still laughing, and going to town on this pretend specialist. *Pow! Pow! Pow!* Until my PJ friend from the other unit steps between us. "Dude, you gotta stop," he said. "You can't do this."

He was right. "Don't ever pretend to be someone you're not, dude," I said to the guy, and held my hand out. He considered it for a moment and we shook.

We staggered off down the road, hailing a cab for the ride back to base.

Back at Bagram, I finished my story and took a few jabs from the guys about how I was lucky I wasn't still in Germany, sitting in the brig. I nodded. It had been silly, even if it was just harmless slap boxing and not actual fighting.

In truth, the flight over had been uneventful. What was memorable on the round-the-world voyage from Anchorage to Afghanistan had been mostly internal. War was a new experience for me. After years of training, I'd finally become a PJ. I was new to the career field. I'd never been deployed. I'd never been on an overseas base. I'd never seen battle. From the moment we met at the section in Anchorage and loaded all our gear onto a flatbed truck with picket sides, I felt I was embarking on a life-changing journey.

I could already feel a change in the way I felt about myself, my team, and my family, and toward life.

There were ten of us traveling together. We took up the whole bed of a big old double-deuce two-ton. We wore khaki-tan flight suits. Mine fit like a condom one size too small. We drove across Anchorage, toward the civilian airport on the other side of town. At the Alaska Airlines counter, we checked our gear bags and carried our rifles to the security point. Our weapons were locked in heavy-duty black cases. We traveled with our own weapons because we had time on them. We knew how they worked. Each PJ has his choice weapon tuned in to specific personal preferences.

I have traveled through Ted Stevens Anchorage International Airport my entire life, but this time I strolled through the concourse with the guys from my unit. In uniform, with a rifle in my case, the experience felt a bit surreal. I was seeing a whole different side of my relatively new career as a PJ.

We traveled cross-country in civilian aircraft. Anchorage to Baltimore, and then over to Europe on a military jet. Before Germany, all I had on was the skintight tan flight suit, and that damn thing wasn't comfortable. The uniform made me feel fat and claustrophobic. None of us wore our regular green PJ suits, which fit us perfectly. Instead, they supplied us a general issue, horrible-fitting thing.

The flight from Germany to Bagram reminded me of a cattle car. We couldn't have been packed any tighter into the C-17. The flight was uneventful, until we began our final approach into Bagram. The jet began the approach and headed right toward Bagram. The timer in my head starts to tick down with the realization that I'm not merely on a long, painful flight. I'm actually about to step foot in a place where violence thrives and real danger is the norm.

Just as we descended for our landing—with the gears dropping out and the flaps adjusted with a familiar, high-pitched hum, the airplane coming down, settling in, sinking—the engines revved, just a little bit, and then I heard a series of small explosions. *Pop! Pop! Pop!*

With my experience in aircraft, I recognized the sound. It was a sequence of flares, shot out of the back of the jet, countermeasures against missiles and RPGs, rocket-propelled grenades. Right away I'm reminded that not only is this aircraft prepared to deter a ground-to-air enemy attack but also those deterrents had actually just deployed. I was flying into a place where a very real enemy would be shooting at me.

Odds are, a large cooking fire or burning trash from a village home beneath the approach path ignited the countermeasures. The flares don't know any better. But whatever set off those mini explosions seconds before landing served as a great final wake-up for me: *Oh-hey! This isn't summer camp, Jimmy!*

One of the other first things I noticed, as Roger, Chris, and my teammates greeted us, was that everything about this place was arid. This part of the world was dry, and super dusty. I could feel the air suck the moisture from my skin, my hair, my mouth, and my clothes. My lips were instantly chapped. I had to fight the urge to lick them. Then there was the thirst. The thirst was immediate and unquenchable.

Roger Sparks, Chris Robertson, Aaron Parcha, Koa Bailey, Jonny Davis, Paul "Bear" Barendregt, and a couple other guys gave us a nice five-star tour of the base and took care of all the military hoop jumping that happens when you first begin a deployment. None of us were particularly fond of that crap. PJs succeed because of a flexible mind-set, which can typically be too restricted when held to the confines of a regimented, by-the-books type of military leadership. PJs operate best when we're left to our own skills and our own judgment calls. So, with our friends showing up and rescuing us from the reception center line, we got to skip out on all the garbage, all the official tours and boring, dry-as-Afghanistan-air instruction and information. Our team told us the important stuff—talk to this guy if you need this, and go here for that. Their tour made the apprehension of coming into the combat zone much easier to bear, almost making that war zone anxiety nonexistent.

Seeing our friends again and listening to their stories put me at ease. They had been having a good time, and there wasn't anything to really be alarmed about. They were doing all sorts of cool missions and got into a couple close scrapes, with some really neat high-profile rescue stuff, but nothing where they were dancing with death on a high frequency. Knowing this gave me some space to breathe.

During the first few hours on base, I felt inundated with people, vehicles, and military aircraft. The base seemed overly crowded and ridiculously dusty. One of the guys explained that the Russians originally built and operated out of Bagram. This base was one of the first places our Special Forces deployed after 9/11. As we cruised around, I could see the different layers and ages, how the place was built and where the base expanded, like rings in a tree, war upon war. Bagram was in an unorthodox place, surrounded by steep mountains and, by my estimate, not at all that secure, but it was to be my new home and I needed to get comfortable.

We bounced down a road that circled the perimeter of the base. All sorts of up-armored vehicles, buses, and small trucks kicked up more dust. Right away I inquired about the crazily decorated trucks and learned that these were what the locals called jingle trucks. Jingle trucks are beautifully decorated, like nothing I had ever seen in America. Imagine a dump truck painted like the Sistine Chapel and you're not even close to what a jingle truck looks like.

Finally, after doing the tour, meeting people, getting some lunch, and finishing the last of our paperwork, we got to go to our section. The not-so-subtle code word for our little headquarters: the PJ section. We like simple.

Chris and the other guys helped us hump our gear and our weapons into the nondescript metal structure. An average soldier on deployment would have a standard issue duffle, but like other special operations teams, the standards aren't always enough for PJs. I carried a half dozen duffle bags full of my own specialized gear. Parachutes, diving equipment, medical equipment, climbing gear. You name it, I had it stuffed in a sack somewhere.

The PJ section was a basic two-story metal building built on a concrete pad. The walls were thin. They sheltered us from the elements but provided no protection from the constant roar of afterburners screaming down the runway. The atmosphere of the section was rowdy, which is often the ambience PJs cultivate. The place bore the weight of a history of the war. Each PJ unit that rotated in and out had been there, so it was like sharing a locker room with a bunch of family. It came with materials handed down from team to team; each crew left their own personality behind, their own little artifacts that gave the space flavor. Without this history, the building would have had that cold military feeling to it, but the previous teams had created a home away from home with all the hilarious and raunchy stuff they plastered to the walls, the goofy items they left, and the traditions they started.

This was what I had devoted the past few years of my life to, and I was there. Boom. The transition seemed so fast it was kind of scary. I didn't know what I didn't know. I was green. I was the FNG, the fucking new guy. I'd been playing with my gear for months. Putting pouches here and there and playing with my weapon and my med-ruck, and I still didn't feel like any of it was in the right spot. Everything seemed awkward. Once I hit Bagram and started using my gear for real and not for training, a few degrees of perceptible change began. At first I felt sloppy, rickety, and scared. I was the new guy in all those war movies. Scared out of my mind. Like I'm going to get shot any time or blown up, scared I would have to get into a firefight. I had no shortage of anxiety, but having my friends there at Bagram helped ease that transition, for sure, and drew the focus away from the oneness of self and toward the collectivism of the team. The team is the key to survival. Teamwork is paramount to success as a pararescueman. This notion is ingrained so deep that each team has a team room. At Bagram, ours was called the Opium Den.

The Opium Den served as our main muster point for the duration of our stay. I didn't question why it was called the Opium Den.

In a strange way, the name made sense. Of course PJs would be housed in a place with such a nonmilitary name. Perhaps it was because we were field paramedics, packing a fair share of opiates for the wounded—or, for the outside perspective, a man would have to be smoking something in order to do what we did for training alone. Whatever the case, we had our own little shack to set up shop.

I stowed my gear in the locker, across from Roger, and joined my team for our orientation and debriefing, which included what to do if our area came under enemy attack, where to take a shower, and most importantly, where to "get huge" (our workout area).

We stood around a big makeshift table, created by rolling together two big cabinets with thick wood tops. Exhausted from the jet lag, I found myself half-listening to the explanations of our new day-to-day operations and the facilities, until the commander pointed out that the base could come under mortar attack at any moment. I snapped to attention. I wasn't in Alaska anymore, and this was war.

Our alert status began right away. We were on standby for any emergency evacuations in the northeastern region of the combat theater, including the nearby mountains, which was why we were there. After the debrief, I stepped out into the blinding Afghan sun and surveyed the surrounding area. Mountains rose up all around, giving the place a familiar feeling. The high peaks reminded me of the mountains buttressing my home city of Anchorage. The comparison stopped with the rugged terrain. These mountains were dry and barren, strikingly less like the mountains of my beloved home and more like the mountains of New Mexico, a place I'd spent a good deal of time training to become a PJ. Vegetation was sparse and trees rare. I grew up playing in mountains covered in green and white. The land in Afghanistan, for as far as I could see, was tan, brown, and upon my initial inspection, it looked almost devoid of life.

I rejoined the team and we spent the rest of the afternoon

unpacking and readying our gear for action. The crew we were there to replace wanted to go home as soon as possible, so they helped us get settled in quickly, get our gear all dialed in, and brought us up to speed on the standard operating procedures.

After the evening brief, we gathered around the table in the Opium Den, as Chris handed out letters and packages from home.

"Mail call, everyone!" He hollered out names as he tossed letters and boxes to various team members.

"Jimmy!" He lobbed me a rectangular box.

I set the box on the table. I was genuinely surprised and excited to already be getting a package from home. I couldn't believe it. Mail is notoriously slow. The entire team watched. My prankster feelers began tingling. The address label was unlike one I had seen, but I had never received mail in a war zone. Maybe things were different here? I pushed aside any thoughts of caution and cut open one end of the box. I folded out the flaps and held my hand out as a clear, open-ended cylinder with a black rubber suction pump tumbled out. I held in my hand . . . a penis pump. A giant one. Laughter erupted around me as I hefted the two-inch-diameter, foot-and-a-half-long plastic tube into the air for all to see.

This was my welcome to the Opium Den. Those who work in emergency medicine know dark and dirty humor is often essential to the job. PJs are no different. As medics, we know a little about laughter and medicine. The team didn't waste any time pranking me, because they knew I would be a good sport. I suspect they also knew I would find a hilarious way to use the "package" to keep up the spirits of the team.

I was never one to pass up an opportunity, and a few days later we came up with a way to break in the flight doctor. He was new to the pararescue community and to our affinity for tomfoolery, but he had been around enough PJs to know we were constantly experimenting with cutting-edge medical equipment. We noticed and appreciated his interest in how we operated and in the equipment we had at our disposal. This made him the perfect target. I removed the labels and put the penis pump back into the box. The next morning I brought the box and a liter of saline in an IV bag up to the flight doc.

"Sir," I said, "I received this new high-altitude IV bag pressure infuser. I just can't seem to figure out how to set it up, and it didn't come with any directions. Do you think you can figure it out?"

"Sure thing. Just leave it on the chair and I'll look at it after I'm done with the paperwork," he said, without looking up from his computer. I placed the cardboard box and bag of saline on an empty chair next to the door and did my best disappearing act.

That evening, I finished a workout and walked from the darkness outside into a brightly lit team room. The flight doc stood at the table in the center of the room, chatting away with Chris. The doc had his back to the door as Ted and I strolled into the room. The cardboard box and bag of saline sat on the table between the two. I made eye contact with Chris as the doctor turned his head to see us enter. When the doc could not see him, Chris smiled ear to ear at me. The doc also smiled at me. A nice guy, and fresh into the military. He was happy and eager to help the mission. He also possessed an active and open mind. Perfect scenario for shenanigans.

"Sorry, Jimmy, I can't seem to figure this thing out," he said as he opened the box and pulled the plastic cylinder out. "I think I understand how this thing is supposed to work, but I just don't think we got the right size." He started to stuff the liter of IV fluid. "There is no way we can get a bag of saline in this thing."

Chris, standing in the doctor's blind spot, turned purple-faced, and barely made it out of the room before he lost it.

Cool as ice, Ted said, "I don't know. Maybe we aren't doing it right, doc. Maybe you gotta lube it up first?" Ted dug in one of the supply bins and tossed the flight doc a single-use packet of petroleum jelly. The doc tore off the top of the foil packet and squeezed a glob of translucent jelly onto his fingertip. Around this time, the door opened and one of our female pilots walked in.

"Holy shit, doc! Is that a penis pump?" the female captain blurted. We doubled over in laughter.

The doc turned bright red and looked down in shock. Penis pump in one hand. Petroleum jelly in the other. He smiled. He got it. We only messed with people we liked.

With the transition complete, we said our good-byes. Chris walked up to me one last time as he was about to depart for Alaska. He gave me another big hug. "Have a good deployment," he said. A head taller than me, he tilted his chin down, stroked the silly-looking Magnum P.I. mustache he'd sprouted during his deployment, and made his prediction: "You know, if *anybody* is going to get shot here, it's going to be you, Jimmy."

"Thanks, Chris," I said with a laugh, nodding in a silent agreement that he was probably right. I gave Chris a big hello-and-good-bye hug, all at once. The cloud of dust and the raw smell of humanity from his uniform captured the moment of reality, that what we were doing in Afghanistan wasn't training.

Of course, Chris was joking about me getting shot, but we both knew that I had the market cornered on crazy luck. That was day-to-day living for me. The more unusual the occurrences in life, the more normal. If life was a lottery of long odds and desperate situations, I drew the winning number every time.

What neither of us realized at that moment, as we said our good-byes, was that Chris's statement was a portent of the things to come. Here is Chris, the first guy who introduced me to the special world of the busiest pararescue unit on the planet, being the first to welcome me to Afghanistan and the war zone, with no way of knowing how close the two of us might come to never seeing each other again.

I'd known this strong-jawed, strong-legged, extreme-endurance mountain racer from my early cross-country running days in high school, before we were PJs. Chris was a country kid from the Susitna

River valley, and I was a city kid from the big, sprawling metropolis of Anchorage. Despite being from rival schools, we met because of a Beastie Boys *Check Your Head* album cover sticker on my water bottle. With similar tastes in music, and being kids who didn't take ourselves too seriously, we hit it off and became friends. We battled as competitors on the ski and running trails, but we were always buddies after the meets. Back then we were just two scrawny runners trying to outdo each other on the racecourses that twisted through the thick birch and spruce forests of Southcentral Alaska. And there, at Bagram, stood Chris, just as he should be, welcoming me to war.

Seeing him in the theater seemed to bring my whole career and life full circle. If anyone was qualified to say I'd be the one on our team who might take a bullet, it was Chris Robertson. He knew me best. Chris witnessed my transformation from pre-PJ all the way to fully operational downrange PJ. He'd seen the whole Jimmy.

2

· · · · · · · · ·

Son of a Survivor

I tossed and turned on the hard black medical cot, trying to keep my eyes shut against the blinding light. Four glaring halogens shined on me from the four corners of the makeshift emergency room. The backs of my eyeballs ached from the synthetic suns that surrounded me. My skull burned with the intensity of a fire poker. I couldn't get comfortable. I heard shuffling around me, and through half-closed eyes I watched the shadows of several medics as they placed a bloodied soldier on the cot beside me.

"Are there more?" I asked, pulling myself to a sitting position. Before I had an answer, I lifted my legs to the edge and steadied myself. "Put the next guy here," I said. I held there for a moment, my hands gripping the side of the cot, my eyes struggling against the floodlights.

My head ached. Each time I opened my eyes, the skin along my forehead screamed with a horrible burning sensation. I lifted a hand to my temple but resisted touching the bandage. The pain surged, intense, searing, as if my scalp was engulfed in fire and someone constantly tore at my hair. The fog of the field surgeon's words echoed in my mind. He said something along the lines of "We stitched it in there. Five stitches. You can get the fragment removed back at Bagram. Make a necklace out of it. You're damn lucky, bro."

I forced a yawn and stretched my jaw, trying to relax the muscles. I stared down at the gray concrete floor covered with boot tracks, marked in blood and grime. Then I saw the big round drops of dried blood on the tops of my shoes. My own blood.

Lucky indeed.

I slid off the cot and stood up. Except for the pain, I felt disconnected from my whole body. I looked around the room, taking in my surroundings. There were rectangular halogen lights on black stands along the sides of the walls. IV poles. Medical cots. I could feel the rush of medical trauma whirling about.

I slid my hands into the cargo pocket on my right leg and pulled out a pair of surgical gloves as they brought the next guy in. "What can I do?" I asked. I sat on the cot's edge. I had a ripping headache, but at this point I knew I wasn't going to die, and I saw them bringing these men in, three of them, and I said, "Bring them right here!" Bandaged and still bloody, I started triaging, working people, getting after it.

"You're supposed to be laying down," one of the navy corpsmen said to me.

"These guys need my bed more than I do," I responded.

I dove in to help with the wounded because this is all I've known in life. I had to help. I was born into a very dynamic situation, to a single mother of two—my younger brother and me. We lived all over the place in Anchorage. Mom went through the men in her life like they were winters. She was a recovering addict, and I grew up tagging along with her to recovery meetings. I was the skinny little towheaded kid sitting in the back of those meetings, usually bored, but quiet. I had no choice but to listen to the struggles and horrors that those unfamiliar adults in the circle persevered through. There was nothing for kids in those smoky meeting halls, and my only source of entertainment came from sucking on the sugar cubes I stole from the blue box near the coffeepot.

It was at those meetings that I heard my mom's horrible, yet incredible, survival story, over and over again. But this wasn't just her story; it was also my grandmother's. And, later in life, I would learn that their story and their strength had become my own. The apple, as it turns out, only took a few bounces from the tree.

Like so many stories told in circles at substance-abuse recovery meetings, there were bits left out. My mom's version was but a sliver of her horrific tragedy, a canned, fifteen-minute summary of an event that lasted hours and changed her life forever. She would have to learn to move forward with her life or allow the haunting memories and survivor's guilt to swallow her. Her story was the kind of tale that, when she told it, anyone in the circle who heard it could nod in understanding of how such an event could lead to drug and alcohol abuse.

My mom had lost most of her family in a boating accident. Her dad, a stepbrother, a brother, a sister, and a best friend. But there was more to the event than just the loss of most of the family.

The real story, the one my grandmother Marian tells, is much more dramatic, one of those classic Alaskan disasters that played out on the front page of every major newspaper in the state at the time. It was only after I returned from Afghanistan that my grandmother shared her version of the day that created the survivors in our family.

One sunny summer day in July 1974, my grandma and her husband, Fred Schultz, were on their twenty-four-foot riverboat with their children, some friends, and their kids. Ten people in all. They were all camped out on the shore of Skilak Lake, on the Kenai Peninsula, and had gone out for a boat ride, when the wind picked up.

The famous Kenai River, with monster king salmon and huge

trout, pours into the northeast side of the lake and drains out the northwestern end. The lake, shaped like a body of a giant helicopter, is fifteen miles long, two miles wide, and more than five hundred feet deep in places, with mountains and a glacier at one end. The waters of Skilak are notoriously cold and turbulent. It isn't unusual to have water temperatures hovering around thirty-eight degrees, even in the summer. The mix of cold water and the glacial ice of the massive Harding Icefield, along with the high mountains that support it and work like a giant wind tunnel, make for a deadly combination that can turn a mirror-smooth lake into the frothing mouth of a monster in an instant. Within minutes, summer warmth combining with the cold can create winds that explode off the ice field in what Alaskans refer to as williwaws—strong gusts that tear down from glacial valleys, often wreaking havoc.

The families were camped where the Kenai drains into the upper part of the lake in a series of gravel bars and fast moving braids. They had been boating up the river to fish. This is my family. My roots. The generation before me, spending a beautiful sunny day together as a healthy, happy Alaskan family.

They fished all day long up the river, and around six that evening called it quits. As my grandma recalls, she wore only a T-shirt, jeans, and hip waders. After a great afternoon of fishing, they packed their gear, donned their life jackets, and boated back down the Kenai. The agile riverboat slipped out through the flat water at the mouth of the river and into Skilak. At first, the lake's surface was only a little choppy, but in mere seconds their fun family outing turned serious and dangerous. The surface of the lake began to boil with huge, rolling waves. Fred, thirty-five and just named officer of the month by the Anchorage police force, had little choice but to try to turn the boat so they could stay closer to shore. The waves built and were soon five and six feet high, cresting and breaking and pushing and lifting. The flat-bottom boat wasn't designed for ocean-sized waves. Before any of them could react, one monster wave hovered over them and another surged at the bow.

"We're going to lose her!" Fred cried as the first wave crashed over the bow and thrust the boat downward. It was one of two things my grandma can remember him saying.

In an instant, everything went under. The next thing she knew, she was plunged into the water. The cold hit her with a jolt. Her rubber hip boots filled and began pulling at her legs like giant tentacles, sucking her down. She kicked off the boots and flailed for the surface. When she erupted from below, everybody was spread out and there were waves, giant waves.

My grandma spotted my grandfather and swam to him. He had been the only one of the ten not wearing a life jacket. She wrapped her arms around him, trying to float and hold him above the water. Fred gurgled and choked. Foam bubbled out of his mouth. He had only the strength to say one last thing to her, these words she would forever carry with her.

"I'm dying. Let me go."

She had to do the unthinkable. With no choice but to free her grip on the man she loved, she let go and began swimming.

The crests rose high over her head, and in the deep troughs she couldn't find the others. The situation was all terror and confusion.

At first, my mom and her best friend, Betty, held on to each other. When my mom saw Fred drown, she realized the severity of their situation. She held on to Betty until her friend slipped from her hands, and she could feel herself slipping away, too.

My grandmother found Justin Koles, a family friend, holding my mom, who was sixteen. The young girl in his arms was unconscious, and Justin held her afloat and swam toward my grandma.

"Take Diane with you," my grandma, always in charge, yelled over the wind and breaking waves. "Swim for shore, and get help."

Justin, twenty-seven, also a policeman, kicked toward the shore, towing my mom.

The cold was taking its toll. Grandma knew she didn't have much time left. With the last of her energy she made her way toward the rocky shore in order to save her own life. She had no idea what had become of their other two boys. All she knew was that her only chance of survival was to get out and find a way to get warm.

She struggled through the waves, her arms and legs so numb she couldn't even feel herself kicking.

When she reached the shore, the waves broke over the top of her and slammed her up against a steep cliff that rose straight up from the water. Her arms and legs barely held enough strength to keep her upright, but adrenaline and fear surged through her. All she could do was begin the steep climb. At this point she wore only a tank top, socks, and jeans, all soaking wet in the wind.

While Grandma was climbing, Justin swam hard, with an arm around my mom. He fought the waves all the way to shore, and by luck he reached a small cove instead of the cliff face. He left my mom on the shore and ran. He sprinted along the shoreline to try to get help. In the meantime, my grandma reached the top of the cliff, not knowing if anyone else had made the swim to shore. She was hypothermic from the extended exposure to the frigid waters, and was trying to get her bearings. The shore of Skilak Lake in that area is rugged, with a dense forest of spruce, birch, and tangled alder brush. She stripped down out of her clothes, wrung out her wet jeans, put them back on, and stuffed leaves and grass inside her clothes to try to stay warm. She continued exploring the terrain until she finally reached an overlook above the cove. Below her, she spotted her daughter lying in the sand. She sprinted madly through the brush to reach my mom. When she arrived, she found my mom still unconscious, with foam bubbling out of her mouth, just like Fred.

Grandma started doing chest compressions on her, yelling over and over, "You're not going to die! You're not going to die!"

With all the carnage on that day, Grandma felt she had to keep Diane from dying, and this was something she could do. She would do something about *this*. She wouldn't lose her girl, too. She worked until my mom's eyes fluttered and she started breathing on her own. But Grandma's daughter still would die if she couldn't get her warm. Grandma found a Zippo lighter in her jeans pocket. The lighter was all wet and wouldn't work. She sat there, holding Diane in her arms, trying to warm her, and then an idea hit her.

She remembered a survival tip she had learned while watching an old show that aired in the early seventies in Alaska, a short program about how to survive if you were caught in the Alaska wilderness. The fifteen-minute segments gave people all these little survival tips, and she realized the episodes kept flashing back to her. That was how she knew to use the grass to stuff into her clothing to create a barrier to keep her warm. The next thing she recalled was how to start a fire with a wet Zippo.

She collected a small pile of tinder. With her trembling hands, she somehow managed to get the lighter apart. She blew on the flint and wick to dry it a bit and then used the sparker to ignite the fuel sponge inside the lighter. Fire. Soon she had my mom warming up by a big burning pile of driftwood, and then she ran down the beach and picked up life jackets that had floated ashore. She hung these up in a tree, so that boaters would see them.

Then, with the fire blazing, she took off on her own to try to find help. She bushwhacked for what felt like hours until she broke out on a rocky overlook where she could survey the lake. She couldn't see any signs of humanity. For a moment she lost it and began to shriek. She screamed into the roaring winds, and the way she tells the story, it felt like her screams were being shoved right back into her mouth. As if the wind that had already swallowed most of her family was just throwing her screams right back at her.

She wailed for a while and then started exploring again, until she realized she had just been walking in circles. Frustrated, disheartened, and exhausted, she sat down, only to feel the vibrations of what she thought was an approaching boat motor. She raced over to the rocky overlook, hoping for help in the form of a fisherman, and she began to get excited. At first she didn't understand or believe what she saw. Instead of a fishing boat, there it was, nearly twelve hours after their boat sank: a giant green helicopter.

Frantic, she waved, and they spotted her. The helo hovered and a man in an orange suit jumped out of the bird, into the lake, and swam over to where she was. He checked her out and said, "We can't hoist out right here. We've got to hike a bit." So they hiked up above the prominence she was on and then they sent down "the bullet," the forest penetrator, a metal seat attached to the hoist cable, and hoisted her up into the helicopter.

Sitting inside were Justin and my mom. They were the only three survivors among the ten souls on that boat. The aircrew flew them to the Soldotna hospital. My mother picked up pneumonia from the water that had penetrated deep into her lungs. My grandmother was treated for hypothermia. It would take a long time for either of them to warm up, an experience I would later share.

"It's really crazy that we got saved by the rescue guys and you went on to become one of them," my grandmother exclaimed, after sharing her version of our story. At first she had a hard time coping with the loss, but she said that what helped her move on was realizing that it's just life, and if you choose to live in Alaska, these things are going to happen.

The remains of my step-uncle, Harold, eight years old, were buried according to his living mother's wishes, and the remains of my aunt Kathy, also eight, were scattered over Sleeping Lady, a mountain north of Anchorage. To this day, my grandmother's husband, Fred, and their nine-year-old son, Danny, remain unrecovered.

The incredible thing is that during this whole struggle, my grandma never once thought she was going to die, never thought about giving up. According to my grandmother, smiling through the hard knocks and embracing the challenges in life are a family tradition. "We're not boring people," she says. "Nothing is ever boring in our family."

I grew up with two notions as the only certainties in my life: nothing is ever boring, and, since that fateful day in July, that I come from a family where hardship and survival go hand in hand.

3

. . . .

Alive Day

I didn't know this at the time, but the wounded army soldiers pouring into Asadabad, the forward operating base, or FOB, I was recovering at, were the guys that an AK-47 bullet had kept me from picking up. My Alaska teammates Aaron Parcha and Doug rescued the men, swooping in under fire and chalking up the first of what would become an impressive list of saves. Their chopper was already shot up when they went in, with my blood still on the floor, and it sustained even more damage when they went back. This time, the helo took a near-fatal shot to the aft that missed the rotor shaft by inches and damaged the helicopter so badly that, once they landed, they couldn't risk moving from the pad in front of the field clinic until serious repairs were made.

Word of my injury and our team's rescue spread. I had the huge bandage on my head, and my uniform was still covered in blood—both others' and my own. So I suppose I stood out. We were no longer the mystery operators in the strange new camo on the FOB. Soldiers were handing me water and slapping me on the back, which I'll admit hurt like hell. After helping out with the wounded, there was a lull. I asked one of the SEAL corpsmen, "I don't need a hospital bed, but is there a place I can just wash up and sit and relax?"

The corpsman said, "Yeah, bro. I got you." He led me back to crash in his room. At Asadabad, the SEALS had their own compound-within-a-compound, secure and armed to the teeth. I washed up, relaxed a bit, and finally called home to say I got hurt but was okay. I called my grandmother first, which probably wasn't the wisest move for a married man. But still, she was the one I had to call first, so I did.

Not long after that, Aaron came to find me. He'd been running rescue missions from the moment he got into my chopper and saw blood all over the floor. Aaron had been out of the loop, waiting for his chopper to be repaired, when my helo arrived, without me. That was when he heard I had been shot, and he put two and two together with the dried blood. He needed to know only one thing, and he got his answer by asking, "Did he walk off the helo?" When the flight engineer told him I insisted on walking, Aaron felt relief. Then, all Aaron and Doug could do was head out and pick up the wounded soldiers still awaiting rescue.

I don't remember what he said when he first saw me, but Aaron's eyes were as intense as I had ever seen them. I had known those eyes since before he'd become a PJ, and with one glance I knew he'd just been in the shit. Hoisting in with gunfire all around. They pulled out several wounded in one load, straining a chopper that, as I mentioned, had sustained serious damage to the tail section. An enemy round completely destroyed one of the .50-caliber guns.

Aaron and I sat around, recapping the action. We met a few of the SEALS. These guys were dressed like locals, bearded and wearing Pashtun clothing, the flowing cloth garments. Under those garments, however, they carried an arsenal that would make an action hero jealous.

One of these guys approached us and pointed to the blood-soaked bandage on my forehead. "Congratulations!" he said. "I've got one, too."

I wasn't so sure how to take his compliment, and the operator was smart enough to understand I was a little slow on the uptake and not following him.

"The day you danced with death, and she didn't take you home," he said. "This is your *alive day*."

November 12, 2010, became my alive day, though that day certainly wasn't my first dance with the pale mistress our new SEAL friend spoke of. My first experience with near-death had happened what felt like a lifetime earlier, when I was a collegiate runner.

I wasn't groomed to be a college athlete. My mom signed me up for track and cross-country running in junior high in the hope that it would curb my teenage overexuberance. I'd always had an abundance of energy, and maybe she thought sprinting through the woods around Anchorage would be a good way for me to burn some of it off. That, or she was hoping I'd take to running and not some expensive sport like hockey or football.

My first varsity race, freshman year, was for the Cook Inlet regional championships. The fastest runners from the biggest schools in Alaska's biggest city were all competing in one meet. I was shy, nervous, and in a bit over my head. My coach at the time was Joe Alward, a positive and encouraging man who played an important role for a kid like me, without a steady father figure. Coach Joe would be one of those influences in my life who helped me learn what my body was capable of enduring and what I could accomplish if I worked hard and always maintained a positive attitude.

After placing thirtieth in the race, I said, between breaths, "Holy cow, Coach Joe, those guys run fast."

Coach Alward turned to me and said, "Don't you worry, Jimmy. You'll be there someday, too." And like most things that had to do with running, Coach Joe was right. With great coaches and teammates, I lettered in three varsity sports my freshman year: cross-country, track, and cross-country skiing.

the ground in exhaustion, landing on the front page of the local paper the next day as reported "casualties." My own day as a running casualty wouldn't arrive for another year. I still had a state championship medal to earn.

That whole week, between regionals and state, I was so nervous. I was trying to be calm, trying not to think about state as state but instead to just think about it as an individual race. This was not the time to change the formula and train in a different way or to approach the race any differently than I had all year, but I do remember a lot of sleepless nights. My mom sensed this, and she splurged and got me a sports massage. The first massage of my life. I remember those warm hands on my tired back and legs felt so good, but the treatment didn't quell my nerves, not one bit.

In those days before the big race, I struggled to focus on school, but I soon figured out how to deal with the stress of the coming race. I had learned one important lesson as a young competitor on the Team Alaska track club. Coach Johnson taught me about mental imagery. He trained me to visualize a race or event before experiencing it, revealing to me a way to mentally prepare and to do all that I could to be ready. What he taught me was not to overthink the coming situation but instead to visualize myself going through these challenges with strength, direction, and purpose.

I learned to visualize goals and to have an awareness of what could happen, and what to do if things weren't going the way I would like them to go. So, those nights before the state championship, I would lie in bed, relax my entire body, and visualize myself running over the course, a trail I had been over hundreds of times. In my head I could see every single turn, hill, rock, and tree. I could see who was going to be around me, which competitors, and at what point in the race I might face obstacles, pain, and then where I would excel.

Coach Johnson introduced me to a life-changing tool. Mental imagery would become something I would utilize throughout the rest of my life when facing challenges, and I believe accessing the

One of the seniors on my team that year would walk away with the state championship. That was Michael Gomez. He was three years older than me and a phenomenal runner. I looked to him for inspiration, and I enjoyed training with him. A gifted athlete, Gomez didn't let his ego get to him. After winning the state championship, he showed me his medal, and I thought to myself, *I want to get one of those someday.*

By my sophomore year I was beginning to really fall in love with running and cross-country skiing, but also with the parks in our town, which are less parklike and mostly heavy forest with trail systems. I also didn't have a vehicle, so I ran or biked everywhere. Anchorage is spread out, with the municipality covering 1,961 square miles. I'm sure there are a few of those square miles I didn't cover on foot or on my bike, but if I wanted to get somewhere, I usually had to do it under my own power. My mom drilled into me a military-style work ethic, and she never failed to say, "Never be late to work, Jimmy. Don't you ever be late to work." I rode an old mountain bike, and when that bike broke, which was often, I had no choice but to transition from my bike to a run. *Never be late for work!*

I also couldn't call at a moment's notice and ask, "Mom? Can you pick me up?" She worked constantly, so her likely response would be simply, "No!"

A single mom with two rambunctious boys to support, she waitressed for years, then eventually went to barber school, became a barber, and went on to open her own salon. She toiled alone to reach that place, kind of an American dream story of her own. Mom was driven, and that determination rubbed off on me. Plus, all my biking and running to cover the wide expanse of our city equated to great lungs and a strong cardio system.

When I wasn't working or training, much of my free time was spent at Kincaid Park, an incredible 1,400-acre park on the southwest edge of town, with nearly forty miles of trail. The park is situated on an old Nike Hercules missile site that once housed more than a hundred soldiers, who maintained an around-the-clock operational alert of the missile battery. Steep bluffs on the perimeter drop down into the tidal monster that is Cook Inlet, and scattered throughout the park are strange concrete structures, covered over with earth, that once concealed missiles and soldiers. Now the buildings contain high-tech ski trail grooming equipment and park vehicles.

This old military installation became my playground. Whenever I could, I ran and skied on the rolling trails through the woods, and even at that young age I felt lucky to live in a place with such a park. Kincaid also kept me out of trouble, which I think was my mother's goal all along.

By my junior year, I started to make a name for myself on the state running scene. My coaches at West High pushed me hard, but still I wanted more. I joined the Team Alaska track club, and under the guidance of Marcus Dunbar and a core group of seriously running-minded athletes, I learned to run fast. We did strenuous workouts in the snow. If you've ever run in deep, soft sand, then you almost know what it is like to run in the snow. It's mostly the same, except harder and colder. Your ankles freeze. Your toes freeze. Soon your feet become these hard blocks you're running on.

It was on those freezing runs that I learned to appreciate and embrace "the suck." They taught me to just keep going. To run through the pain and discomfort. To enjoy that feeling of your body working hard, coming alive, and to understand that, after the freezing first fifteen minutes or so, you start to feel the hot, moist air coming off your body, up around your neck, and things start to feel good. Sacrificing comforts, I chose training year-round, and this is when my running made dramatic improvements.

Junior year, I placed third at state for cross-country running. By the beginning of my senior year, the local sports reporters knew me on a first-name basis, and coaches and runners on the other teams

knew who I was, and had me favored to win. My senior year started out with a roar. Girls were paying attention to me. I had a truck. I felt free. I was feeling confident and doing well. My teammate John Angst and I pushed each other in a good-natured battle for first. We had a great team, a tight family that meshed well and encouraged each other. The energy from John and me helped pick the whole team up.

I was running strong. Every race felt better than the last. When I stepped up to the starting line, for the other runners, it became a race for second place. I had no clue what was to come in a year's time. No indicators that the next race could be my last. As far as I knew, I was in the best shape of my life. In the entire state of Alaska, during my senior year, I was the guy everyone wanted to beat.

The most epic race, one that stands out to me, was the regional meet at Kincaid. Reporter Doyle Woody's caption below the cover photo in the *Anchorage Daily News* the next day would read like a war correspondent's report: "Casualties littered the finish area, some runners falling to the ground in exhaustion, others being helped to their feet at the finish chute, and still more bent over, chests heaving, hands resting on wobbly knees."

For years I had watched people win that race and had dreamed of winning the regional title, and there I was. I was really going to win. I couldn't believe it. The feeling of everyone screaming for m[e] gave me goose bumps. I stuck my hands out to the side, coming u[p] the final chute, hitting the hands of hundreds of complete strange[rs.] I crossed the finish line and ran right into the big arms of Coa[ch] Joe. That was a very happy moment for me in running. My co[ach] spent more time with me than a lot of the father figures in my [life,] so I had a really strong bond with him. The reward of sharing [that] moment with him was special for both of us, and I think he re[ally.] He was an Alaskan guy, too, and, like me, he didn't have a p[erfect] life as a kid. Running was something we had in common. S[haring] the victory with him meant everything.

My opponents crossed the line not long after me, colla[psing] power of the brain in this manner has become a huge key to my success. I didn't know it then, as a high school senior interested mostly in girls and running, but I'd locked on to an important life skill: mentally rehearse scenarios and come up with ways to find success and ways to overcome hardship, because no matter how good you think you are, there are always unforeseeable challenges out there that will trip you up when you least expect and when you're not prepared. You're going to fall on your face. Expect the fall, and be prepared for it. Spot your landing.

Race day arrived. A chilly fall wind rustled the remaining leaves on the trees. Only a few from our school had qualified for state, so instead of the whole huge team, only a couple of us stepped up to the starting line. I felt pretty alone, and I knew I had an enormous target on my back. Five kilometers away from my last high school race finish in Alaska.

A stampede of hundreds of runners started on a giant soccer field next to Palmer High School's football field and funneled into a trail wide enough for a Honda Civic. I remember busting out to try to stay up with the front-runners, on an uncharacteristically fast start. But when I got in there with the front pack, the leader set a much slower pace than I wanted, and I started to get frustrated and antsy. I made my move early in the second lap, and once I took the lead I never surrendered. We blasted into some nice rolling hills through the woods, with some gentle uphill climbing, and then hit a drastic downhill that made a curve, so that we were all gaining speed and taking this sharp turn to the right, and then we came out of it and rolled to a left and then another right. The downhill led into a series of spaghetti turns and then emptied back out next to the football field. This was the setup for three laps that would bring the race to five kilometers.

The spectators were standing three deep, walling the course, cheering, their yelling intensified with each lap. In the final kilometer, high-fiving people in the finish chute, I lost my focus, and I looked back and caught a glimpse of someone in red sprinting hard for the line. This snapped my focus back and I powered to the finish line. I won that 5K, with a time of 16:32. Five seconds ahead of my next competitor.

Winning state was one of those moments in life where one of my own dreams had come true. My mom was there, wearing this crazy big fur coat. Total Alaskana. I remember being kind of embarrassed at her choice of coat. I was with the runners and their parents and they were all dressed in expensive high-tech gear, like polypro and Gore-Tex, not this old-school fur stuff.

But being on top of the podium, that very day—I couldn't believe it. There was no way I would have ever believed it. If you had told me, during my freshman year, that I would become the state champion for running, I would have said you were crazy. At the same time, I had to be kind of humble. That night I had to go back to work at Carrs and keep bagging people's groceries. I didn't have time in my life to sit and dwell on my win. The success felt good, though, and I started taking running even more seriously.

At home, I think my mom started being a little easier on me. She rode my ass pretty hard most of my life, and she always kept me busy, because I was a high-energy boy. She kept me out of trouble by keeping me busy, and for the most part that worked. Through high school, I worked. My mom made me; she was a smart lady. I had energy to burn and we didn't have a lot of money. In her mind, sports and school and a job would keep me out of trouble. I started out as a lawn mower, then a grocery bagger, and then worked as a cashier and janitor. Then, with the reputation as a runner, I landed a coveted job working at Skinny Raven, a popular high-end running-shoe store.

My only shot at college came from my legs and my athletic record, not my brain and my academic record. I did average in school. I did okay, but I would get distracted. I made honor roll a few times, but then I wasn't all that concerned with my grade point average. I barely got Cs. I was always eligible to compete for sports and was never on the academic watch list. Now I'm older and I respect education a lot more than I did then. I didn't really value education because it was thrown in my face as something I had to do. Ironically, now as an adult who understands how the world works, I really appreciate the opportunities education affords.

My first major break to establish the trajectory of my life came in the way of acceptance into the US Naval Academy. The academy was an incredible opportunity, but I wasn't really mature enough for it. The academy appointment was an overwhelming lifestyle change at a crazy time—and initially it wasn't my idea. My mom crafted that plan. It was very clear there wasn't money in our family for me to go to college. If I was going to go to school, I was going to have to pay tuition myself or get a scholarship, and as an athlete my best bet was a scholarship. The academy was more my mom's dream, and if they accepted me, then the government would pay for an Ivy League education for me and I would be guaranteed a job after I graduated. I understood the opportunities and finally convinced myself that the naval academy wouldn't be that bad, because I would be running at the collegiate level. The whole thing sounded better when I realized I could run—and perhaps become a helicopter pilot or a rescue diver.

On the day of my going away party, I left work at Skinny Raven and drove out to the Kincaid Chalet. My mom had planned a great party, and all the cute girls were there. That should have been a sign for me. I'd be saying good-bye to my favorite park, my family, Alaska, and women. I pretended to be excited, but I wasn't.

Perhaps at some level I knew that my heart just wasn't into leaving Alaska.

At Annapolis, my family stood at the big gate, waving and yelling good-bye. My mom, my brother, Chris, and my stepdad. I had this strange feeling of dread. I can't explain it beyond that.

A month or two later, my mom sent me a package with some snacks and photos. I had to open the package in front of everyone, share the food inside, and read her letter aloud. Then I flipped through the photos. In the last of the photos I found this totally depressing photo of my mom, standing at the gate, crying and sad.

I really wasn't happy at the academy. When you are new to the school, you are a plebe, and you have all your rights taken away, just like at basic training, but it's a different model. Instead of trained professional instructors breaking you down and beating you emotionally for a strategic and clear military purpose, it was my peers. These young men, just a year or two ahead of me, were laying the hate down on me, based on what was dropped on them as plebes. There appears to be no real strategy, no rhyme or reason to this abuse—and these are also people who, later on, I'm supposed to look in the eye and respect and salute?

Being a plebe, the only way I could level the playing field was on the racecourse. Once we slipped on the running shoes, the status fell away. I ran on the cross-country team and the track team and held my own, but in school I seemed to face one disappointment after another. For example, I had my shot at learning about being a rescue swimmer during some training, but it turned out the water wasn't my friend. I was a terrible swimmer and I hated every moment in the water. Swimming was ridiculously hard. I was horrible in the pool, heavy-legged and half-panicked. On my feet I could breathe whenever I felt like it; in swimming I had to govern my oxygen consumption against my breathing rate. My thoughts of being a rescue diver drowned there, you could say.

Running was where I felt comfortable. We had a cool outfit: a yellow singlet, with blue NAVY across the front. We wore these very short shorts. I later would learn those skimpy things have always been in the military, perhaps as far back as when Washington crossed the Delaware. Those shorts are everywhere in the navy and are called silky Soffe shorts. I would later hear them called ranger panties. Every branch of the military wears them, and whoever Soffe is, her family must be rolling in the dough.

On the navy team, I got to explore the East Coast, a whole new world for a kid from Alaska. Cross-country was my favorite part of my time in the academy, but when that season ended, my choices as a runner were limited: indoor track or outdoor track?

I hate track. Running on a track is boring. Flat. Predictable. I need hills. Twists. Obstacles. I need challenges. I prefer activities that require me to be mentally engaged, but it was run or be stuck in Annapolis being bossed around by some asshole a few years older than me. So I started running indoor racing.

For a little while I enjoyed my new sport. I felt like I ran incredibly fast, because the indoor tracks were half the size of a normal track and I felt quick. But when you're a long-distance runner, the round and round and round shit gets old after a while. A race that normally took four laps or eight laps on an outdoor track became eight or sixteen. And even though my time was going to be roughly the same, the monotony was mind numbing. Still, I ran my laps and was doing fairly well for a freshman.

The Harvard track would spell the end of my navy running days. Harvard designed this very cool and unique tuned and springy surface, based on biomechanics, to reduce injuries and improve performance. Inside a large enclosed gymnasium, with bleachers on the side, the footfalls of the people running on the track echoed like thunder. When the long-distance competitors ran past in a big pack, it created a loud, syncopated rumble. *Boom. Boom. Boom.*

I don't remember how many events I was supposed to do that day, or how many I even participated in, because there are some definite holes in my memory of the day. However, I do remember the sensation of the floor creaking and bowing under my feet and being strong under my shoes, and the sound of thunder around me and echoing off the walls from the pack. And I'm in the pack, but I'm trying to hang on and stay with them. My grip was tenuous, and they were pulling away from me. Time slowed. I watched as guys who I always beat in practice dropped me like a bad habit. I'm hearing the pack get ahead of me, and in my mind I'm strained. I was giving it everything I had. I was suffocating. My chest vibrated. My heart seemed on the verge of bursting with each rapid beat. My chest exploded over and over again. I felt my neck and shoulders starting to tighten, and a stabbing pain shot through my back, and I tried so hard to keep going. I could feel the thunder of the pack starting to catch me from behind.

What the fuck? I'm getting lapped? Me? Lapped?

My memory is fuzzy from there. I have these strange visions of seeing myself, as if shot on a grainy surveillance video. I'm coughing and vomiting. I staggered off the track toward my coach. I think I said, "I don't feel good."

His voice came back warbling and distorted, "You-u-u don't lo-o-ok good!"

The black of a tunnel circled all I could see. The tunnel tightened, and then everything went dark.

That was about it.

My first alive day.

The event at Harvard led to a battery of nonstop medical exams. The doctors concluded that I had suffered a minor heart attack, but they couldn't nail down the cause. I was placed on "restricted" status. The military wasn't sure what to do with me yet, and with the holiday right around the corner, they sent me home. Home to Alaska. Home to winter.

Being surrounded by snow-covered mountains eased the sense of anxiety I felt about my heart, but I'd never known Alaska as someone who was medically restricted. I wasn't used to just looking out the window at the beauty; I was used to being in it—sweating, racing, flying through the wintery woods on skis, with my heart pounding and a huge grin on my face. I tried to be positive about my situation, but as an active nineteen-year-old with so much uncertainty ahead of me, I struggled. Alaska is dark in December, and depression can easily take root. I did the only thing I knew to keep it at bay. I snuck out, slipped on my skis, and hit the trails.

After the holiday break, I flew back to Annapolis, and the medical exams continued. The military medical team had me do this ridiculous stress test. They pointed me to a treadmill, had me get on it, and hooked me up to a batch of monitors. Their system wasn't set up for a collegiate-level athlete. The technician kept adjusting the treadmill, finally setting the device to the maximum slope and at the maximum speed. I ran hard for twenty minutes and my heart rate wasn't getting above 120.

The doctor looked at me and said, "This isn't doing anything. Do you think you could replicate that event?"

"I'm pretty sure I can," I said.

By then, I knew what sort of workouts set my heart off.

"I've got an idea," the doctor said. He brought out this strange-looking device with a snarl of thin wires and a little box the size of four packs of cigarettes. "This is a portable electrocardiograph," he said. "I want you to wear it for twenty-four hours, then bring it back to us. Between now and then I want you to do a hard workout, but not so hard you die. Got it?"

Always one to appreciate humor, I nodded, and said, "Yes, sir," but I won't lie. I was a bit scared. Someone like me isn't supposed to have heart problems.

The heart monitor had twelve leads that attached to my chest, with the wires looping around my back to connect to the small box. I wore this uncomfortable mesh tank top over the contraption to keep all the wires in place. I've never felt so weird or gross wearing anything in my life as I did that day when I left the doctor's office. I looked like Dynamo in Arnold Schwarzenegger's *The Running Man*, the big funny-looking fat guy with the metallic circuit board outfit.

Almost always one to follow directions, like a good little boy, I immediately went out and did an intensely hard workout involving interval training around a track. I would sprint as hard as I could for half a lap, then slow to my 5K race pace for half a lap, then repeat. I could not shower while being monitored, so I went to bed dirty. I somehow slept with the device on, and then I dropped it back off early in the morning, thinking nothing of it, not really expecting any answers.

Later that day I was sitting in class, and these navy medics came trotting into our classroom carrying a litter. *Something really must be wrong with someone,* I thought.

"Midshipman Settle?" one of the men called out.

I raised my hand.

"James Settle, come with us," he commanded.

I waved off their offer of the stretcher and followed them to the van. I didn't have a chance to collect my things, pack a bag. Nothing. They delivered me to the airport and flew me straight to Bethesda Naval Medical Center. That was the first time I was on a military airplane. On this aircraft, everyone sat pointed toward the tail. There I was, with just the clothing on my back. No money. No change of underwear. Nothing but a nagging feeling that something must be really wrong with me, but no idea what the hell was going on.

They put me up in military lodging, and someone told me my appointment would be the next day. All that rush and sense of urgency, yet I had an entire day to kill. My first real taste of the classic hurry-up-and-wait military way, but because of the rush, all I had to wear was my academy uniform, which threw people off. The naval academy's plebe uniforms have insignias that almost look like a real rank, but everything is the wrong size and doesn't look right. People weren't sure what to make of me. Enlisted personnel who had been doing the military thing for a while would see me and not know how to react. Officers seemed just as perplexed. I was an outsider.

I felt so isolated and alone and I wanted to say, "Hey, I don't know what I'm doing! Don't look at me!" Years later, as a PJ, I would gain a better understanding of what it is to wear a real uniform that people don't know how to react to.

That first day, I ate out of the vending machine. I didn't know where the chow hall was. I was so green I didn't even know how to ask for the chow hall. I only had the few coins in my pocket.

I was starving by the time they came and picked me up for the doctor the next day. This was the first time I met the man who would explain what the hell was going on with me and how he would fix it.

Unlike any of the other physicians I had seen to that point, this doctor was cool. Young and kind of hip, the doctor was really easy to be around. The man was relaxed, and this helped relax me. I would find later on, as a PJ working with all types in the hospital setting, this is a pretty good attitude to have—as a PJ, as a PA, as an MD, but especially as a cardiovascular surgeon. Just be cool. A lot of specialized physicians can be pompous assholes. Not this surgeon. He was nice. He sat me down in his office and laid it all out for me.

"Here is what I think is wrong, James," he said. "Your heart has been a strong and very active muscle your entire life. It is has been firing and firing, and the muscle tissue has mutated to produce an extra electrical node. The human heart is supposed to have two, but your heart has three. What we call SVT Supraventricular tachycardia."

He went on to explain the situation to me in the most basic terms. When the heart is doing its normal acoustical rhythms, you should hear it as *lub-dub, lub-dub, lub-dub,* and feel it in your pulse as that steady *thump-thump, thump-thump.*

As the doctor explained, having an extra electrical node not connected to my brain could be a problem. When the third electrical node received a signal, it would tell the muscle tissue around it to fire, generating another electrical pulse. This made my heart start bumping out of rhythm, and the ability to move blood decreased. And as you might guess, that's bad.

What the doctor wanted to do (and I would be one of the first to get this procedure, which seems crazy now) was to go in through my femoral artery with a laser probe. The plan was for him to identify the node that wasn't supposed to be there, stop my heart, then zap the pesky node. This would create scar tissue, so that even if it did receive a signal, it wouldn't be able to transmit. When all this was done, he would restart my heart.

My mom and my grandma flew down and arrived that day. They had to travel from Alaska to Bethesda and couldn't get there for the initial briefing, but they were there that afternoon and the medical staff explained the procedure. That night a dark funk hung in the air between us as we left the hospital. We went out to eat at some greasy spoon within walking distance of the hospital. I felt an immense guilt. I knew it was hard for my mom and grandmother to fly down on such short notice. Both were barbers, and no one has ever heard of a rich barber. Every day my mother was away from work, she lost money. I also knew they had to pay the walk-up ticket price with no reservations. A ticket like that from Alaska is about as painful as it gets. I felt guilty for being a burden and adding such expense and stress.

The next morning, when I arrived at the hospital, I was directed to get dressed in the hospital gown. It felt liberating to take off the uniform I had been wearing for three days. Before I went into pre-op, the doctor said, "Two things about this procedure: One, we will play any music you want to listen to, because you are going to be semiconscious. You aren't going to remember a whole lot. It won't hurt. We'll take the pain away, but you will be semiconscious. We're going to be working on you and I'll be checking in with you. And two, if you hear the AC/DC song 'Hell's Bells,' that means everything has gone well and the operation is a success. 'Hell's Bells' and you're going to be fit to fight."

This gave me something new to ponder. The thought of my own choice of tunes took away my anxiety about the procedure. I was really thinking about what music I wanted, and when I got into pre-op I asked the cute nurse prepping me, "How about some Beastie Boys?"

She smiled. "Hell yeah," she said. "We have the Beastie Boys. I'll tell the doctor." She left for a moment and I attempted to relax. She returned with a tray. It was mostly empty except for some alcohol wipes, a bottle of iodine, and a Bic razor. I thought, *Well, isn't that weird?*

I wore only a white gown, lying on the gurney in this sterile hospital hallway. The cute young nurse reached down and flipped my gown up, exposing my genitals. The move caught me completely off guard. It was like having a fantasy granted, but in the Twilight Zone.

"What are you doing?" I asked, not sure if I should be excited or scared.

She gave a slight nod of apology, saying, "Well, I've got to get you ready for surgery. This is pre-op." She picked up the razor. "I have to shave you."

So here was this cute woman lifting a razor toward my groin. I hadn't really had sex that many times, at this point in my life, and although I was about to endure a life-altering surgery, this moment with the nurse was far scarier—not to mention cold. I tried to think of something funny to say, like "He's a grower not a shower!" Instead, I said nothing. I looked away as she set to work shaving my most intimate of areas with a disposable Bic razor. This was far from any sexual fantasy I could have ever imagined. Had the doctors attached a heart monitor at that moment, my heart rate would no doubt have been off the charts. To me, at that point, this was the most horrific thing to happen in my life.

After those few very uncomfortable moments, I was taken into surgery. I felt cold, and bright lights blinded my vision. The room appeared to have an upper gallery behind glass, where an audience was seated. The doctor explained that these spectators were present to observe and learn about the procedure about to be performed. The room was crammed full of beeping and whirring equipment. All around me the performers of this dance efficiently attached probes and placed a mask on my face. Someone poked me with an IV, and from there my memory gets fuzzy. The drugs they administered worked well. Early on in the procedure, I felt a little sting inside me and I said, "I felt that."

Someone said, "You felt that? Give him more."

Whatever they pushed into my system hit me quick, and the rest is a surreal haze in my mind, but I remember the experience of them stopping my heart. I don't recall what was said, but I remember when the doctor indicated that he was ready to do his thing, and they stopped my heart. What I remember most was not being able to breathe, an overpowering, crushing weight on my chest, grasping my whole being like a fist squeezing cookie dough. I couldn't breathe. I couldn't move. I remember that feeling as clear as if it happened yesterday. The intense pressure, suffocation, inability to breathe, crushing weight, and complete paralysis is something I will never forget. I could make a dumb joke here about a heart-stopping moment, but in reality, at that instant, my life force hung in the balance. I had no choice but to be cool and not panic. This experience and choice of action would come in handy a few years later.

The surgeon completed his work, and the aftermath and recovery is one part comedy and two parts horror story. I can't really recall awaking to "Hell's Bells," but the music was there somewhere in the drug-induced state. As they wheeled me to my recovery room, an explosively bright fluorescent fluid moved up my body from below my feet, over my head. *How strange,* I thought, *fluorescent lights seem brighter when you're riding a gurney down a hall.*

Once I was brought into my recovery room, the floating heads attached to the colorful scrubs surrounding me started to move me from the gurney to the hospital bed. Up to this point in my life, I'd never really been drunk or high, and I was feeling disconnected from reality, to say the least. Almost as if I could float over my own body. I remember trying to bring my vision to focus on the wall beside me. I was having difficulty concentrating because I didn't understand what I was seeing. The institutional white paint was changing colors, with red spots and blotches, like a moving Rorschach test. I found the red wall beautiful. The changing coloring captivated me. The spots got bigger and bigger, turning red, growing and growing on the wall. I felt a surge of warmth.

A sudden self-conscious thought hit me: *Oh, no! I peed myself!* I couldn't speak, but I also didn't want to say anything, because I had just lost control and could only manage one thought: *How embarrassing!*

I was still hallucinating, and higher than Denali, and I realized the warmth and wet feeling had spread through my entire groin area. *I really pissed myself?*

I turned my attention to my abdominal area, very slowly, ashamed and wondering what people would think of me, trying to make sense of everything. Here stood this giant of a black man, a large male nurse, his mouth moving in slow motion, yelling over his shoulder, as his huge muscular arms pressed down on my legs with all his might. His face was intense, his lips were moving, but I couldn't hear what he was yelling, or anything anyone said.

I didn't feel pain. I wasn't worried about this nurse and didn't think about why his hands were colored the same as the splotches on the wall. Disconnected, I fought for consciousness as the room became chaotic and filled with frantic people. I thought, *Is this really happening? What is this? What the hell is going on right now?* Detached from the reality of the situation, unable to help myself, and losing a massive amount blood, I passed out.

I awoke to pain all over my body and a new, pressing weight on my hips. I couldn't move my lower half. For a moment I panicked. *Something went wrong? Have I've lost my legs? Am I paralyzed?*

It turns out I wasn't paralyzed; the surgery had been a success. What went wrong was the transfer from the gurney to my hospital bed. The move didn't go as smoothly as hoped, and one of the sutures on my femoral artery popped. This was my first exposure to an arterial bleed, and it happened to be my own femoral. I had to be stitched back up. The weight on my pelvic area was sandbags, to keep me from moving.

I don't remember how long I was there. I don't know how long I slept in the recovery room. But it was long enough that the damp winter weather and the stress of her son having heart surgery caused my mom to have an epic asthma attack and need her own hospitalization. My grandma stayed by my side as long as she could.

It was during this time that I learned what "recovery" means. Overnight, I went from collegiate-level runner to a guy who almost needed to learn how to walk again. I went from an athlete who felt capable of anything to a broken shell of a young man. I had to learn to take it really easy, and taking it easy was not something I had ever known. In order to reach my heart, the surgeon had to go through the muscles of my hip flexors, so recovery took what felt like forever. It would be a long time before I was even close to being back to the strength I had before the surgery.

Back at the naval academy, once I could walk again, my future looked grim. I tried to run but nothing felt the same. My grand ambition of being a helicopter pilot or a Navy SEAL clearly wasn't going to happen. My future was now going to be restricted.

Restricted. I wasn't thinking how valuable that navy education would be later in life, or about my life in the long term. I was nineteen. I had zero interest in being a navy desk jockey. I joined the military to do something sexy. I was too young to realize that I could use the opportunity to pursue engineering or something else with fantastic career options, something applicable in the civilian world. At that age, I didn't have the brains to accept such an incredible education for free, not with that caveat of "restricted." As wiser men than me have said, "Youth is wasted on the young."

My friends were back in Alaska or at colleges, out partying and having all sorts of fun. In my mind, my dream of a cool job had just died, and running, the focus of my life for years, was gone. I could stay on for a few more years or part ways.

I walked away from the US Naval Academy with little more than the scars of surgery, but I was alive.

4

. . . .

Shoe Guy

The navy offered to buy me a plane ticket home to Alaska or give me the cash equivalent. My mom was not stoked I left the academy. In fact, she was very pissed off. She was so mad, I wasn't welcome to come home. I took the cash and an honorable discharge.

I got in touch with another one of the few men who had been a strong and positive influence in my life, Coach Harry Johnson. Coach said, "Well, Jimmy, this works out pretty good." His daughter Heidi, my age, was also leaving her school. He needed somebody to help her move her stuff from Minnesota to her uncle's place in Texas. He wanted someone to drive her Jeep because she had already had several speeding tickets.

I helped Heidi move to Beaumont, Texas, and that was my first experience with the South. For an Alaskan kid, it was a stark contrast to my beloved home. Texas had two things this Alaskan does not do well with: snakes and heat. Humid, humid heat.

My time in Beaumont also led me to learning the basics of construction. I wasn't running, and for the first time in my life I started to pack on weight. As the state champion, I stood five foot eleven and weighed 140 pounds. In the coming years, as a nonathlete, I would balloon to 180.

Eventually, I migrated back up to Alaska. I missed the trails, the people, and the mountains. When I saw Kincaid Park and the trails around the city, I realized that not running was killing me. I couldn't let my fear of my heart failing me keep me from what I loved. So I started running again, but this time I was heavy and slow. I was also flat broke and without much of a future ahead of me.

I enrolled at the University of Alaska Anchorage and set my sights on running on their cross-country team under the leadership of Coach Michal Friess, but I had a way to go before I would be a competitor again.

The Anchorage Heart Run, in May of 1998, would mark my return to the Anchorage running scene. It was a money raiser for the American Heart Association. I didn't win the race, but I came in twelfth, with a time of 16:42 for a 5K, almost a minute short of my personal record of 15:49. The place won me the title of Mended Heart winner, the highest place for a runner with a heart-related surgery or deficit. My time was a record for the Mended Heart category, and I would repeat that title for a record four years in a row.

I made UAA's cross-country team the next year. Physically, my heart was doing fine, but somewhere in the time between the naval academy and taking out school loans, I began to lose my competitive drive. I moved in with my brother and was taking a full class load, plus working out twice a day and working part-time at the gym and pool. I failed to manage my time, and within a few years I burned out. I needed a break from school and competitive running. I start working full-time back at Skinny Raven.

The next few years were, without a doubt, some of the most humbling for me. It's one thing to be fitting people for shoes when you are in high school, but quite another to be kneeling down at a customer's feet and have her recognize you from newscasts a few years earlier. More than once I heard, "Hey! Weren't you the runner who won state a few years back?" All I could do was smile and give pointers on what shoe would work best. Maybe offer a little training advice. I was beginning to feel as though all the promise was being sucked from my life.

Then I met a girl who had run collegiately, had finished school, and had recently moved back to Alaska. We hit it off, and I couldn't let it look like I was going to settle for being a shoe salesman. I was more than this. I needed to make a change in my life, but I just didn't know what that change would be.

Early one fall morning, two hours before sunrise, I was driving from my new girlfriend's apartment to a run-down split-level bachelor pad where I lived with five other dudes. As I drove across town, contemplating this new stirring in my chest that was so different and scary for my heart, but in a very different way, I heard on the radio that a passenger jet had just crashed into one of the twin towers in New York City. This was around five in the morning in Alaska, and when I arrived at our apartment, I flipped on the TV and saw the smoking tower. I ran upstairs and woke all my roommates up.

We were in the living room, crowded around the television, when the second jet hit. Something about the sight mesmerized me, and I was caught off guard by the emotions that welled up inside me. I had worn a uniform, of sorts, and had run for the navy, and now we were under attack. I felt a sense of duty and obligation, one that I'd never known before.

The phone rang. The call was for one of my roommates, a Ranger using the GI Bill and fresh out of the army. When he hung up he turned to us and said, "They don't know what the hell is happening, but they're calling everybody back to base."

As he disappeared out the door, I couldn't help but think how things had turned out. I would have been just out of the naval academy. With or without my heart condition, I could have been helping my country. Instead, I had to pack my lunch and head off to sell shoes.

As with so many Americans, things changed for me that day. I don't think I sold a single pair of shoes. Nobody was in downtown Anchorage. I thought of going for a run right down the middle of the city streets during my break. I needed to run. I needed to do something with the energy and anxiety I felt. I didn't know what to do.

I also didn't know that those attacks would plant a seed that took nearly five years to germinate—I saw the lanes of opportunity ahead of me and I wasn't too excited about what there was to see. The military seemed like the only chance for me, but I knew then that my heart surgery, my job profile, all that would be in my record. My navy time would be recognized, but I didn't do anything of value for our country. Plus, after the disappointing academy experience, I didn't have a fire for the military in any way. My experience as a powerless plebe had left me thinking I didn't possess the discipline it would take, anyway.

I was wrong.

I would spend the next few years in love with the runner girl. She came from a big, adventurous, and rambunctious family with six kids. I fit in well and they treated me like family. We moved in together, in a small fixer-upper. I worked hard at the shoe store and moved my way up the ladder to midlevel manager.

My salary had increased, and I was doing a little better financially, but being a shoe guy wasn't satisfying. Something was missing from my life. Then, one day, the door to the store chimed. I looked up from some orders and in walked a man who almost looked like Chris Robertson.

"Jimmy!"

"Chris?" I asked, unsure how to match the handsome, brown-haired, muscular man with my memory of the lanky boy-faced runner I knew from years earlier. We shook hands and then spent the next half hour catching up. Like mine, Chris's path had included some college, and then he joined the National Guard and became a part of the biathlon ski team. What really caught my ear was the part about him becoming what he called a "PJ."

"A PJ? That sounds sexy," I said, and I gave him a cat growl. "What's a PJ?"

"Pararescuemen," he replied, and he then filled me in on what sounded like the coolest job description I'd ever heard in my entire life, something along the lines of "We jump out of planes and helicopters to save people."

I gave Chris a military discount and he left the store with a new pair of running shoes tucked under his arm and the promise to return with pictures. It had been great to see him. His stories and his unique line of work intrigued me and at the same time depressed me. Chris jumped out of planes and saved people for a living. He was soaring and saving human lives. I was a shoe guy—literally the bottom of the world.

In the following months, Chris kept coming to visit. Sometimes he brought members of his team and sometimes he came alone. Each time, he brought photos and stories, and then one day he brought in his laptop and said, "I'm just going to show you a whole bunch of pictures from being a PJ." Images flashed on his screen of mountaintops, glaciers, and all sorts of cool military gadgets and weapons. There was a great picture of him and a few other PJ's wearing tie-dyed Moose's Tooth T-shirts while posing with their weapons and mustaches, leaning against the firepower of a mini-gun mounted on a helicopter in an exotic desert backdrop. He participated in these amazing training exercises all over Alaska, and he'd been through specialized courses that sounded like the training I'd only heard about SEALS and Rangers doing. It all had the twist of something outside the box that struck a chord deep within me.

At some point, Chris took me to "the section." Originally, before being used by the PJs, the building was an armory for the Alaska Army National Guard. When you pulled in from the street, it looked like a single-story structure with American and Alaskan flags on poles attached to the faded yellow concrete walls. A cluster of birch trees stood out front, with the occasional moose browsing. The only indication of what the building contained was a moose-size PJ sign just outside the entrance. The hand-painted version of the PJ logo had a blond-haired guardian angel with large white wings, her arms wrapped around a black globe with fine white lines of latitude and longitude. The words "That others may live" were written in black beneath her.

The PJ section blew my mind. They had been working out of the building since 1992. This was the home of the 212th, the busiest pararescue team in the United States. The building itself was funky and contained layers of character, perfectly fitting the personality of the Anchorage neighborhood of Spenard and the spirit of the Alaska PJs. Rough. Tough. And not so pretty. Underestimated on the outside and overexcelling and performing on the inside.

The section was a firehouse on steroids. Each PJ had his own "cage," an eight-by-eight-foot chain-link box with an eight-foot ceiling, loaded with tens of thousands of dollars' worth of personalized and top-of-the-line outdoor equipment. Think of a Batcave that would give Batman wet dreams. Here, the PJs stored their rescue and tactical gear, planned their missions, trained, debriefed, slept, and socialized.

And did they ever know how to socialize.

To encourage fraternization and to ensure decompression after stressful missions, the section had a hot tub and a keg. It was actually someone's duty to maintain an adequate supply of beer in the kegerator at all times. Team members were issued giant tan ceramic beer steins with the name and logo of the parachuting angel and the globe on the side.

I knew, the moment I first walked into the section, that I wanted to be a part of this life. It wasn't just the incredible amount of gear, suited for every Alaskan outdoor sport imaginable, or the inspirational job description. No, the 212th offered something that I had only really known superficially as an athlete in high school, on my running teams—a tight-knit and highly functioning family.

My first introduction to the pararescue community was as a guest. A fan. An outsider. I knew most of the PJs at the 212th because

I had been fitting them for shoes, but I barely felt cool enough to hang out at the section. Chris Robertson invited me as his guest. I was accepted openly. I found a place I wanted to be. This was everything I wanted in life. But the moment I decided to get after it, to attempt to become a PJ, everything about my relationship and my interactions at the section, and with the PJs there, shifted dramatically.

5

. . . .

The PAST

Once I made my intention to become a PJ evident, I entered what is called the "toad" phase of becoming a PJ. This is the stage of PJ life where you are at the outer ring of the inner circle. You are not a fan anymore; you are trying to be part of the team. As a toad, I was attempting to advance to the next level, cone, but I was in a stage of development where I wasn't in the air force and I hadn't completed the rigorous physical tests or attended any courses. The PJ world was all conceptual to me at that point. A cone is a PJ or combat rescue officer (CRO) trainee who has passed the tough initial Physical Ability and Stamina Test (PAST) and the initial selection phase. I would have to become a cone before I could even begin dreaming of becoming a PJ.

As a toad or a cone, I couldn't just come and go at the section anymore. I had to earn my entrance and exits from the building. This was called "doing your ins and outs." On the outside of the building, right next to the front door, hung a pull-up bar. Even in the winter, no matter how frozen, trainees did fifteen pull-ups. There also was a "training opportunity" you were required to perform whenever you entered the building: fifty push-ups, in addition to the traditional offering of respect—one for pararescue, one for teamwork, one for fallen comrades, and then one for any sergeant, officer, or man standing within sight who had earned the maroon beret of a PJ.

After the fifty-odd push-ups, I did my best to become invisible, which wasn't easy, because we did our push-ups just inside the main door, in the middle of a four-way intersection. To the left was the team room, to the right was the command area, and straight ahead was the cage area, deeper inside the building. One of the hallways always had someone coming or going. As a trainee, the ultimate goal is to avoid contact with anyone in possession of a maroon beret. If I encountered someone, I needed to make sure I was on point and had my shit in order and my appearance wired tight, because an aspiring PJ had to be prepared to be grilled on all things pararescue, including the PJ creed, historical PJs, and even the Pledge of Allegiance. Failure to satisfy the inquisitor would result in lessons reinforced with sweat. Push-ups, flutter kicks, burpees, and much-more-creative physical rewards awaited any cones who lacked the appropriate motivation or knowledge.

A quick example of this happened to one of my friends, Jeremy Maddamma. A cone like me, he stumbled upon a PJ and was asked, "What's the Pledge of Allegiance?" Nervous and under pressure, Maddamma, that poor guy, experienced a very brief moment of brain vapor lock and didn't have an answer. He paid the man that day—endless push-ups and an essay on what the Pledge meant and who wrote it.

As a trainee, I wanted to be low profile and so squared away that if someone did come at me they were going to just walk on by and not pick on me. I learned how to be invisible—invisible through excellent performance, not by slacking or hiding out. The PJs have a word for slacking: *scurving*. Scurving is an insult. I didn't want to be called a scurve. Yet, in order to survive, a good deal of tactical scurving has to happen. I had to learn the moments to scurve, in order to save energy and survive.

The entrance to the old building was a heavy steel door, locked at all times. To gain entry, authorized personnel used an electronic pass card or had to be buzzed in. As a trainee who had yet to pass the PAST, I didn't have a pass card, so every time I visited I had to get buzzed into the building. That meant someone knew I was there, and they were at least listening and watching. Perfect form was a must, and I had to be loud when performing the requisite exercises. Enthusiasm was a must. Every single push-up was counted out loud and proud. All the way to fifty. Then one for teamwork, one for pararescue, one for fallen comrades, and one for any maroon beret walking around. For a new guy, this was an intimidating and challenging number of push-ups. My arms would shake as they reached their physical limits after dropping for set after set of push-ups. My knees would be twitching, back and chest on the verge of cramping, and yet I needed to sound and look determined.

I've always been a motivated dude, and it's easy for me to dig deep in matters of physical endurance, especially self-driven, self-inflicted pain. Running, too. I have always enjoyed the challenge that comes from pushing myself hard. But man, the push-ups were never-ending and every day. Sometimes the mentor would become bored watching me do push-ups, would yawn, check his watch, and send me on my way.

The next most common physical training exercise was the flutter kick. Flutter kicks are a four-count exercise designed to strengthen the quads, hip flexors, core, and abdomen in order to prepare for the long swim sessions at combat dive school. The starting position is on your back, legs straight out, toes pointed. Feet six inches above the ground. Then, one at a time, you bring them all the way up: "Six to thirty-six inches, men!" Each leg goes from six to thirty-six inches twice to count as one flutter kick. Flutter kicks burn white hot in your belly and legs after a while.

Another favorite was the jack-up. This is where you do a handstand against the wall and start pushing out presses of your own body weight, down until your head hits the ground and then back up. The jack-up. One night, while I was at the section late as a cone and the PJs were socializing, I had a PJ—Douggie Fresh, as I called him—tell me to do a hundred of those. "Jack your feet up and knock out a hundred." I deserved it and saw it coming. He hated being called Douggie Fresh, especially from a cone.

I was sold. For the first time since my freshman year of high school, when Michael Gomez showed me his state medal, another nearly impossible goal began to form in my mind. I began to dream and have visions of myself doing something other than selling shoes. But three major obstacles blocked my path. I knew from my naval academy experience that I was not a strong swimmer. Also, I may have been a speedy runner, but I wasn't confident enough in my physical condition to consider taking the PAST. And finally, there was my actual past. At the time, PJ trainees didn't have to be enlisted in the air force, and I was still a civilian. In all likelihood, my old military record would keep me out of service. My heart had healed. The surgery was deemed a success. But would that "restricted" label the navy placed upon me a few years earlier come back to haunt me?

I wouldn't know unless I tried.

The first thing I needed to do was hire a swim coach and prepare myself for the PAST.

There is a PAST required for different branches and specialties in the military, each with differing requirements, but in the end the tests are all trying to do the same thing: make sure each soldier is at a specific physical fitness level. The PAST for becoming a PJ is tough, because it has to be. This initial fitness exam involves running, swimming, pull-ups, push-ups, sit-ups, and flutter kicks. And that is only the PAST. A regular entry-level PAST exists for those interested in applying as a PJ in the active duty air force, and then there is the Alaskan PAST. As you might imagine, the Alaskan standards are both higher and tougher.

The Alaska team's test, the toughest of all PJ entrance exams in the country, is the equivalent to the graduation standards for the Air Force Pararescue Indoctrination Course, or INDOC. INDOC is the first nine-week course in what is called "the pipeline." As far as special operations training goes, the pipeline is the longest course in the world and touts an 80 percent attrition rate. The Alaskan rate of attrition is lower, but that is because of how selective and tough the local team is in selecting candidates to pass on to INDOC. The Alaskan squad wants to make sure you can pass the final graduation standards for INDOC before they give you their blessing.

I trained for an entire year before I took the test for the first time. Running was natural for me, but I had to learn how to swim with efficiency and speed. Growing up in Alaska, I didn't really do much swimming. The water is predictably cold—horribly cold. Staying in the water for long periods of time is just not what most Alaskans do, not even on the hottest summer days.

If I wanted to be a PJ, I needed to learn how to survive four twenty-five-meter underwater swims, with two minutes for each length of the pool, followed by a five-minute break and then a fifteen-hundred-meter surface swim in under thirty-four minutes. Then a thirty-minute rest and a three-mile run in under 22:30. Then a fifteen-minute break, followed by calisthenics. I figured I could survive the running, and the pull-ups, flutter kicks, sit-ups, and push-ups (ten pull-ups in under a minute, more than sixty flutter kicks in two minutes, at least sixty-five sit-ups in two minutes, and a minimum of fifty push-ups in two minutes). But for the swimming portion I would need serious help. With little money to spare, I hired a private coach. Several days a week, for an hour before work in the morning, I would slip into the pool. It took me about a year before I felt comfortable and even remotely prepared to attempt the PAST. Passing on the first time seemed important to me. I had Chris Robertson essentially sponsoring me, and I didn't want to let him down.

All the hard work paid off, because I passed the test on the first try. My initial success with the PAST was in a way also redemptive for Chris. All this time, he had been basically saying, "This is a guy we want on the team. I think Jimmy has what it takes, and he's a great dude." Or, at least, that is what I imagined he was saying. But the truth was, I didn't want my buddy to have to eat his words before I even had the chance to jump into the pool at INDOC.

Aside from the Alaskan version of the PAST, the 212th had put together an additional screening. Perhaps "voluntary Alaska torture" would be a better term. This was a sort of mock extended training day, or a wintery all-day version of INDOC's "Hell Night." For my extended training day, all the new cones were instructed to show up at the section before sunrise and were told to "be ready." Ready for anything. "Anything" essentially meant endless hours of physical and mental exertion specifically designed to push us to failure and beyond. The cones at the time were, from rank down, Major Bryan Adrian, Lieutenant Koa Ali Bailey, Staff Sergeant Jeremy Maddamma, Senior Airman Zach Kline, and then me. I didn't have a rank yet, because I hadn't even made it through basic training.

I stepped into the section before six o'clock that cold winter morning. Maddamma was already there, geared up and ready to go. Maddamma is one of those guys with striking eyes that appear to have the ability to examine your soul. He's intense, but also one of the nicest and most accepting guys I've ever met. Intelligent and capable, Maddamma came from the cutthroat streets of Cleveland, Ohio. He started his air force career as a firefighter. I learned many things from him, and we would eventually end up serving together in Afghanistan. He's a stout five foot eight, thick-muscled, and covered in detailed tattoos. A cone at the time, he had already passed through INDOC and been through combat dive school. Action-figure fit, Maddamma was in the physical condition you reach after a year of constant, rigorous PJ training, all day long, every day. Each muscle begins to have definition, shape, and some cut to it.

Then came Koa Bailey, an officer, an Alaska boy like myself. Koa starred as Chugiak High School's quarterback, playing on the football team not far from my hometown. After high school he went on to be a quarterback in college, before joining the air force. He was just a few inches taller than me, at six foot one, handsome, and with beautiful brown skin, a nod to his Pacific Islander heritage. Koa didn't party like the rest of us, but he was fun to be around, and motivating.

Zach Kline was next to arrive. Another cone who stood over six feet tall, Zach possessed a gigantic chin and was built like a spider monkey. An incredible climber, Zach can hang off a ledge by his pinky until the ledge grows tired of his weight. The guy is a wizard with rope systems and knows just about every knot a rope can make. The only things more twisted than his climbing ropes are his humor and love of practical jokes.

The only cone older than me was Major Bryan Adrian. Major Adrian piloted C-130s for the Colorado National Guard. He flew gunships and at some point became a special operations C-130 pilot, with endorsements beyond those of the standard C-130 pilot. He became interested in the combat rescue officer career path while PJs were jumping out of the back of the planes he piloted.

Before this hell day, I hadn't been around Major Adrian a whole lot, and this day was the first time I would work closely with him. I didn't know this at the time, but his friendship and mentorship of me would transform my understanding of what dedication to becoming a PJ means. Prior to this experience, I had never been exposed to a man who served in the military as long as Major Adrian. He was coming into cone life at over forty. This was old for the career field, but he was still a stud. Major Adrian stood at least six feet tall and close to two hundred pounds of solid muscle. I expected that, at some point during the day, we would be doing buddy carries with him, and I was thinking, *Fuck that guy is heavy. Solid. No fat on him! Who could carry him?*

In fact, I think I was the chubbiest cone there that early morning, with just a little bit of a beer belly left from my hiatus from serious running.

Hours before sunrise, standing out front of the section, we did our pull-ups. Our breath erupted from our mouths like clouds from a steam engine. It mixed with the light snow flurries that fell under the orange streetlight above. Once inside, Tellsworth and Romspert, the PJs leading the training, threw green ALICE frame rucksacks at us. Tellsworth said, "Okay, everybody, you're going to fill these rucks with gear, and don't forget your pool gear." We grabbed swimming essentials: mask, snorkel, fins, weight belt, buoyancy compensator vest, and some ropes. We threw all that into the rucksack, with a couple MRE rations, some water, and an extra uniform.

Once we were ready, Romspert said, "Okay, gents, let's weigh these bags. Everybody is going to have seventy pounds." I set my ruck on the scale and he said, "Nope! Add some plates from the gym until you hit seventy." Whatever poundage we didn't have in our ruck, they added, using the big heavy-weight metal plates from the gym.

Once our rucks all weighed enough, we threw them into the bed of the PJ six pax, a four-door long bed F-350. *Pax* is a military term for "passengers," so this is a truck that can fit six. Tellsworth and Romspert loaded into the warm cab. We lowly cones rode with our gear.

It was cold as hell in the back of that truck. The air stung at my nostrils. I'd been out on the trails skiing the night before, and my skis had little glide, so I knew the temperature couldn't be but a few degrees above zero. I wasn't sure where they were taking us or what exactly we were going to do, but I knew the pool was involved somehow, and I suspected the day would be as tough as anything I had endured in my life to that point.

I had been told that National Geographic released a series about the pararescue training pipeline, but I intentionally did not watch any of those episodes. I like the challenge of surprise and the unknown, and I didn't want to psych myself out. My naïveté and ignorance of what was to come left me raw, a virgin for the challenges the day would bring. I wanted it that way.

The drive took us from Spenard through the sleeping city of Anchorage. From inside the truck topper, we couldn't see which tree-lined streets we were on, or which of the countless strip malls we were passing. Like kidnap victims, we had no idea where they were taking us. Anchorage midwinter in the morning is dark. Six in the morning could be midnight. The only indicator of morning would be the roadside coffee stands, open, with cars in a line, waiting for a latte. We bumped along in the cold, dark bed for about twenty minutes, and then suddenly we come to a hard stop.

The frosted rear window of the topper opened, the tailgate dropped. "Get out, cones!" Romspert said.

We bailed out and glanced around. In a second I realized we were in a parking lot at the base of Arctic Valley, an incredibly long and steep mountain road. Switchbacks cut back and forth up the steep grade until the road terminated in a high mountain valley. On one side of the valley sat a run-down ski operation that might have been a nice resort back in the seventies. Arctic Valley Road ended at the top of the pass. Situated right above the valley, at four thousand feet, is a Cold War relic, an abandoned Nike Hercules missile site called Site Summit.

Previously, as a civilian runner, I had trained on this road countless times to really challenge myself. Then, I wore top-of-the-line running shoes and a T-shirt, and I trained with seasoned running friends in perfect weather. On even the best of days, a run up Arctic Valley Road is daunting. It's a hell of a drive just to get up the mountain. In my prime running shape I could reach the top pass in about an hour. When I ran that particular road, I relished the climb to the top. I knew the payoff view up the alpine valleys, with Anchorage and the ocean below, would be worth every grueling footstep. The green of the willows, the twisted black spruce, and the alpine tundra melded with the backdrop of jagged peaks to create the world that meant so much to me, both as an athlete and as an Alaskan. In a place like Arctic Valley, you can see that you're perched right on the edge of an immense wilderness. You're looking from the top of one mountain, out across a sea of mountaintops. The view isn't necessarily one mountain and then another; it's more like rapids made of rock and snow, flowing and almost alive.

But this was different. For my first foray with a team of cones, I would be headed up toward my idea of heaven, but in hellish conditions.

"Rucks on!" Tellsworth yelled to us. We scrambled and hoisted the impossibly heavy packs onto our backs. "Get humping. There is a helo waiting for you guys at the top! You've got an hour. Go! Go!"

Major Adrian and I looked at each other. "Well," he said, "let's get this thing going."

I had backpacked before, but I had never rucked military style before, not with seventy pounds. I'd run up that mountain without weight on my back countless times, and those climbs were plenty challenging by themselves. To run it with a seventy-pound pack? Brutal. Absolutely brutal. On the easiest day a strong runner going up that mountain is sucking wind within five minutes. The intensity and elevation gain get steeper and steeper for the entire distance.

I had my doubts that we could make it up the mountain with those packs in an hour. No way. This was part of the cone selection process. It isn't about getting guys to quit from fatigue so much as it is about watching to see how they deal with the impossible. How a man accustomed to success and achievement most of his life deals with failure.

We formed up as a group and started the journey up the mountain. The instructors loaded up in the truck and drove on ahead. We lost sight of them as soon as they rounded the first switchback.

At first, all I could think about was the incredible weight digging into my shoulders and Jack Frost nipping at my exposed face.

We must have looked pretty pathetic. We were doing our best, under the circumstances, trying to run with all this heavy shit on. Cars full of skiers and snowboarders heading up for first tracks of the day honked as they passed. Faces peered through foggy windows, trying to comprehend our motivation, as we pounded up the snow-covered incline.

Believe me, we struggled. Within minutes we were sucking wind. Sweat formed on our faces and crystalized on our eyebrows and lashes. To this point in my life, even with all my race training and preparation for the PAST, I had never done anything like what we did that morning. We tried to move at double-time speed: tick tock, tick tock, tick tock, left right, left right, left right. That might have been the tempo of our feet, but our stride length against the elevation gain was only maybe a foot. Left. Left. Left. Almost a sad hopping shuffle. There was no way we were going to make that chopper at the pass, but still, we had to try.

I think it was Romspert who told us he wanted us to "jody" while we trudged up the mountain, to keep everyone in step. In any military movie you've ever seen, marching men usually sing or call out cadences as they march. Apparently *jody* is a term from the late 1930s, based on an unsavory character from old blues songs, who stole the wives of soldiers away at war. I remembered a few songs from my days in the academy, and never being one to pass up a chance for a laugh, I added a few of my own, tailoring them to the painful situation at hand and the imaginary ski bunnies awaiting us at the top.

We were almost in a zone, in cadence and a pretty good rhythm, when we came to the first switchback, a little over a mile into the trek. As we made a right hairpin turn, the PJs were standing in the road. The moment we rounded the corner they ambushed us with a single word: "*Drop!*"

In the PJ trainee world, when you hear the word *drop*, you stop whatever you are doing and immediately assume the standard horizontal position: on the ground, on your face.

Ah shit! I thought.

We had been marching in formation, so when we hit the ground we were this scrambling bundle of packs and boots, trying to crab walk around one another so everyone had room.

Romspert hollers, "Start knocking them out, boys!"

I've got gloves on, but the ground is frozen hard, packed snow and ice. Of course we've got to do fifty, plus one for teamwork, one for fallen comrades, one for pararescue, and for the PJs standing over us. All this with seventy-pound rucks flopping on our backs. This is the first drop session of the day, and already my chest is on fire, my arms jiggly and threatening to give out, my kneecaps dancing. We must have looked pathetic, because before we could finish, Romspert yelled, "Jack up your feet!"

Then we start knocking out flutter kicks until a car comes and we have to get out of the road. A moment of reprieve, and then Tellsworth got creative. "All right, you guys, I want to see you duck walking! Go!" So (again, we're wearing our rucks) we're doing duck walks up the hill and back down. A duck walk is a deep lunge, something like a normal lunge, but the duck keeps the hips and knees low. You never come out of it and rise up, as you would in a normal lunge. The duck walk is an amazing inguinal and core workout.

We duck walked up the road, back down, and back up. Then they told us to drop our rucks. This was welcome news. I tore my pack off and felt so light I almost started to fly. Then they yelled, "Bear crawls." We dropped down on the frozen road and began crawling. "You're bears. Be bears! I can't hear you!"

We started grumbling and growling like camouflaged teddy bears. I remember growling and saying, "*Grr grr,* I'm a big bear. I just came out of hibernation! I'm hungry. *Grr. Grr.*" It was an attempt to maintain a degree of humor in the moment. The PJs' stoic gazes showed no expression of amusement with my Yogi Bear impression.

In the cone world, when you're performing physical acts of training under the direction of a maroon beret, it's called being smoked. They smoked us there on the side of the road for a good half an hour, all the while yelling at us for how slow we had been getting there. "We're only a quarter of the way into this! You guys should have been here ten minutes ago!"

Somewhere during those moments of torture, Koa turned to me and said, "We got this, Jimmy!"

During my years as a runner on a team, I had developed a notion of myself as someone who could keep team members motivated during the hard times. On the march up the mountain I was cheerleading and trying to bust jokes to keep our morale up. Koa was even better than me at this, in terms of leadership. Koa worked wonders that day, motivating us through those hard times, revealing his leadership skills, and for a newbie like me, this was encouraging to see.

Koa, perhaps from his years of grueling football training, had clearly cracked the code. It's simple. You turn around and say to the guy struggling behind you, "Come on, buddy, you can do this!" In helping others, you take your mind off your own pain. By trying to help your buddy, you find it is easier for you. Koa is one of the guys who figured that out early. He's very good at encouraging his teammates to tap into their own potential. He's a really inspiring leader, who preaches teamwork. I would learn to embrace and hone the art of teamwork in the days and years to come.

When Tellsworth and Romspert were satisfied with the smoke session, they ordered us to get our rucks back on and get back to charging up the hill. We were really only making the first major turn up the valley. Normally, this is a breathless spot, in terms of beauty, but for us it was breathless because we were gasping for air. Our breath was creating our own little weather formation, with clouds of steam pouring from our mouths and rising from our bodies. We pushed up the steep, snowy road, each step taking more effort than the last. We reached a clearing overlooking the Anchorage skyline. Of course, the PJs were there to smoke us again.

They ordered us to drop our packs. I was glad to be free of the ruck, but in that moment I learned an important lesson about PJ training. Training challenges are loaded with tricks. When an event seems like it might get easier, you learn to expect that things are about to get more complex. The SEALS have a saying that captures this concept succinctly: "The only easy day was yesterday." PJ training, as with all Special Operations training, follows a similar mind-set.

I learned, at that moment, to never expect things to get easier.

One moment they're yelling at us to drop our rucks and I'm thinking, *Yes!*, and then the next two words out of the Romspert's mouth are, "Buddy carries!"

A buddy carry is just like a fireman's carry. Your buddy gloms on to your back and shoulders like some kind of human leech. Then you pack his ass up the mountain. In my case, the buddy was Major Adrian.

I dropped my seventy-pound pack only to pick up a two-hundred-pound mountain of muscle. It didn't take more than a few steps for me to vow to never again wishfully think that things would get easier.

Here we were, on the side of a mountain, in this nice little clearing of snow-covered spruce and birch, doing buddy carries up and down the steep slope. For all the pain and effort and anguish, I realized something that would make all the difference for my survival in the pipeline. I looked around, soaked in the beauty of my surroundings, the feeling of building camaraderie among these really cool guys struggling with me, and in that moment it came to me: *I love this shit.*

The yell of Romspert ripped me from my little out-of-body dream state, as would often happen during the ensuing years of training. "You guys," Romspert said, "are going even slower than you were before! Ruck back up! You need to get up to the pass in fifteen minutes!"

We were trying. We really were. At this point, Zach Kline started to lag a bit. He was about to crash on us. In my years of running, I recognized this as a blood sugar crash. I had experienced and witnessed enough crashes in races and workouts that I possessed a certain level of paranoia about a crash happening to me. So I made sure I carried a supply of little foil energy packets, or GU packets, stashed in pockets all over my body. GU was, at the time, a popular sports energy supplement. It's a gel with the consistency of cake frosting. You rip the top off of the small foil packet and push the contents into your mouth. Chase with water and repeat.

I handed Zach one packet of orange flavor and another of chocolate. We ended up walking for a while, letting him recover, and that slowed us down, but it wasn't like we were going leave him behind. Although this training was about individual performance, it was also about working as a single unit and doing what it took to finish as a team. We would rather help Zach recover and get through the training day together as a team than as individuals.

The PJs came down off the top of the mountain and intercepted us with the six pax, and they smoked us for a while. There was no chopper. The adding of a chopper to the training scenario was all about turning up that level of anxiety and excitement. "You guys have taken too long and busted the timeline," Tellsworth said. "Load up."

We didn't summit the mountain, but we had made it pretty far, all things considered. This day was designed to inoculate us against the toughest times of the pipeline. This career and this training program certainly teach you how to accept failure. You can't win one hundred percent of the time, and the PJ pipeline starts by setting you up for abject failure. That morning's march up Arctic Valley Road was a perfect example. They started with the mountain march in an attempt to weed us out. But none of us quit on the mountain.

We loaded up in the back of the truck and were told, "Dig into your MREs. You've got half an hour."

We speculated on what challenges could be next on the agenda. It was cold and uncomfortable, but we made it work. We strung out and laid across the truck bed, alternating feet to head in a zipper fashion, sitting on our rucksacks to provide warmth and insulation from the frigid metal of the truck bed. The rucks, with the big weight plates in them, provided little cushion from the jolting of the F-350 down that potholed gravel road. On the ruck up the hill, I was burning up, hot and sweaty. On the truck ride, no longer working my body, I started to shiver and had to dig into my ruck to layer up. Sweating in the cold of winter is not a good idea. I needed to get my shivering under control and be ready for what-ever they threw at us next.

We had no idea, so we ate.

We tore into our MREs as if we'd forgotten to transform back to humans after the bear crawls. That was my first time eating an MRE, and I was excited. I felt like I had accomplished something cool. My first time eating an MRE, and I remember thinking silly Jimmy thoughts. *I'm sure glad that hiking part is over. That stuff was hard!*

They drove us straight to the pool on Fort Richardson army base for my first taste of war in the water. We bailed out of the truck with our rucks, hustled into the pool locker room, and switched into pool clothes. They had secured the pool for our use only, though there were lifeguards and people in the bleachers, observing.

I'd been in the pool with fellow cones who had more pipeline experience. We would work together, training each other for the events and schools to come, so that when the instructors brought the pain, we kind of had an idea how to respond. The bottom line was that you knew the instructors were going to come at you harder than your buddies would.

The PJs came on strong because they knew the pool could really crack a cone. They needed to crack us or bring us as close to cracking as possible. That day in the pool is mostly a blur, but there are a few key moments I'll never forget.

We're standing on the gutter of the pool, all lined up. We're wearing our weight belts, buoyancy compensator vests, and dive masks. We were in a push-up position—the task was to do push-ups and, when they said go, jump in the water. Swim under water to the far side, touch the crack on the bottom, and come up. The only time you were allowed to come up for air was when you had touched the crack on the far side.

This was a new event for me, so I tried my best to copy the other cones, in an attempt to look like I knew what I was doing. At the order, I jumped in and . . . I'd never done this before, and I was wearing this honking big dive mask. I launched, arms stretched out, shooting out with my legs to get as far as I can, with air in my lungs for depth and distance. I flew out, thinking I had made an impressive dive. And then impact. *Boom!*

My dive angle was wrong. My face smooshed against the concrete-like surface of the water and my mask erupted in red. *Wham.* My nose was a blood geyser. I wasn't quitting, though. I swam for the crack, touched it, climbed out of the pool, and returned to the push-up position. And Romspert yells, "Jimmy! You're bleeding. Get the hell out of here!"

I jumped up and ran into the bathroom and plugged my nose up with tissue. My nose continued gushing for ten or fifteen minutes, giving me a strange kind of relief. We'd already been in the pool for a long time, and exhaustion and stress had started to creep in on me. This was a hectic, intense environment, and some of these were new events for me. My bloody nose offered a welcome little break.

While I was sitting with my nose plugged with bloody toilet paper, there was another incident in the pool. It happened to the only guy in our group of cones who wound up quitting. We'll call him Frodo, because he's the first guy I'd ever seen who lost consciousness under water.

The PJs had the guys doing another underwater event, and Frodo lost consciousness. He went limp, and they pulled him up and out, onto the side of the pool. They gave him a couple slaps and he snapped awake and muttered some nonsense.

Frodo had visited the wizard.

"Visiting the wizard" is a term the PJs use for someone who passes out under water. Humans need oxygen to survive. Swimming under water for long periods of time without taking a breath of air can cause one to use up all the oxygen floating in the bloodstream. Your body communicates the urgency and need for air as it uses up its reserves. To be successful, you must make peace with the discomfort of "guppying" for air as the diaphragm desperately tries to initiate air exchange, unaware that the airway is under water.

To break the surface prematurely will bring greater pain on the surface, from instructors, than if you pass out. Passing out can lead to a visit to the wizard. I had heard from the more experienced cones that visits to the wizard are a regular thing to witness if and when I made it to INDOC.

First I had to survive the rest of this hell day.

With Frodo's wizard visit, the PJs gave everyone a time-out and treated him until he was back to normal. I'd finished bleeding, and they cleared me to get back in the pool, just in time for buddy breathing. I was partnered up with Maddamma.

The PJs seemed to take special interest in ripping on Maddamma. They gave him special attention because he was the cone furthest along the pipeline in our group. At this point in his game, he'd already been through INDOC and combat dive school, so he had his combat dive certification. He tried to convince the PJs that he didn't need to do the pool work, but they thought otherwise.

Jeremy Maddamma and I floated, faces underwater. The goal in buddy breathing is to pass a single snorkel back and forth. Jeremy passed to me. I cleared the snorkel by blowing out the water, took a breath, and I passed to him. He gave it back to me and I got "capped" by a tough PJ's hand, placed right over the top of the snorkel, blocking any air. I passed the snorkel back to Jeremy and he got capped. He passed back to me and I got capped, then he got capped and again passed back to me. Capped yet again, I popped to the surface. I inhaled the biggest breath of air I've ever taken. As soon as I broke the surface, the PJ on top screamed at me, "Get your face in the water!"

I stuck my face back under, but as soon as I did, I popped back up. I took another big breath and dove back down. This whole time, Maddamma was trying to feed me the snorkel and was probably thinking I'm the biggest jackass he's ever been in the pool with.

To clear the snorkel, you have to forcefully exhale—you almost spit air into the snorkel to jettison the water out—and then you can take one quick breath. *Poof!* You exhale. Then you take one quick sip of air and pass the snorkel. Your buddy gets a sip and then, in theory, he should pass the snorkel back. But I didn't know what the hell I was doing. I couldn't relax and slow my heart rate. I kept popping up like an old-school toaster—you know, when you're trying to toast two slices back to back and the damn thing just won't stay down?

Up. Down. Up. Down.

I struggled, frustrated and almost on the verge of panic. I couldn't breathe. Those guys pounded on me. I needed air. I couldn't get my breath. My lungs screamed for air. I had to pop. Up again. Down. Up again. Down. The whole time, the PJs were screaming at me, "Get your face in the water! Breathe off the snorkel! Get your face in the water!"

Finally, the whistle blew. I struggled to get my shit together. The PJ challenging us said, "What the hell is going on? Have you done this before, Jimmy?"

And I responded, "Not really. Kind of. But not really, I guess."

"You guess? Okay. Keep your face in the water, breathe off the snorkel, pass it to your buddy. You got it? Stay under!"

"Hooyah, sir!" I said, trying to sound military, despite having never been to basic training and being scared as hell.

So we did it again. And again. When they got tired of buddy breathing, we moved to all sorts of fun stuff that involved nearly drowning. It all went on for what seemed like hours.

As it turned out, that day of torture in the pool would be really handy for me. Once I had survived the buddy breathing session, I knew I might be able to survive the rest of the day. The fear and anxiety began to dissipate.

In retrospect, the smoke session in the pool was one of the most challenging training days of my life. I had a sense of fear that was new to me. Not necessarily a fear of dying but a fear that I might not be able to handle the challenges required to earn my own maroon beret. Plus, I wasn't being challenged by strangers. I was being challenged by potential teammates. In many ways, the impossible march up Arctic Valley and the near-drownings in the pool were me pledging to a fraternity. I've never done that, so maybe it's a horrible analogy, but it was definitely an initial test to gain entrance to an exclusive brotherhood. These were my first baby steps into a rite of passage, and I had to survive if I wanted the 212's support.

After the pool session, we loaded right into the bed of the truck. Our faces clearly displayed the deep utter exhaustion of fighting for our lives underwater. Very little was said as we bumped down the road to our next objective. Mostly we nibbled on snacks and rested. Once again the truck stopped. The sound of the doors opening and closing signaled an end to the brief period of relaxation. The bed of the truck opened, and once again we climbed out, this time back in front of the section, where the day had started. We had completed a day with many challenges that must have been entertaining to see.

The grand finale was a series of ATV races. A PJ would sit on the seat and steer a four-wheeler with the transmission in neutral. We were set up with five quads, which the cones pushed in laps around the section. The race was competitive; the jockeys commanded all the speed they could from the "conemobile," with much glee. The task was hard, but a fun kind of hard.

I successfully completed the day, but I didn't do it alone or in a vacuum. We finished as a team, and a strong team it was: Major Adrian, Koa Bailey, Zach Kline, and Jeremy Maddamma. All of these fine men would continue on, all of us plunging into the PJ/CRO pipeline, ready to sacrifice everything—and the only one of these five not to don the maroon beret would die trying.

One more obstacle posed a daunting roadblock in my path to the pipeline. I had lived through the extended training day, had successfully completed the PAST, but what about my actual past, and that little bit about my former heart condition? Would it keep me from heading off to basic training? All I could do was take the entrance physical and see whether my navy military record would flag me as ineligible.

When it came to my official application to the air force, I thought I would let my navy record speak for itself. I didn't lie about the heart thing, but I definitely didn't voluntarily mention that little piece of trivia. I figured that if I passed the entrance physical—and I would, since I was in pretty good shape—I stood a chance.

I had two things going for me. I was in excellent health, and I was entering just at the moment when military health records were beginning to go digital. My heart passed with flying colors, and before I knew it, I was on a jet headed to Lackland Air Force Base in San Antonio, Texas, for basic training, early in the fall of 2005.

6

·········

Basic Contraband

The thought of basic training put my stomach in a cluster of knots tighter than anything Zach Kline or Roger Sparks could tie, but not for the reasons you would think. The PJs and other cones who had been through basic had filled me with an impending sense of dread. I wasn't worried about the pressure or the stress. I wasn't worried about some asshole drill sergeant harassing me. No, my biggest concern was the coming ten weeks of physical fitness—or rather, the lack thereof. Essentially, basic would be too easy. I'd get out of shape.

Ten weeks of a much-restricted physical fitness regime would be torture. It wasn't at all what I was used to. I needed to be in the best shape of my life, heading into INDOC. During basic training, there was no swimming. The running was very structured, and slow by the standard I needed to be at when I walked through the PJ schoolhouse door on day one. I would need to find a time and a place to stay fit.

I found time to sneak in the extra exercises while I was on night watch. When everyone else was asleep, I'd go into the bathroom and work out in silence, doing push-ups, sit-ups, and flutter kicks. What concerned me the most was my inability to do pull-ups. I could do push-ups and sit-ups, and I would sacrifice sleep to maintain as much of a physical edge as I could, but there wasn't any place or time for me to get in the pull-ups I needed.

Our basic training quarters were three stories tall. The bottom floor held the instructors, offices, and the cafeteria. My flight was on the third floor, and I volunteered for any and all night watch duty. The task on night duty was to make sure no one was trying to kill themselves, fornicate, or sneak in or out. In reality, the main task of night duty was to let instructors in the door, because the place is locked down.

As CQ, charge of quarters (or "watch"), my job was to patrol our small bunk room. The room was mostly bed space, the walls lined with lockers. Rows of bunks ran down the middle, with openings at each end. I sat at a desk on the inside of a steel door at the top of the stairwell. Next to that door was the latrine door. Inside the bathroom we had a bank of unused urinals—unused because we didn't want to clean them. We had to clean the bathrooms every day, and we all mutually agreed, *Nobody pisses in the urinals.* Every morning we cleaned the sinks, shitters, and showers.

I didn't want to do push-ups and sit-ups in the bunk area where everyone was sleeping, and I didn't want anyone stumbling to the bathroom late at night to trip on me. And, to be honest, I didn't want anyone to see me. I was kind of working out in secret. I also didn't want to draw attention to myself. One thing I knew from my previous military time and my toad days around the PJs was that I didn't want to draw extra attention to myself. No one needed to know I felt like I wasn't getting enough exercise.

Night watch posed one problem. Two people were always on duty, so I couldn't really get around the fact that the person on watch with me knew I was working out extra. A few wanted to join me at first. One was this fat kid named Eddie. Eddie seemed motivated, the first night, and I think he imagined he would be all badass, but the morning after, when I asked if he was ready for another night, he said, "No way, dude. I'm too sore. I can't do that shit anymore."

So I trained alone during the middle of the night, working up a sweat in, of all places, the bathroom showers. The showers were the perfect place to work out because it was the cleanest floor in the bathroom. We cleaned the bathroom each morning after we took showers, and then the room sat all day, unused. We would wake up in the morning, go do physical training, or PT, take showers, change into our uniforms, and grab breakfast. After chow, we did all the dorm cleaning. At the end of the day, the shower floors, by my estimate, were cleaner than any space available. I had my own little private workout room.

The one thing I couldn't practice at basic were pull-ups, and it would come back to haunt me. We did pull-ups only a couple of times a week. When we were running laps, they would have us do only five. I needed to be doing fifteen, but the way they had the pull-up routine structured, there was no room for sneaking in extras. Not long after I completed basic, the military began introducing basic training classes composed of people who wanted to try out for one of the air force's more physically demanding schools, like pararescue, combat control, SERE, or explosive ordnance disposal. But, of course, with my typical luck, this new basic course wasn't in place when I needed it. I was in with everyone else, where the standard for pull-ups for the lowest level was zero, slightly lower than the fifteen I felt I would need at INDOC.

Because of my navy experience, I didn't stress out like most people at basic. I knew the game. Fold your underwear a special way because they are going to yell at you if you don't. Don't ask why, just do it, and do it as quick as you can, and then help the guy next to you. The navy experience, as much as I didn't really enjoy my time there, was probably a really good thing.

Aside from not getting any swimming in and not having a place to do pull-ups, the second most stressful thing for me was my drill instructor. My drill instructor wasn't cruel or unfair or aggressive.

No. She was gorgeous. The kind of beautiful that both intimidated and flustered guys. Barely five foot five, and fiery. A hot Asian-Latina-white mix of lovely. If Lucy Liu, Jennifer Lopez, and Marilyn Monroe all mothered the same girl, she still wouldn't be as striking as this woman.

On one of the very first days, while we were getting our hair butchered, the overwhelming need to urinate hit me full force. Completely embarrassed, and about to explode, I approached her. "Drill Sergeant, I have to go to the bathroom. *Please* can I go pee?"

She told me to go ask the building next door. So I sprinted over and asked if I could use the bathroom, but the jerks there simply told me no. So I waddled back to the barber's and told the drill sergeant, "They said no."

She shrugged and said, "Well, I guess you have to hold it."

The three barbers took about half an hour to trim the rest of the flight. I did my best to hold it, and my bladder began to throb. The march back to our building was less than a mile, but it may as well have been on the other side of the world. I'm dying, hitting one of those physical states where the sound of a dripping faucet alone would send a big warm stream down the front of my uniform. Sharp, stabbing pains shot up and down my back; the pressure was like someone was standing on my bladder. I couldn't stand fully erect because the tension on my bladder was too great. I was having a hard time staying in step. Near tears, I saw ahead a small bank of portable toilets.

I stopped, without permission, and begged to use the bathroom. My sergeant halted the rest of the forty-person flight and let me use the outhouse, and if she didn't believe I had to go before, she thoroughly believed when I was done. Everyone could hear the steady blasting stream of piss hitting the plastic urinal. The relief was near orgasmic. My muscles relaxed. I could breathe again. I even felt a little taller and a bit lighter. After I finished, I sprinted back into formation, and one of the guys said, "Jesus Christ! That was a long piss. That took forever!"

Shortly after that, the drill sergeant awarded me the distinction of being our flight's guidon, the dude marching in the front of the flight with the flag. I was selected because I broke the number one rule of any sort of military training: don't stick out. Every moment we marched I was trying to remember if the flag needed to be this way or that way . . . and talk about nervous. I was a lightning rod for every drill instructor's special attention. I was bad enough that drill instructors from other flights would get in my face—not just sometimes but all the time. Most likely because I was the worst guidon in the history of guidons. They were correct, and most of the time I agreed with their belief that I was the last person who should be leading a march.

I hated my role, but small joys can help one endure. Being yelled at wasn't exactly pleasant, but when my drill sergeant stood close, her pretty face inches from mine, her volume turned up to eleven, she was the slightest scent of anything remotely female in a sea of man funk. It was, in a word, heaven. Since she was shorter than me, it was easy to look over her head as she verbally corrected me. When I did look down, I thought, *Wow. She's not so bad. At least this isn't some dude with tobacco-stained teeth and stinky coffee breath. This is pretty good! I think she likes me.*

At the end of the day, we would gather for mail call. This was a special time for trainees. We were starving for anything from the outside. A letter from home or a box from a special person would briefly allow us to escape the rigors of our long days. Packages were handed out first, then letters. All packages were opened in front of the entire class and were closely observed by the instructors, on the lookout for contraband.

I received a handful of letters from loved ones during basic training, but I only received one package, shortly after Thanksgiving, at the end of a cold day of training. We were dressed in gray PT sweats and seated on the cold hard floor outside the drill instructors' office. Like Santa, our instructor hefted a large sack bulging with boxes and letters. She pulled the first package out and called someone's name. He stood at attention next to the instructor as she handed him a small box. The trainee tore into the box to reveal a chocolate orange. He broke it up and passed the pieces to everyone. I sat there, enjoying the delicious chocolate as it melted on my tongue. Not expecting a package, I drifted with the moment of sweet chocolate ecstasy, and then I heard my name being repeated and looked up to see the instructor looking me dead in the eyes across the room.

"Hey, Settle," she repeated. "Do want this package or should I just throw it away?"

Surprised, I sprang up and danced my way through the web of feet and legs as she dangled the box over a garbage can. I wondered who had mailed me a box and what might be in it.

"Airman Settle reporting ma'am!" I snapped to attention next to her and she handed me a package about the size of a shoe box. I noticed the box had something heavy and loose in it that made an audible *thunk* as I tilted it back and forth in my hands while reading the address label.

I expected to see a return address from California, where my grandmother had moved, presents from my mom, or brownies from my brother in Alaska. The name I saw on the return label wasn't any of these. In fact, I didn't recognize the name or address at all. My instructor perceived my hesitation as me needing her help. She snatched the box out of my hand, pulled out a knife, and cut the tape on the top. The object inside made more noise, bouncing around as she handed the box back to me.

With a mild degree of trepidation, I opened the lid slowly, and peered inside. Already confused about why a stranger would send me a package, especially during basic training, I grew increasingly confounded when I pulled out a handful of blue nitrile examination gloves. My peers began to giggle, and a subdued chatter among them began to fill the room. Sweat formed up and down my back as I reached back into the box. I turned to see my instructor eyeing me suspiciously. I pulled out a large, blue-lidded jar of Vaseline.

I began to suspect an epic prank about to explode. Then I pulled out several glossy magazines. I took me a moment to understand what I held in my hand. Pictures of muscle-bound men in suggestive poses with other muscle-bound men.

My instructor and I made this connection at exactly the same time. I immediately dropped the magazines back into the box.

"Contraband. Definitely contraband!" she said, and the entire room erupted in laughter. "Settle, push-ups! On your face! *Now!*"

I dropped to the floor and counted out push-ups while she threatened the same for anyone who thought this was funny. She made a quick phone call and hauled me and the box into the commandant's office. I stood at attention, sweaty and red-faced, as I was interrogated. I had no idea who sent me the box or why they had sent me gloves, lube, and homoerotic pornography. Deep inside, though, I was doing my best to contain how funny it all was. I grew up with a pretty graphic and active family concept of humor. The package contents had a funny implied meaning to me, but the true comedy came from observing the reactions of the series of instructors that rotated through the commandant's office over the next hour or so.

I was returned to my barracks after promising to shape up, and I was told, "You better make sure you don't get any more packages like that or you're through." It was late and everyone was already sleeping as I brushed my teeth and prepared for bed. I didn't need to do push-ups in secret that night.

The guy on night watch came, poked his head in the bathroom door. "Dude, that was awesome," he said, smiling, then turned and left. I splashed water on my face, looked in the mirror, and let the laughter fly.

At some point, perhaps after the porn incident, my drill sergeant somehow keyed into the fact I was going to INDOC, and she did her best to attempt to train me to actually be a good guidon. We were learning how to march for the final graduation ceremony, which for many is a big deal. You march in front of your families. Generals and important people are present. She made a horrible selection, but she was stuck with me. She really should have found someone else for the job. She worked extra, gave me additional time to go downstairs and practice twirls and whirls and fancy stuff with the flag, but it didn't work. I was bad. Beyond bad. There was a point, the day before graduation, when she got in my face and screamed, "Why are you so bad at this, Settle?"

And I yelled back in frustration, "I don't know."

"Well, just don't fuck it up tomorrow!"

"Okay! I'll try!"

But I did.

The next day, in front of all the families and important people, after a series of commands, would come my big test. We rehearsed over and over, and I knew what I had to do, but in the stress of the situation, I blew it. When the instructors gave a "Parade rest!" command, which means you go from standing like a stick to standing like a tepee, with the flagpole at an angle, I thought they were going to say "Present arms!," which is like giving a big hello salute. When they say "Parade rest!," you go into tepee mode and you tilt the flag out just a little bit, but when they say "Present arms!," you raise that flag up as high as you can and you whip it down as hard as you can with a *snap!* And so they said "Parade rest!" and I whipped that flag up high for all—and I mean *all*—to see. *Shit!* There was no recovery after that.

My drill sergeant approached me following the ceremony and said, "It's a good thing you're graduating." I didn't know if that was a threat or a pickup line. I was afraid to ask. Later, I heard about a drill sergeant at Lackland who lost her job for posing in *Playboy*. I can neither confirm nor deny that this was her.

Basic was me trying to keep my edge and my positive attitude, because I was headed straight from basic to INDOC. The way the dates lined up, I was going to be missing the introductory, "easy" week. I would be leaving basic and diving right into week one of INDOC. As a result of the time I spent at night in the shower maintaining my fitness in preparation for INDOC, I was awarded the top male physical performer for the entire air force basic training class. I got a Warhawk certificate and coin for it, Top PT Scorer, but I was in no way ready for what was coming. I would be hitting the ground with a crash out there and would be expected not just to catch up but to be accelerating. The program is set on a crawl, walk, run basis. It doesn't plateau and wait for people to catch up. Every day, the INDOC cadre would be bringing a little more pain than the last.

7

. . . .

Keep Your Chin Up

I missed the pretraining week of INDOC. This is where all the cadre, the instructors, demonstrate all the drills and exercises you'll be facing, but without their withering "harassment." I missed that week and had been struggling to stay in shape at basic, so I was already off on the wrong foot and potentially in trouble from day one.

Fortunately for me, Major Adrian from my Alaska team landed in the same INDOC class as I did. He came to my rescue. He met me in the courtyard the first evening, when I arrived at the dorms that house the PJ trainees. We practiced commands and appropriate responses before I had a chance to screw up in front of the INDOC cadre. He was a major and I was a brand-new airman, right out of boot camp. My ears were still wet, while he was a seasoned military man. My squad sergeant probably should have been out there with me, but Major Adrian, instead of delegating that responsibility, took it as his own.

He helped me tape all my gear up the right way and make sure everything I owned was labeled properly. He showed me how to take white medical tape and put it on the inside of my dive mask with my name facing out through the glass, and then also on the inside. Then he did all the exercises and drills they were going to make us do, stuff that I had never done before: grass and gorilla drills, leaping lizards, donkey kicks, scorpions. Major Adrian spent a good two hours out there, when he could have just relaxed and ordered someone else to prepare me. Or he could have opted to just let me flounder the next morning. Instead, being the leader and brother he was, he got me all spun up himself. I would be ready to go in the morning, thanks to him.

When we finished our workout and were headed into the dormitory, I turned and thanked him. He threw one of his giant arms around my shoulders and said, "Hey man, I'm going to take care of you. You take care of me. We're going to take care of each other. We're going to rock this, Jimmy."

The next morning, my first day of INDOC, nearly a hundred men stood at attention on the large concrete pad. Two giant green painted feet covered the cement beneath our feet. Each of the trainees appeared to be a fine, nearly perfect specimen, each at the top of his game physically, each with his eyes on the prize. Every one of us knew we might not be standing there in ten weeks, but we knew we couldn't entertain those thoughts, not that early on. We all knew the staggering numbers. In each class of eighty to one hundred trainees, at best only twenty will finish. Sometimes less. Sometimes zero. The attrition rates for INDOC are 80 to 90 percent.

The numbers standing on that pad the first day would get whittled down very drastically by the end of the pipeline, and even further with all the additional courses one must take to acquire the maroon beret of a PJ. The SEALS have their trident; the marines have their eagle, globe, and anchor; the Army Special Forces have their Green Berets; and the PJs have the maroon beret. That maroon beret is the goal of every man who reaches INDOC. A beret in any of the special operations units is a coveted item, and one of the primary things that makes any object a coveted one is how hard that particular object is to obtain.

Those first ten weeks at INDOC are just that: indoctrination into this particular branch of the Special Forces. From sunup to sundown, the job of the instructors is to do two things: to prepare the few who will make it and to weed out those who are unfit for the maroon beret.

Elimination happens in a couple different ways. You can fail to meet standards and be unable to progress during the INDOC fitness standard evaluations that every trainee must meet, every week, to progress through the course. If you fail an evaluation, you are given a second chance. If you fail the second attempt, then sayonara! You're out. If you're lucky and the cadre of instructors likes you, there is a chance you'll get invited back. An invite to return for a second attempt at INDOC is called "being recycled." If they don't ask you back? Time to think of a new career field.

Failure to meet standards can happen in other ways, too, and the practice extends beyond INDOC and into subsequent courses. It could be the inability to meet the stringent academic standards. If you're not maintaining your general academic standards, dive school standards, paramedic academics, or the free fall standards, then that poor performance can get you kicked out, too.

INDOC is incredibly tough. It's ten weeks that are designed to make recruits quit, and most of them do. They quit by failing to meet standards, or they choose the most popular route of all: self-elimination. Soldiers have few choices in the military. INDOC is different. As a trainee, you are allowed to leave the course at any time your heart desires. There are two ways to self-eliminate. One is called "quitting by action." This occurs when you simply stop doing what the instructors are telling you to do. This happens all the time. The body and the mind conspire and suddenly you're unable to jump back in the pool or unable to take another step. The cadre will yell at you and get in your face and insist you carry out the task at hand, and if you don't or you just simply can't? You've "quit by action."

Everyone tells him- or herself, *I'm never going to quit. I'm never going to say I quit.* But the rigors and trials of INDOC will take men to the point where mind, soul, and body cannot go on any further. I've seen the biggest, toughest guys you've ever met in your life come apart in the pool. Early on, I saw a man who I thought would skate through INDOC totally collapse inward like a dying star. As he sat on the edge of the pool, he couldn't make those words come out of his mouth. He was frozen, in a catatonic state, sitting and staring off into space, rocking slightly, crying. Most who reach their cracking point don't get back in the pool or don't get back underwater, or they can't seem to put their boots back on and pick up their ruck. When you start to believe the words of doubt in your mind that are telling you *I'm not doing it anymore, I'm over this,* you are quitting by action.

The second, and manliest, way to quit involves a small air horn. A small plastic cone screwed on to a can of compressed air. At INDOC, whether you're in the pool or trudging around Lackland carrying a telephone pole or a long, heavy steel rail, the air horn is present. If you're done, if INDOC has broken you, or if you've realized you don't have what it takes, or if you're scared and don't want to spend another moment struggling for air at the bottom of the pool . . . the ever-present air horn awaits you. All you need to do is walk over and grab the damn thing, hold it up in front of your classmates. They might try to stop you, if they see you. They might call out to you, try to give you that little bit of moral support you need. Even the cadre might question you: "Are you sure you want to do this?"

But, for most, by that point quitting has infiltrated the mind like some sort of contagion. Few can turn back once the horn has been picked up. A decision has been made.

Once you give that one loud blast—*honk!*—and say, "I quit!," it's over. Go grab your shit from the dorm, go sit outside in the court-yard, and wait until the bus comes to get you and take you away from the crucible of fire.

And sometimes the contagion will spread to others, in succession, like waves of a plague.

Honk. Honk. Honk. Trainees quitting left and right.

Look what you started.

Sometimes three or four people quit at the same time. In the pool house, the first couple weeks, it sounded like a traffic jam with the all the horn honking. So much noise echoing off the glass walls and ceiling. *Honk. Honk. Honk.*

This system of elimination is in place the whole way through the PJ pipeline. Until you are a beret-toting PJ, you can be dropped for failure to meet standards or by self-elimination. Every day is an evaluation day. Every day, that air horn sits waiting.

That morning, my first day at INDOC, I didn't know I would be witness to so much emotional turmoil. Men melt under the pressure. Guys twice as strong, twice as successful, and seemingly much more put together than me would suddenly quit. We joked and laughed at breakfast and by lunchtime those men were gone.

I don't remember exactly how many guys started on day one of my first class, but when we sat around the eight-lane pool, wearing Speedos and T-shirts with our names stenciled on them, elbow to elbow, we went almost halfway around. Easily eighty to a hundred hopeful pararescue candidates jumped in the water that first day. And those first couple of days, the buses kept coming for the ones who chose to pick up the horn.

Sometimes, in the middle of the night, guys would get into their own heads, and once or twice during the week, I awoke to find them dressed in their blues, their formal uniform, instead of the normal PT gear we wore to get our morning sweat on. A guy dressed in his blues uniform in the morning meant only one thing. He was formally quitting. The next move for a trainee in his uniform was the walk of shame over to the schoolhouse to inform the cadre he'd quit.

This was crazy to me. Each time, I felt bad for those guys. They'd given so much of themselves. So much time and energy to get to that point. They would be returning home, having to explain to their families why they quit. Perhaps coming up with excuses, or maybe just telling them the truth: *INDOC is impossible.*

But I didn't quit. I was stubborn. And there was something about INDOC that I found exciting, and even fun. I visualized my success. I saw myself completing the physical challenges ahead of me. I imagined ways to work around the problems and obstacles ahead.

I never once visualized myself crawling out of the pool, hobbling over to the air horn, and letting a blast of air signal that INDOC had weeded me out, too. There was to be no quitting for me. I couldn't see myself returning to the shoe store. I also didn't see myself enlisted but *not* a PJ. I also wasn't about to let down Chris Robertson, the Alaska PJs, or other cones who were rooting for me. Plus, I had Major Adrian going through INDOC by my side. I wasn't quitting.

The irony about quitting at INDOC is this: at the schoolhouse, where all the instruction and indoor physical standards testing takes place, there is a green sign with white letters, right between the exit sign and the top of the doorjamb, that reads, "Never quit." Each time out of the building, we would jump up, touch that sign, and yell, "Hooyah! Never quit!" For some, these were hollow words, spoken out of duty. For others, "Hooyah! Never quit!" was a battle cry of fierce devotion.

I knew that if I was going to get eliminated from INDOC it would be due to one thing and one thing only: pull-ups.

At the end of training days, early on, it was clear who was seriously dedicated by the way people maintained their edge. Most times, guys would go to bed early. No partying. The dedicated wanted their full physical and mental reserves for the challenges, which build as the weeks progress. You had to be prepared, when the instructors had a wild hair up their butt and decided to run you extra hard. Those were the days when you could tell who was taking care of themselves and who was just barely getting by.

I was supremely focused on how I lived my life during INDOC, too. I wasn't superstitious, per se, but I wouldn't sleep comfortably unless my bag was packed and I was ready to rock and roll at a moment's notice. I knew there was a strong chance those instructors could bust in through the doors at any time in the middle of the night, and they would have us out there on the pad doing PT, and I better have my gear squared away or it was not going to be good. The time to be packing a bag is not when somebody is yelling, or when the rest of my team is doing push-ups while they wait for me. These were important lessons, which would come in handy downrange in Afghanistan. You want to have all your gear wired tight, so when you're in the middle of action your stuff is ready to go.

During my time as a trainee, one of the prevailing topics of conversation among cones at INDOC was about Hell Night, an extended training day, similar to my experience with the Alaska team. Every class experiences Hell Night. No two classes have the same day or challenges. One class made it all the way to the final week before Hell Night descended upon them. For other classes, Hell Night came as early as week two. Cones would gather around meals or late at night in the dorms and speculate on when our Hell Night would come and what it might be like.

The extensive training by the Alaska team had psychologically prepared me for Hell Night. I felt nervous, but confident. I experienced the Alaskan version and survived it, and that success gave me a lot more faith in myself and in what I could endure. I wasn't as intimidated by Hell Night as long as I was prepared for it. I had my ruck packed and, as far as superstitions went, I always had extra food and socks in my bag, because I knew the night was going to be as savage as they come. The comforts of a little food and some dry socks can make all the difference.

My first real Hell Night came on a Monday, right before the half-way point in the training. Mondays consist of an entire day of evaluations. They were always a grueling day in and of themselves, requiring your best effort to meet the escalating standards. Imagine an entire day of running, swimming, push-ups, sit-ups, pull-ups, and more.

I approached each event as if it was a world championship event, but the day didn't go as planned for me. I failed to meet the pull-up standard. I would have a second chance later in the week, but the first taste of failure was unpleasant. Pull-ups came early in the day, so I had to compartmentalize the frustration over the failure until after I got through the rest of the day's evals.

We were all drained by evening, and the instructors were casual. Right before we were released for the day's final push-ups and sent to dinner, the cadre formed us up and, very casually, said, "Good job today, guys. Good job. But why don't you just go out on the pad and *get ready for Hell Night*!"

Then shit went crazy.

I remember my heart sinking. I thought, *Oh, no! No! Not now!*

Since they don't tell you when Hell Night will be, it's a surprise and a complete mindfuck. They totally leave you in the dark and catch you off guard. I remember being scared but excited. I think just the idea that it was Hell Night was more difficult to handle than the actual activities it entailed.

We started out on the pad, doing endless calisthenics. The cadre took turns blasting us with water and smoking us. We started off with push-ups, where my arms, legs, and knee caps jiggled, and every time I went down I wasn't sure if my arms could push me back up. When they were tired of watching us suffer, they flopped us over for flutter kicks. But now we were wearing combat boots, and those things got heavy. Just a couple hundred of these flutter kicks are muscle destroyers. They chew up your legs until they are noodles. But they weren't done with us, not by a long shot. They had us get back on our faces, cranking out more push-ups. It went on until every muscle was cooked. Then came the command to gear up and get ready to run. Trying to figure out how to get up and run after that workout, commanding my numb legs to keep moving, proved challenging indeed.

We moved like molasses, so the instructors pulled out a training aid called "the log." These were two giant telephone poles, each painted with green feet on the ends. These are team-building training aids—heavy and huge. A telephone pole requires a team effort to move. We lifted the log in unison onto our shoulders. Everyone zippered in on either side. Walking required synchronization, because if someone was out of step it could be catastrophic for everyone. The count always started with your outside foot, then your inside foot. The jodies always went, "You're in. You're out. You're in. You're out." And the songs went from there.

At first, this was fun. We were motivated and tough. Someone would yell, "Yeah! Let's go boys! Let's get some!" Then, after about an hour, the flames of motivation began to wither. Our once loud chants devolved into muted words of encouragement: "Okay, boys. We can do this. Come on." And then, still later, as there seemed to be no relief from the oppressive weight of the log, motivation began to wane and our thoughts became *What the fuck are we doing? I didn't even know humans could move poles like this. We could have built a log cabin by now with all the wood we've moved.*

The cadre had an array of these training aids. From the log, we moved to the steel railroad track; we zippered up and carried it the same way. I realized, during these log- and rail-carrying events, that it paid to be average size. The really tall guys carried a disproportionate amount of weight. The little guys, on the other hand, had a hard time even reaching the log. The log and rails were terrible for them.

Then came the Zodiac, a fifteen-foot rubber boat with no motor. One cadre would sit inside what he called his Cadre Cadillac.

Naturally, the cadre wanted us to jody everywhere we went, and when we sang songs he didn't like, he would yell, "Change the radio station, cones!"

We got smoked there on the pad and around the schoolhouse for hours, but no one quit. This was just the warm-up, though. It wasn't until we got to the pool that things really started to happen. Bear in mind, we'd already been in the water all day, performing evaluations, so even the most pool-savvy dudes were done with being in the pool that day. But we were trying to get that maroon beret and you've got to man up! The cadre tightened the screws by making us wear our uniforms into the pool, turning the lights off, and putting glow sticks on us to make sure they could see when we stopped moving.

As we got into the pool, I remember being scared shitless. Swimming under water for twenty-five meters on one breath with a uniform on seemed impossible. Looking down through my mask at the bottom of the pool after I launched, I realized instantly that my uniform was a real drag. Normally when I swam under water I could rocket across the pool, but not fully clothed. I would sweep my arm for a forward stroke and glide, but my forward progress was nonexistent. Usually I could glide for two or three seconds on a stroke, but there was no gliding with my uniform.

As soon as I stopped moving my arms, my body stopped moving. *Oh shit . . . This is going to be a long night.* The additional drag made swimming under water across the pool brutal. Every stroke was like swimming through concrete. The increased drag and effort brought a craving for air almost immediately. I couldn't get the hang of it at first, and I think the instructors loved the hell out of our slow asses, because they swarmed all over the place and constantly sharked us, hitting and grabbing us, and then latching on and taking a ride on our uniforms as we pulled them through the water. Swimming across the bottom of the pool, I felt like a sea turtle with hungry sharks swooping in on me.

Above the surface, it was a deafening, chaotic mess. There were sirens, people screaming, whistles, and overall pandemonium. Trainees filled the pool when we started, but the horrors in the water went on for several hours. And, as if the pool could leak men, it did. Finally the cadre ordered us out of the water, yelling, "Gear up for a ruck march!" As we scrambled to move out, I noticed that our ranks had thinned significantly. Loading our rucks onto our backs outside the pool house was the first time we had a chance to look around to see who had survived the pool session.

There was no time to ponder the losses to our group, because the cadre once again began pushing us. We marched double time to the golf course with all our gear on our backs, and then to a new place, the obstacle course. They gave us a few minutes to wolf down an MRE dinner there in the grass as the sun dimmed toward night. Then they sent us into the obstacle course, which proved to be more fun than hellish. I caught the tail end of a fiery sunset, the sky a swirl of clouds, light and dark. I stole moments on the crazy log, rope, and steel structure to look around, to take in the sky and the surreal scene before me. We ran the course for a couple hours, and I remember thinking, *This isn't so bad. I can deal with this.*

Once again, I fooled myself into thinking things might get easier.

The cadre yelled, "Gear back up, boys! To the pool!" We rucked several miles across the sleeping air force base, back to the pool. Each step was just pure dread. Rucking is like going backpacking with some of your friends, but we're all moving at a seven-minute-mile pace, double time. Normally it can be sort of a fun feeling, running in a group like that, but this was running in a pack of dread. We knew that with every step we were getting closer to the real pain. With each footfall, the horrors of the dark pool house returned.

The real water torture was coming. That first pool session was bad. The next would be worse, guaranteed. It was difficult to push away thoughts of impending doom. Were we marching into our own demise or would we somehow survive? I had a notion that the cadre were about to really drop the hammer.

I was right.

As soon as we arrived for our second round in the water, the stress inoculation began. At one point, I stuck my head out of the water and, amid the cadre's screaming and the strobe lights flashing, I saw the instructors grabbing all our rucks and emptying them into the pool. We had to dive in and find our own personal gear, over and over.

"You guys are not doing it fast enough! Do it again!" they shouted.

In hindsight, that exercise wasn't all that bad. At first it was every man for himself, sifting through the floating and sinking gear that littered the pool. Eventually, though, we began to work as a team to gather our stuff, working to identify one another's belongings. Not like the underwaters in your battle dress uniform, your BDU, where the sharks are hanging on you, where there is no teammate to help and survival is your own responsibility.

Then came buddy breathing with the snorkel. The instructors work hard to deny you a breath of air or to strip the snorkel out of your hands. You have to stay under the surface the entire time. Unlike my extended training day back in Alaska, the cadre would do their best to deny every and any breath of air. I had to stay under the whole time. If I popped my head up, like I did that day in Alaska? Failure. Drop the snorkel? Failure. Let go of my buddy? You guessed it: failure.

And if your buddy does any of those things, it's a failure for both of you. So it's not just an individual event to push yourself, you also have to make sure your buddy gets there too. *Hooyah teamwork!* As the intensity of the training escalates during buddy breathing, your body and mind scream for air. You want that snorkel back as fast as you can get it, because you want air, you need air. But the fastest way to get air to yourself is to get it to your friend as fast as you can. That is the only way to survive the hell of buddy breathing.

In constant motion, you grab the snorkel and force it back and forth, to and from your buddy. Sometimes, when you're taking just the teeniest sip of air off the mouthpiece and you've pushed all the water out with the last bit of air in your lungs, given out the last remaining giblet of air you've got, the instructor puts his hand over the top just as you inhale. Now there is no air coming into your lungs. Time to pass the snorkel to your buddy, right now. You fight your basic human thoughts of self-preservation: *I need air! I need air!* The way to get oxygen is completely counterintuitive. You must give away your only source of air. It's a mental game as much as a test of fortitude, and this particular session was extremely brutal.

Multiple instructors hovered in the water over each pair of cones, hammering us over and over. They allowed for no recovery time. Normally, between sessions, there would be a minute or two of recovery, but the only recovery period came when the instructors rotated. When they changed positions, we floated with a snorkel.

This was the fiercest buddy breathing session I'd ever been a part of, and I was not alone. I managed to stay in the pool, and I passed the snorkel back and forth with my buddy. All around us, cones dropped like flies. The cones who didn't quit stayed in the pool, as did the bloodthirsty cadre. Eventually it got to the point where there were more and more instructors per pair of trainees. Men were quitting left and right.

We called it the meat grinder the next morning, because it just chewed so many people up. They quit by failure. They quit by action.

"I can't do it anymore!"

"Fuck this. I'm done!"

"I quit."

"I quit."

"I quit."

Some just sat on the side of the pool, muttering, "I quit."

Quitting became a contagion. Every time I popped my head out of the water and took an assessment of what was going on around me, there were fewer and fewer cones left in the water.

This is crazy! That guy? Where is that guy? Another one gone?

The pool is often referred to as the great equalizer. The quitting

fueled me. Some of the guys who quit were dudes I thought were
sure things.

And damn. They quit. But I'm still here.

It was almost a relief. I knew the physical pain manifesting
itself with the mental anguish was temporary, and I was succeed-
ing at not succumbing to the weakness.

After what seemed like an eternity in the pool, we were once
again ordered out—and told to board a bus. We scrambled as quickly
as we could away from the horrors of the pool and on to the next
challenge. Once we were on the bus, it was clear that our numbers
had been slashed. We'd lost so many that every guy could have his
own seat. The bus took us around base and eventually stopped at
the front of the schoolhouse. We spilled out of the bus and quickly
organized our rucks in neat rows as we did our "ins," pull-ups and
push-ups. Then we scurried into the schoolhouse, delirious and
loopy. We stood at attention as the cadre entered. The tension in
the air was palpable. *What the hell did the cadre have in mind now?* I
feared we would get a smoke session on the pull-up bar.

The mountain of a man who had been leading the cadre that
night tossed a small cardboard box at the feet of what remained of
our class. He ordered the lead cone to open the box and pass out
what was inside. *What trickery is afoot now?* As the box came around
to me, I saw the contents. The blue fabric, the coveted blue ascot,
the symbol that a cone has survived Hell Night.

"Congratulations, cones!"

We did it.

I survived Hell Night. But those damn pull-ups had spelled
trouble for me. I had failed to reach the previous week's standard
for pull-ups. We would retest the following Monday. I had one
chance left.

Major Adrian was the only guy I knew with a car, and Sunday
morning was the only day we knew we weren't going to get messed

with by the instructors. A guy could almost relax, if he weren't so exhausted and beat up.

Major Adrian started a tradition, taking us for Sunday breakfast at the Medina Diner, a little greasy spoon right outside the gate. He always gave me a ride. Without Major Adrian, I'd be stuck eating at the chow hall seven days a week. Bellying up to the chow trough gets old really quick. Some of the guys in the pipeline would get food delivered, and it smelled good. I understood the need to eat some nonmilitary chow, but at the same time, I wasn't gambling with the bloating and pipe-cleaning food delivered in grease-soaked bags. I probably passed up quite a few decent meals during INDOC because I wanted to make sure that I wasn't going to screw myself, digestively speaking. I did my best to make wise dietary decisions. Every day but Sunday I stuck to the basics delivered at the mess hall. Sunday was the exception. I'd hop in Major Adrian's ride and within minutes would be gorging myself on some hearty food. Biscuits and gravy with scrambled eggs and bacon. If I was feeling extra sporty, I might add a few waffles on top of that.

I would estimate we were eating well over five or six thousand calories a day. We were physically active from five in the morning until five at night on a good day, often later. In the evenings, we worked right up until chow time, and sometimes beyond.

I'm not complaining about that. I wanted the challenges. I wanted INDOC to be difficult. I didn't want my time there to be easy. I wanted to earn my place on the team. I wanted to earn that beret, not just have it handed to me for being handsome. I wanted to look at other guys who had earned the beret and know that I was a peer, a brother.

Those Sunday mornings with Major Adrian were special. He exemplified true leadership. The team flowed really well under his guidance. We sat around the breakfast table, reflecting on where we'd come and what we had left. We had made it through Hell Night, and midterms loomed. Sometimes, in my memory, I sit at that table across from Major Adrian, wishing I had taken a few more moments to really absorb how special that diner time was for all of us.

Midterm day arrived and I ran the five-miler with ease. The first event of the eval was the running, and I never stressed my footwork. While on the track below the schoolhouse, I worked to keep myself in the upper third of the group, to make sure I passed and to make sure my pace would be on target.

After the run, the cadre took the times and wrote them down on a clipboard. I don't recall what my finishing time was, but I was well within the time frame. We did a five-minute cool-down stretch, then jogged as a group up the little hill toward the schoolhouse. We removed our shoes at the concrete pad. Cones, any time they are on the pad, unless they are doing some kind of work, take off their shoes. The pad is kept in a state of cleanliness unlike any other concrete block on the planet. The "set backs" and those who are waiting to go or are injured are tasked with cleaning the pad every day.

From there we trotted inside in our stocking feet. In the middle of this room, on the left wall, were the pull-up bars and wrestling mat floors. On the right was a gym area with free weights, dumbbells, machines, kettlebells, and CrossFit gear. Beyond that area, straight back, was the cadre area, a place where students weren't allowed unless they were going to quit or the cadre hauled their asses back for some reason or another.

The schoolhouse floor was foam, rubberized, with an enormous PJ pararescue logo around the middle. This is where the academic portion of the training is combined with the physical. When you're not in the pool or in the gym or crawling through mud and having a hose sprayed in your face, you're studying. On the periphery of the wall in the main gym room were pull-up bars. A few feet below the ceiling, but above the pull-up bars, was the requisite PJ reading material. These were three sentences the cadre would often point out and demand to have read back to them. The black block letters of the PJ creed around the perimeter read, "It is my duty as a pararescueman to save life and to aid the injured. I will be prepared at all times to perform my assigned duties quickly and efficiently, placing these duties before personal desires and comforts. These things I do that others may live."

The first fitness level standard in the gym was push-ups.

I had finally started feeling like I could handle the eighth week, the final standard test for push-ups. I wasn't worried about those seventy-five push-ups, and because of all my cross-country skiing, I crushed the sit-ups. I only had to pace myself and make sure I didn't do a full burnout, but as long as I kept a good pace going, and kept breathing, I could pretty much go hard the entire two minutes and get well past the required eighty sit-ups needed in the final week.

And then the pull-ups.

At fitness evaluation time, the team forms up, lining up with the pull-up bars, an even number across. At my turn, I stood before the pull-up bar and waited for the commands.

Everything during INDOC is command driven. Perhaps I left that out. *Everything* is command driven. The command came.

"Cones! Ready! All right, gentlemen. The first event is pull-ups. Today's standard is eleven. You must meet the standard in sixty seconds. A pull-up is from a dead hang, totally straight arms, and pull up. No kipping. No wiggling your feet. No kicking your legs. No rocking your hips. Just a straight pull-up until your chin clears the bar and you look down and make eye contact with your instructor. Then all the way back down to a dead hang. That is one pull-up! You have sixty seconds to complete eleven pull-ups. Cones, take your positions!"

At that command, I took a quick couple steps to the pull-up bar and turned around, my back facing the wall. I could see my instructor and the faces of my classmates. I jumped up, and once everyone was in position, in a dead hang, the cadre yelled, "Cones! Begin!"

I tried to start off strong, and to keep track, but the instructors counted silently, using one of those silver clickers you see bouncers use at the door of a bar. *Click. Click. Click.* If you don't hear a click, the pull-up, for whatever reason, doesn't count. Sometimes you can hear it click, and at the same time there are these damn clicks all around the room. It sounds like you're in a watchmaker's shop.

I struggled. I pulled as hard as I could, giving everything I had. In my head I counted fourteen. But it was probably more like twelve, and the last three were hard-earned, where I shook and barely reached the bar. I tried with every ounce of life I had left, giving that bar all that I could muster. My hips wanted to engage and rock up, because I knew if I could get a little jerk I could get my chin up there and score that final pull-up.

But pull-ups, done in required military form, must each start from a complete dead hang, and after just a few, the muscles tire out. The pull-up is a difficult exercise in the best of circumstances.

I managed to get up to the bar in the final seconds, but I rocked a little at the end, just as the lead instructor yelled out, "Time!"

The cadre watching me said, "Whoa! Almost there, Settle! If you'd have just gotten that last one!"

I dropped down to the floor. Stunned. Not quite sure what the cadre meant. We stood at attention, and everyone the room remained dead quiet. I think everyone knew. The main instructor walked down the line with the clipboard and called out each of our names to the instructor.

"I've got Settle."

"What are his numbers?"

"Ten."

My heart sank.

Ten.

I needed eleven.

My teammates said things like "It's okay, Jimmy! You can do it!"

The events went on, and the thing is, even if you fail to reach a standard, you still have to continue performing. If you want to have a chance at staying in the pipeline, you don't quit. Even if you failed and are technically out of the course. Not if you want a second shot at

INDOC. I demolished the remaining events for the day. I had to show the cadre that I had the spirit and the can-do attitude of a PJ. I wasn't going to let failure hold me down. I knew I had to earn the right to return.

I also knew I'd failed, and this was my second time failing the pull-ups. My guts twisted up on themselves, but I knew I had to put my feelings in a bottle and put that bottle into a fuel can and use that as energy to make it through the rest of the day. I couldn't let the negative energy bring me down. I'd done that before, in running, converting negative angst into positive performance. There were times I just hated life, and I took it out on running. I transformed into a runner that way. This was one of those times where I crushed the rest of the day.

If you're red on something twice, meaning you failed to meet a standard the second time, you get recycled. The failure was a shock. I knew I wasn't good at pull-ups, but I wasn't ready to have such a simple exercise kill my dream.

At the end of the day the instructor, Sergeant Pack, approached me. "Settle. See me at the schoolhouse. Need to talk to you."

"Hooyah, Sergeant," I said.

I stayed behind at the schoolhouse after we finished the day. The rest of the class took off. I approached the cadre area. When I reached the line on the floor, the designated "Do not cross" area, I read the instructions posted on the wall, the rules of how to enter. It felt very *Wizard of Oz*-like. I followed the instructions—knocked three times on the wall and then announced myself.

"Airman Settle, to see Sergeant Pack!"

"Hold on, Settle," he replied. "I'll be right there."

To put it bluntly, Sergeant Pack is a giant of a man. I liked to call him Mount Pack. The man is huge. At least ten feet tall and two tons of muscle. He looks like one of those strongmen you see on television, the kind of guy who could tie a rope around his waist and pull a 747 jetliner. Sergeant Pack is a PJ version of one of those men. It was incredible to watch him do just about anything. Despite his enormous size and scary aggressiveness in the water, however, as a human, Mount Pack was as good as they come. He instantly made me comfortable when I stepped into the room.

He sat me down, studied me for a moment, and then said, "Good job today. Bummer on the pull-ups, though." I nodded. I didn't know what to say, but I felt a level of relief that he and the other cadre recognized how hard I had worked after my failure on the bar.

"Do you want to try again?" he asked.

"Hooyah, Sergeant, I sure do."

"Okay, so you'll be set back. You've got one more shot. We'll see you in a couple weeks."

It was that easy. He didn't' make me feel bad. He didn't sweat me.

I hustled back to my dorm room and dropped off my gear. I was devastated, but not inconsolable. I had a second shot, and I knew I could do it.

I sought out Major Adrian. He was my Alaska cone team leader *and* someone I liked, respected, and worked well with. He also knew me, understood where I was coming from. I knew he could mentor me through the setback process. He immediately made me feel better.

"Man, you got this," he said. "I know you can do this. *You* know you can do this. No problem. Just keep working on those pull-ups. Keep your chin up. You got this, Jimmy. You got this."

8

· · · · · · · · ·

Major Adrian

My talk with Major Adrian gave me the balls and confidence to call the Alaska team back home. I was nervous and disappointed, and I was sure they would feel the same way, sending me all the way from Alaska to fail out because of a few lousy pull-ups.

Within seconds, talking to my chief, I felt relief. Essentially he said, "No big deal. We'll just keep you down there, keep you training. Keep your head up. Hang in there, buddy."

I'm sure Major Adrian must have set the tone that allowed me to get my second chance. He must have called and told them I was a motivated dude, and trying hard. I suspect he had already paved the way for the home support in allowing me my second shot at INDOC. His kindness, guidance, and friendship made all the difference, and it only added to the jolt I was soon to get.

They granted me a couple days of leave before I would be recycled. I wanted time to regroup, rest my aching body, and take a little break from the endless physical and mental rigors of INDOC. On my first day of leave, driving to the airport to pick up a friend coming to visit from Alaska, my cell phone rang.

It was Chris.

I'd been wondering how long it would take for word to spread of my failure. "Jim," he said. "I'm really sorry. I heard about what happened and I'm just really sorry, man."

I could tell from the serious tone of Chris's voice that he was doing all he could to support me. Little did he know that I was doing fine. The setback was only going to improve my chances, as I saw it. I tried to let him know I would be okay.

"Well, thanks, buddy," I said. "I appreciate your concern. I'm going to be okay. I got this, Chris." There was that sense of brotherhood again. I loved it. That kind of compassion and care meant everything to me. Family. These PJs were the best sort of humans. I was in the right place.

"Well, good," he said. "Don't quit or anything. You can do this. I just feel really bad." And he just kept going on and on, and then there seemed to be this disproportionate sense of concern for me, especially for me being set back for some damn pull-ups. I actually expected Chris to be saying things more along the lines of "Come on, you big fat pussy! Get your chin up to the bar!"

But he wasn't. His tone held this deep, serious concern. Perhaps he'd heard something about me and was worried I was taking the setback as more than a setback?

I'm not sure when or how it happened, but at some point in the conversation we both figured out we weren't talking about the same thing. My memory of the exact words from this point on is a bit gray. My vision blurred and I actually had to pull over to the side of the road and put the car in park.

"What exactly are you talking about, Chris?" I asked.

"Major Adrian," Chris said. "What are you talking about?"

"Being set back for . . . What about the major?" I asked.

Silence.

"Chris?" I said. "Chris?"

My mind couldn't quite piece together what the silence meant. Major Adrian didn't quit. I knew that. I couldn't even find the words to ask Chris what the hell he wasn't saying.

"You haven't heard? Shit. Oh, shit. I'm sorry, Jimmy. The major. Adrian is gone."

The rest of the conversation, the exact details of what was said in those minutes, was mostly lost in a pool of tears. This whole time I thought Chris was talking to me about being set back, but he was actually calling to express condolences about the loss of Major Adrian. The major had died, just hours earlier, during a training event in the pool. Chris assumed I was there in the water. That I witnessed his death. I could have been—I *should* have been there—but I wasn't.

The news sent me into shock. I couldn't even process how to feel. No one saw it coming. I think later they determined he died of heart problems. A heart too big, too generous, too kind. They said he died under water. I don't know the full details. Everything I know about his loss is cone rumors and gossip. But what I do know for a fact was that he went unconscious under water and never came back.

Major Adrian was a hell of a man. A beast. A strong man. I'll tell you what, if that is how he died, I know he died doing something he really wanted. It sounds messed up, but he died trying to achieve a dream. He had a goal and he gave everything trying to reach it. Not many people are lucky enough to die that way, to go out doing what they want, chasing a dream. Too many of us are dying terribly slow and painful deaths, letting our dreams wither away without ever taking so much as a step toward achieving them.

That weekend they had a memorial service at the church next to the dorms where we'd all been living and struggling together. Everyone was there, all the cones and all the instructors. Some of the Alaskan team came down, too.

Major Adrian's departure left a void for many of us.

I learned something about pararescue. It is an awesome career, and there are some great men, but the field is a high-stakes game.

I think people forget what we willingly do to ourselves in order to save perfect strangers. Even in training, we were living to that motto, "That others may live." Think about what that means. To be a PJ you're willing to sacrifice your own life so that others may live. Those are easy words to say, but to put a creed like that to the test? Not many people have, and not many people will.

The loss shook me, but I tried to turn the pain into something positive, just as Major Adrian would have wanted. I kept the flyer from his funeral taped in my dorm closet. I told myself, *I've got to do this for Major Adrian.*

Later, when I got back up to Alaska, there were pictures of him on the walls. The 212th had accepted him as a brother and missed him as a brother, and even though he technically didn't complete the pipeline or get his beret, he earned it.

Major Adrian never gave up.

I vowed to myself to do the same.

In the weeks that followed the loss of my friend, I became a pull-up machine. I had an advantage: the failure came in an area that I knew I could improve. I knew that, for a few weeks before the next class, I could really work the bar.

By the time I got my second and final shot at INDOC, I would be able to do more than twenty pull-ups, something that seemed impossible a month earlier.

In a way, the setback was a minor blessing, because now I knew I could pass the first half of INDOC. I had that in the bag. The only thing that had slowed me down was something physical, which I had taken care of, so now it was mostly learning the new academic material in the second half. I've left out all the technical and academic components of INDOC. They work your mind just as hard as your body. My setback reduced the stress of wondering whether I could make it through the first four weeks.

When I began INDOC for the second time, I owned the pull-up

bar, in addition to entering the course without the same level of anxiety and stress. This little advantage gave me the mental freedom to help cheer on my classmates and really be encouraging and positive. The first half of INDOC, on the second go-round, would almost be fun. Almost. Those first few weeks were a turning point for me.

During my second tour of INDOC, I grew to admire the instructors, one of whom was called Yo-Yo. And he was exactly that for us, a yo-yo. Whenever we were down and hurting, he worked his Yo-Yo magic and brought us up again. I found this member of the cadre to be as inspirational as any man I've worked with. When things got really bad, Yo-Yo would call us out, make us all form up, and then he would give these crazy motivational speeches. Most of the time, instructors put you in formation only to diminish your humanity in preparation for more push-ups, more flutter kicks, and another smoke session in the pool or with the telephone pole. But not Yo-Yo. When that guy spoke, you listened.

Yo-Yo would gather us, allow us to catch our breath, and say something like "Hey, *Yo!* I came out of nowhere. You guys can do this, too, man. Yo, yo, yo, just a little bit of heart is all it takes, a little bit of heart! Come on, boys!" You *wanted* to do push-ups for Yo-Yo. You wanted to please him. He was as cool as an instructor could get.

I didn't mind working for people who earned my respect through action and character, as opposed to working for people who demanded mandatory respect. But the feelings of joy quickly wore off. Despite all that I had hoped, the second time around wasn't any easier. My claim to fame for INDOC? I earned the blue ascot, the little blue neck scarf that came with surviving Hell Night, twice.

The big difference about the second Hell Night came at the end. Four thirty in the morning, and they had us all lined up on the pad. We were allowed to go, but only if we could make the instructors laugh.

My hand shot up like a surrender flag.

"Airman Settle!"

"Hooyah, Sergeant! I got one!"

"It had better be funny."

"Hooyah, Sergeant! What did one saggy boob say to the other saggy boob?"

The cadre shrugged his giant shoulders.

"You'd better perk up or people are going to think we're nuts!"

They laughed and excused me.

I had survived my second Hell Night, but others weren't so lucky. The class was 06-003, affectionately called Ballz 3, and it was a huge class of cadets, more than my first. A couple majors, a captain, a couple lieutenants, one of whom would go on to become a very good friend of mine: Lieutenant Brock Roden. I didn't know it at the time, but we would go through many of the courses in the pipeline together, and he would eventually become an Alaska PJ himself.

Brock was one of only two officers to graduate with Ballz 3 at INDOC. Brock exuded what I can only describe as a sort of Zen existence. He was calm. Never stressed. He treated the anxiety and stress of INDOC very philosophically.

Fortunately for me, the two of us were assigned as partners on the culminating event at INDOC. The final event for the entire eight weeks would be the toughest: buddy breathing. This whole course, the cadre had been pounding us in the water, but for the final, the intensity and duration would be taken to a whole new level. At this point, the instructors kept us underwater for almost the entire time we were in the pool. It seemed to be a contest for them, to see if we would crack. Forcing us to stay beneath the surface and constantly threatening our air source was the most effective way for them to challenge our stress thresholds. The closest the instructors could come to simulating combat was to scare us nearly to death.

We all knew they were going to challenge us to hang on until the bitter end, there in the pool that afternoon. We knew it was going to be as tough as anything we'd done to that point. I was so close to finishing; I told myself I would drown before I would ever blast the air horn on the final event. I told myself I would hang on, and as we prepared, I thought about Major Adrian, who had died in that same damn pool. I told myself I would hold on for him.

At eval time, everyone sat with their back to the pool, in rows, with each guy's legs wrapped around the guy in front of him. "Nut to butt," they call it. There was no room for being uncomfortable about being cozy with another man, and by the end of INDOC the nut-to-butt position becomes preferable on cold days, because you can absorb the other guy's body heat to stay warm.

Brock and I dropped into the water with our single snorkel, knowing that, as soon as the whistle blew, the water battle would be instant and violent. We swam up to our instructor—Sergeant Pack, of all people. We might have been lucky drawing each other as partners, but we drew the short straw in terms of sharks. Sergeant Pack became liquid fear in the pool. One impossibly strong man and several minutes without oxygen stood between Brock and me and graduating INDOC.

The whistle blast sent us under. We barely got one pass of the snorkel before Pack tried to snatch it. With all his strength, he yanked and tore, trying to get that tube of life out of our hands. But this was only his first strike, and Sergeant Pack, the beast, grabbed our snorkel and spun us into a full alligator death roll, followed by a powerful drive to the bottom of the pool. Then, as suddenly as he had hit us, he disappeared. But only for a moment. We approached the surface, and Brock cleared the snorkel. Pack capped the top. Then I took the snorkel, cleared it, and Pack capped it.

Now we were running on no air, and before Brock could make another attempt to clear the tube, Pack alligator-rolled us and dragged us to the depths of the pool for a second time. Now, on the bottom with no air refill, having exhausted a significant portion of the air supply in our lungs in the failed attempts to clear the snorkel, we were in trouble. We gripped each other and the snorkel.

We held on for our lives and our futures. One screwup and we were done.

The clock ticked. Pack hammered. We used up our oxygen. We were running out of time. Things didn't look good, but neither of us was going to quit. But then again, nothing is certain when your brain screams for oxygen. Your lungs will start to contract. You'll try to recirculate the air in your lungs by swallowing and contracting the muscles in your chest and abs. But the air that is left is useless. Your body screams for oxygen. Your brain starts to shut down. The edges of your vision blur and darken. You have but seconds. You will surface and breathe, or perhaps you'll take that little visit to the wizard.

At this point we had no masks, and the water around us churned with bubbles and chaos, and we could only feel the impacts from Pack slamming the water with his giant arms. The slaps from his mighty fists hit like bombs going off near our skulls. *Boom! Boom! Boom!* Mount Pack continued destroying the water around our heads. He tossed us like toys in a toddler's tub. I'm not certain, but I think he was actually having fun. We had been under at least two minutes, enduring total harassment, and we were oxygen-deprived, bordering on a hypoxic state. Unconsciousness loomed.

Then it happened.

I felt the hit first, but I was deliriously close to not being certain of anything. Then I felt it again. A tap on the top of the head.

Brock and I both erupted out of the water, giving big giant roars of celebration. This was a moment of sheer excitement combined with pure relief. We had passed the hardest event and we had survived the toughest instructor. The feeling of excitement, happiness, and accomplishment surpassed winning a state championship, because I got to share the moment with Brock. Surviving that carnage was intense, and we did it together.

In some ways, someone might argue that it isn't fair to be judged in your final INDOC event as a pair. If your buddy screws up, then you're both done. I would argue it is the only fair way to be certain someone is truly ready for the PJ pipeline. Buddy breathing comes down to you being willing to pass the snorkel and to not let go of your teammate. Survival is about making sure your partner survives the event. There it is. That PJ motto again: "That others may live."

Only nine of us received the pararescue trainee sweats with the green feet logo on the right chest and right side of the leg. The sweats made it official. I was a an INDOC graduate and a PJ trainee and on the path to earning my beret.

9

· · · · · · · · · ·

Operation Green Feet

For as long as I can remember, I have wanted to jump out of an airplane. It was the parachute on the PJ logo that initially caught my eye. The *para-* in "pararescue" puts parachuting right in the job title. I couldn't get to the Army Airborne School fast enough, but the way it works is, once you enter the pipeline, you also hit half a dozen other schools and courses as positions become available.

Lucky for me, my first school after INDOC was Airborne. I packed my bags and headed to Fort Benning, Georgia. When I reported in, I was assigned a barracks room with three army men. Our class size had to be close to two hundred men and women. The first thing I noticed in the dorm was that the doors to all the rooms had been removed, which seemed strange.

On the first day, I was given my room assignment and was issued a green wool blanket, a pillow, and linens. I hauled the bedding and my gear up to the second-floor room. I threw the sheets and blanket on an open top bunk and started unpacking into my locker. I took out my shower gear and closed and locked my locker. By the time I finished my shower, someone had swiped my fine bedding materials. Perhaps that was why the doors had been removed. *Welcome to the army!*

That first night I slept in my PT gear and used a wadded-up sweatshirt top for a pillow. The next morning, we started early. The cadre strutted up and down the formation like cats stalking prey. Black ball caps distinguished the Airborne cadre from the fresh meat. These "black hats" collectively referred to us as "legs"—because anyone who can't jump out of airplanes has to use his legs to get around. The Airborne black hats also loved to use the word *boots* to refer to a form of physical strength conditioning. They would holler at us when we needed correction, "Beat your boots, you dirty, nasty legs!" To beat your boots, you begin by standing erect. Then, while maintaining a vertically erect upper body, you bend at the knees and hips until your hands can slap your ankles, and then you return to the fully upright position. The black hats ensured that our leg muscles had the strength to absorb the impact of an airborne landing.

Next came my first introduction to a chow hall, US Army style, which is an adventure in the army way. For some reason, which I'm sure in theory is related to jumping from an airplane, in classic "military intelligence," we were allowed only one food item per hand. Piece of toast for your left. Glass of orange juice for your right. Don't even think about throwing a banana onto a plate of institutional scrambled eggs and grabbing a coffee. *Are you insane, man?* One item. Per hand. Period!

The chow hall chief, a man with too much time on his own hands, will raise his voice and stop you cold in your tracks if you try to slip by on this. You will be directed, in no uncertain terms, to return all items that break the one-item-per-hand rule. Of course, you are invited to get back in line, to make another trip, for two more items. Having a quick breakfast could involve three or more trips from the food line to the seating area.

And the food? Let me just say, we don't have the best military in the world due to our cuisine. The whole base at times seemed to smell of high-protein army-diet farts that, oddly, were not that much different from the smell of the food they served us.

Before and after breakfast, the black hats had us form up on what they called the "wires." These are big steel cables bolted to the ground to serve as reference marks for formation. We did a lot of standing on those damn wires. Hours. The boredom on the wires would lead to silly games, like tossing small pebbles into helmets, and to adding to the already fragrant aroma as the morning meal churned in our bellies and that famous Georgia heat began to rise.

Airborne school could be called "I wish I wasn't born" school, with all the waiting. I almost quit just from all the standing around and doing nothing for hours and hours. But, for some, the waiting caused a fair bit of anxiety. Technically, there were two hundred "volunteers" in my Airborne school class, but plenty of them possessed zero interest in the whole jumping-out-of-airplanes thing. The first week of Airborne involved hours of ground training and waiting for ground training. Basically, the black hats were teaching us how to land. They taught us the parachute landing fall, or PLF.

The PLF is a graceful crunch into the earth. In classic military training form, the Airborne instructors followed a crawl, walk, run format, just as the cadre at INDOC had done. The first day or two was the crawl phase, the easiest tier of the training program. They had us get "jocked up," with realistic training parachute packs harnessed to our bodies and a reserve parachute across the belly, just as if we would be parachuting. We practiced jumping off boxes and doing PLF landings in deep pits of pea gravel. This was sweaty and dusty work. Up on the boxes. Down in the gravel. Repeat. Repeat. As the training progressed, we started to jump from taller and taller objects. Soon we were launching from airplane mock-ups and towers high in the sky. The black hats turned up the heat and the height.

After ground week, we began tower week. Here, they would have us jumping from giant towers. We were going to be working on learning how to jump out of aircraft, to deal with twists in the paracords, and then to stick our landings. On my first trip up, we jogged as a formation divided into columns called "chalks." As we approached, I could see the towers with steel cables attached to the top and anchored, about one hundred feet away, in a giant dirt berm. We split into chalks and went to our assigned towers. Each tower was constructed mostly of wood two-by-fours and plywood, creating a loud, echoing racket of people riding the zip line down from the top. Every time someone jumped, you could hear the pulleys clanging on the steel cable, resounding through the tower like old church bells.

Most of us were really excited to ride our first Airborne zip line. The guys in line behind me knew each other. Every time someone jumped onto the zip line they would cheer like frat boys. I was behind an army female who grew less and less excited about the training as we made our way up the stairs to the launchpad. At first she was friendly and social, but after the first person went and we heard the *clang* and *thud* and the sound of steel cables, her demeanor shut down. I watched as her anxiety increased with each *clang, thump,* and *zip.* After each series of noises, we took one more step up the stairs of the tower. I could just feel the dread building in her.

"It's going to be fine," I said.

She didn't reply.

After about midway up, we were high enough that the ground began to look far away. Around this point, her nerve began to waver, and she was clearly having second thoughts about earning her jump wings. I joined the soldiers around her, in support. We encouraged and cheered her on. At first we were simply saying calming and encouraging things—"This ain't nothing" or "You got this." But by the time we could see the top and the launching platform, our words fell on deaf ears. She was pale and on the verge of tears, but not ready to quit.

She didn't like being up there, but she still put on the harness, her helmet, and her gloves when it was her turn to jock up. By the time she stepped up to the edge of the platform to jump, though, she stopped cold. She didn't just hesitate on the edge; the poor girl froze. Solid. The earth waited far below us, and jumping from that height isn't natural. She just couldn't do it.

I'd seen men fail by inaction, but I had little experience around women in combat training roles. I was a bit worried about how the instructors would treat her refusal to jump. It didn't take but a second for me to see how Airborne deals with such moments.

The kind and loving black hat gently showed her the most efficient way off his tower. With the bottom of his boot.

She screamed the whole way down and hit the landing hill in a billowing cloud of dust.

The instructor turned to me with the smile of a man who loves his job.

"Will you be requiring assistance this morning?" he asked.

I answered with a smile and jumped before he could even think to lift his boot off the deck.

I jumped, and for the first half second from the tower, there was a brief feeling of weightlessness. This was immediately followed by the feeling of compression as the steel cable caught my weight and the downward energy from my fall became converted into horizontal speed. The first time, things happened fast and furious and there was no moment to take things in. The giant dirt berms that the cables were anchored into raced up toward me so fast that I barely got my feet up in time to make my PLF and keep from becoming a crumpled pile of broken air force property.

The weekend following the first week at jump school, I hung out with other PJ trainees who had just graduated from Airborne. So, naturally, we partied. A few friends of note were there: Brock, Reach, Wilson, McGraw, and a guy named Schumacher, or Schu. Some of these were guys I had survived INDOC with. That night, we closed down the bar, and on the way home we decided to get some food at a late-night greasy spoon. Our server was a full-figured, beautiful-as-life black woman. She described the specials and then warned us, in her rich Southern accent, "The milk shake machine is out of order."

Without any thought for my surroundings, half drunk, I exclaimed, "But your milk shake brings all the boys to the yard!"

The table exploded in laughter. Without missing a beat, she leaned down toward me and said, "You can't handle my milk shake, honey."

And she was probably right.

"Beat your boots!" they yelled out to us, rousing us from our beds in the predawn morning of our first jump. We had to jock up before the sun rose. The jump required being rigged up in our parachute harnesses.

They had us in a big hall, all lined up by chalks, on hard wooden benches in a converted giant airplane hangar. A black hat instructed us flatly, "Once you get jocked up and inspected, you can't leave." We weren't allowed to stand or to walk around. All we could do was talk quietly and watch the instructional video looping over and over on itself.

The problem with periods of forced sitting is that the human body, my body in particular, likes to process the fluids I intake at a pretty high rate. After the first couple hours, the urge to piss began rising like the tide at Turnagain Arm back home. Fast and unstoppable. The black hats had made the morning sound as though we were jocking up and jumping that minute. Instead, we'd been thrust into the classic military hurry-up-and-wait.

"This is happening right now. Get jocked up and let's go! Hurry up," they yelled. And then we sat. One hour became two, and then four. Waiting. Waiting. There I am, trying to be a cool guy in the PJ pipeline, and I'm on the verge of pissing my pants in front of

God, country, and a bunch of army folks who are itching for something to clown the air force guy with. Was taking a piss going to count as failure? Was this another military test of endurance?

I couldn't handle it anymore. I rose, but barely. I could barely stand.

"Can I go to the bathroom please?" I asked the first black hat.

"No, Air Force," he said. "We'll have to re-JMPI you. Sit down."

JMPI meant jumpmaster preinspection, where the jumpmaster inspects all buckles, straps, and pins and makes sure that you are good to go. And the jumpmaster takes his job very seriously. I guess the jumpmasters at Airborne were a little too busy to come deal with guys who couldn't sit for four hours without needing to step into a bathroom.

I waited some more. Then I asked again. I received another no.

Finally, on the verge of pissing myself, I stood up and started walking. I walked, though it might have been a little more of a hobble, over to the bathroom. There, by some force of divine intervention, I encountered a black hat in an air force uniform.

He said, "Hey! Where are you going?"

"I really have to go to the latrine," I pleaded.

"Cool. Right over there. What are you training for? What pipeline are you in?"

In the air force, there are only a handful of jobs that involve jumping. The two most common are PJ and combat controller. I knew he had a pretty good guess as to which I hoped to be.

"PJ, Sergeant," I said, trying not to sound like a ten-year-old girl.

"Good luck," he said. I'm pretty sure he meant in the pipeline, not whether I would make it to the urinal or not.

In I went, did my thing, and he inspected my chute upon return. Within minutes I was back to my spot. It was that easy. Army control, exemplified, but it was also a little lesson, and a recurring theme in my military career. I can't tell you how many times I wished for a catheter tip with a hose, to just run it down my leg and feel that relief.

After I relieved myself and returned to my spot, I realized that I had started something, and other people began getting up too. The black hats got angry, and one of them shouted, "Hey! You guys have to get reinspected!" The boots didn't care. I'd started a urinal mutiny.

Not long after that, we finally made our way out to load up on the airplane.

We all carried on our backs the T-10, the old-school green army parachute. They look like they are right from World War II. We carried the reserve parachute on our bellies, and that beast was heavy, the harness tight and confining as hell.

When it was our turn to load onto the airplane, four chalks loaded, two on each side of the aircraft. The airplane would jettison people out of the back, on both sides of the airplane, one after another. It would take two passes over the airfield to get everybody out.

This was the first time I had ever been on a C-130, and I heard the auxiliary generator outside supplying power to the aircraft. We walked up the ramp in formation, four lines, up and into the back of the airplane. We shuffled in and sat down. The cargo area was lined and divided down the middle with green canvas seats, making four rows of canvas seats, one row for each chalk. Two rows for one door, two rows for the other door.

All the compression from the weight and straps makes for an uncomfortable ride on the thin, narrow canvas seats. The aluminum bar cut into the back of my legs and the weight of the parachute pressed down on my guts and bladder. Between the weight and my nerves, if I didn't feel like I needed to go pee before, I definitely did then.

They shut off the auxiliary generator and started the motors. Those engines on the C-130s are workhorses. The props sprang to life and the whole world started vibrating. I couldn't help smiling so big my cheeks hurt.

Oh baby! I'm about to jump out of a perfectly good airplane.

C-130s have been around for a long time, and I couldn't help but wonder where this plane had flown, what action it had seen. I started to feel a bit nervous, but not nervous like I couldn't do it. This was that nervous excitement before a big race. The difference? I couldn't believe I was about to jump out of a plane. As my job. This was my job.

At that moment I was the luckiest man in America. Jumping out of airplanes was something that I always wanted to do, but I never really had the guts to go do it on my own, out of personal interest. There was also the fact that I was always broke. Poor people don't jump out of airplanes on their own dime. To have the opportunity, as my job, was phenomenal and a bit unbelievable to me. I was super stoked to be there. I was not really afraid. I knew I wasn't going to die or anything like that. But my heart picked up the pace significantly when the jumpmaster gave us our first signal.

I didn't intentionally put myself into the position I was in, but I happened to be one of the last people to board, so this made me the first person out the door on my side, on the first jump pass. First guy out the door, on my first jump ever. *Hell yeah!*

"Stand up!" the jumpmaster commanded. He held out his open right hand, fingers pointed toward the ground. He raised his hand halfway, in a sweeping motion, with the palm facing up. Then the jumpmaster made a fishhook with his index finger and raised it over his head. "Hook up!"

At this point, you hook up the metal clasp you've been holding in your lap the whole time, clipping it to a steel wire hanging above you. The metal hook is attached to several feet of one-inch yellow webbing. This webbing, called a static line, is a tether from the airplane to the parachute on your back. When you jump, the static line pays out as you fall from the plane. Once you reach a certain point, that static line yanks the parachute out of the pack tray, deploying it. The static line stays with the aircraft as it flies away. Jumper and parachute deploy together and you float happily to the ground.

That's the plan.

If the main parachute doesn't work, you have plan B: the reserve chute on your belly.

If the reserve chute fails?

There is no plan C.

I was first chalk on the first lift. The jumpmaster opened the door. He looked at me and yelled over the roaring wind billowing past, "Are you scared? Come here!" He waved me forward. I stood in the doorway and he grabbed my arm. He faked shoving me out of the plane. "Hey, you scared? You scared?" he asked, grinning.

"No, sir! This is cool! I like this!" I yelled in reply.

I leaned forward and looked out of the aircraft, soaking in the adrenaline. The C-130 cruised along at 130 miles per hour. We flew at 1,200 feet but, for some reason, that seemed closer to the ground than I expected. I thought, *I don't know if there is a lot of room for error. A guy could get hurt or die if something goes wrong here!*

I could see people going about their lives below us. I could see the houses. I could make out the individual trees and shrubs. We passed over neighborhoods, schools, and baseball diamonds as we lined up on the drop zone, the DZ. Normal people, living normal lives below. *That used to be me. This is crazy.*

The flight engineer for the C-130 was air force. Since I was one of the few air force guys on the airplane, he waved to me and yelled, "Hey, man, look at this." He had his flight suit on, and on his suit he had the classic Velcro name tape. I don't recall what his name was, but he smiled and then peeled off the Velcro to reveal red embroidered words underneath. It simply read, "STD FREE." I laughed. My first jump, my first introduction to an air force morale patch— and to aircrew. They can be some seriously goofy people. He slapped me on the back and yelled something about luck.

I moved back to my spot at the door.

The sequence of events goes like this: You jump out of the plane with your feet and knees together like you mean it. You wait for that big tug from the static line. Then you count to three. One. Two.

Three. After the g-forces of the opening sequences slow down, you look up to inspect your canopy and check for twists, or funny looking burbles, or gremlins, or anything crazy. If you see any of that stuff, you'd better try to do something about it, and quick. If you see a really scary mess above your head, you have only a few moments to decide to activate your emergency reserve, and then you ride that sucker down. That's the name of that game. A little different from what I would learn at free fall school, but that is how it works at Airborne school.

Luckily, I never had to ride the reserve option.

My adrenaline surged. A couple minutes now; weeks of mind-numbing training was on the verge of actually being used. I don't think I ever thought I would actually get to jump from a plane, and there I was. And since I would be the first one out, I had the privilege of watching the ground below for those final minutes, as we came in on our approach to the drop zone.

The jumpmaster must have sensed how excited and happy I was to be there. He smiled and slapped me on the back. "Get some!" he said.

The jump light turned green and he yelled, "Go!"

This was it.

I took a deep breath and launched.

As we had practiced, I held my chin to my chest. Feet and knees together. Hands on the reserve parachute on my belly. I tumbled down and then felt the jerk of the parachute, the hard yank pulling me into myself. I looked up toward the giant green airplane with men falling out of both sides. One. Two. Three. They streamed out like little ants.

My canopy expanded and untwisted itself, and then I saw them. The risers were all twisted.

Shit! Shit! Shit! This isn't good! My risers!

I'd say my stomach dropped, but I was dropping with it.

The parachute canopy comes to two connection points, one on each shoulder, and these are the risers. Sometimes they can twist around on each other and make it really difficult to steer, and sometimes the tangled risers can make a descent deadly.

What I saw above me looked like a hammock twisted in on itself. Instead of the lines being open in an umbrella fashion, they were wound tight. The black hats had warned us that this could happen, and for a brief moment my heart thudded rapidly in my chest and I could feel the tinges of panic. *Oh no! What is going to happen?*

I kept my cool and remembered my training. The black hats had drilled us on how to identify many potential problems while parachuting and how to take rapid, lifesaving action. To deal with this situation, they had taught us to "work it." You do this by pulling apart the risers near your neck and bicycle kicking.

As soon as I identified the problem, I did just that. I grabbed the risers as high as I could. They had twisted almost completely down the length of the lines, to near my neck. I started bicycle kicking for my life. At the same time, I pulled down and out. Slowly, I began to unwind. Once that started happening, I felt relief. I worked the problem almost until I hit the ground. The world revolved as I spun in circles under the canopy. The risers straightened out and I was able to line up for a landing.

The situation turned out okay, but at the time I wasn't so sure about my predicament. My training made all the difference, but, I'll admit, that moment of realization came as a surprise. As much as they taught us, I wasn't ready for it. But I worked the problem, and the next thing I knew, the ground was coming quick. I could hear the black hats below.

"Feet and knees together, Airborne!" they bellowed at us from the ground. This was a phrase they yelled frequently, and for good reason, as I would learn later in free fall school.

The earth raced up to greet me. I held my feet and knees together and hit the dirt. Hard. This was tilled-up, rocky dirt. There was a road in the middle, and you didn't want to hit that, but every now and then somebody would. I aimed for the soft dirt. You can steer these particular chutes a little, direct your descent somewhat, but it isn't like steering a car. You don't have a whole lot to work with. I managed to hit the plowed-up dirt of the field, but what I missed was enjoying the ride down. Too much of my time in the air had been consumed with the tangled risers.

That was my first jump. And I would get my shot at enjoying the ride back to earth. Before graduating Airborne I would complete a total of five jumps, a couple of them at night. Night jumps would become my favorite. I loved jumping into the black sky. The world is different at night. I felt like I was a secret agent every time we did night jumps.

That was Airborne. The one school where they mass-produce a high volume of jumpers. They can churn out hundreds of jumpers each month, all of whom execute five static line jumps to earn an Airborne badge. Later, I would hear operators call these soldiers "five-jump chumps," because there is literally an army of men who go to Airborne school but only ever jump at the school. This is the only time they will parachute during their entire career. They earn that patch, and they can look cool: "I'm Airborne!" Some even walk around with the swagger of Airborne, though they've only got the five jumps. More than once, I heard someone say, "That's a five-jump chump right there, boys."

At the end of Airborne school, the Friday after our last jump, with graduation the next day, my PJ trainee friend John and I pulled a prank that could have cost us our careers. The idea, like so many not-so-smart ideas, occurred to us after a few beers. John and I decided it would be an awesome idea to climb one of the 250-foot drop towers that stand in the middle courtyard, between all the Airborne dorms. The towers look like a cross between a giant high-tension electrical tower and a scary ride at the fair. On top, four arms (one for each face of the tower) reach away from the center like arms on a metal giant.

Fueled with a little liquid courage, we thought it would be cool if, in the middle of the night, we did our own little covert special ops mission. Something big. Something that sent a message. Something that said, "The PJs were here!"

It was a genius idea, and beautifully executed. Around midnight, in a silly stupor, we free-climbed the outside of the structure until we reached a point where we had access to the inside, to the internal ladder. Earlier in the evening, using a bedsheet, several cans of green spray paint, and cardboard stencils, John and I had done a little covert art project, which we would put on display. The whole mission was sketchy and fraught with pitfalls.

The towers were very exposed. Traffic on base seemed busy for the late hour. At times, as we climbed, we froze in place and pressed ourselves against the structure. Any one of the cars driving underneath us might slow down, the driver looking up, and we would be busted.

"Did they see us?" John asked, as a car stopped underneath us and the red of taillights illuminated the ground below.

"I don't know," I said. "Wait for a minute." The brake lights dimmed as the car once again began to drive away. Up we went, all 250 feet. At the top, I handed John the prize.

When we reached the pinnacle, John shimmied out on one of the four releasing arms that stretched almost a hundred feet away from the core of the tower. The arms bring four people at a time to the top of the tower. The tower is designed to bring you up on an open parachute, allowing for a drop of 250 feet, so you can experience landing with a parachute already deployed.

At the tip of the arm, John and I draped our flag, and it fell perfectly and unfurled beautifully. Then we free-climbed all the way back down, gave each other high fives, crawled into our separate bunks and went to sleep.

Formation occurred before first light the next morning. As the sun rose, illuminating the base, there was our flag, proudly waving.

You couldn't miss it.

A big white PJ flag; a pair of giant green feet.

John and I grinned at each other. *Yeah! We did it! We didn't get busted!*

But it wasn't very long before the black hats were popping out and pointing at the flag and looking at each other and stomping back into the main building. At about this same time, John and I began to realize we weren't quite as brilliant as we had thought.

There were no PJs in line for the class behind us, and the group ahead had already graduated and departed before us.

John and I were the only two PJs in Airborne school. Perhaps the only two PJs within several hundred miles.

Through the extensive use of powerful, all-intrusive army investigative efforts and the sheer might of military intelligence, the supersleuths were able to narrow the suspect pool to two people.

John and I were brothers. There was solidarity between us, and we were good friends. We wouldn't rat on each other, and we would never crack. But there was a second big problem with our plan. We did this prank, and we executed it flawlessly, but we pulled our awesome prank one day too early. If we had waited one more day, perhaps until after we had graduated and had gotten our jump pins, we could have skipped out of town, been gone, and never landed in so much trouble.

Then again, we also would have been denied the reaction of people when they saw those two green feet hanging from their army tower. People were screaming. Screaming!

"Who did that? Who put that up there!"

"There are only two PJ trainees!"

John and I were on our faces all day, doing push-ups, push-ups, and then more push-ups. "Go report to this person!" they would yell. Push-ups. "Go report to that person!" Push-ups. We did push-ups the whole way up the entire chain of command. And the whole way, each person of higher rank would ask, "Did you guys do this?"

And we would say, "No, sir!"

We just denied, denied, denied. Maybe if they had us do math, we would have cracked.

We weren't just denying the green feet flag. Someone had also spray painted smaller green feet all over the training structures. We denied this, too.

Our denial continued, until we got all the way to the Army Airborne commandant. I'm sure he was a colonel or higher rank, and the first thing he did was to put us into the push-up position in his office. We started banging out push-ups while he dialed the commandant of our schoolhouse back at Lackland. He put our commandant on speakerphone and apprised him of the situation.

Our buttholes puckered up tight. It was all fun and games until we heard our commandant's voice on the phone. Now we were concerned, and suddenly we saw that our little prank could spell the end of our careers. Also, we were sweating—not from the push-ups but from all the black hats' threats about felony charges for defacing military property. We began to worry that some of those threats might have real merit.

Our commandant addressed us over the phone. He said, "Hey, boys, I admire your prank. And I admire your ability to maintain integrity." (This comment would make more sense to me later, because it fell in line with the SERE training that I was about to receive—namely, when being interrogated, deny everything!) Here we were, on our faces in the Airborne commandant's office, and our own commandant said, "Go on. Just tell them what they want to hear, so you can return to Lackland."

"Yes, sir," we replied.

He hung up the phone, and with that command, John and I capitulated. "We did it, sir."

And the commandant yelled, "Goddamn it. You boys!" He was pissed, but oddly relieved and happy. What he said next would have floored the two of us, were we not already actually on the floor. "You two are true specimens of physicality. I'm impressed with what you did. I think it's cool. The problem is, those other two or three hundred knuckle draggers out there are going to think they can do that kind of shit, too. And they aren't nearly as physically fit as you are, and someone is going to get hurt if they try."

We agreed. It was cool.

He continued, "How did you guys do that? They sent out a climbing team with ropes and carabiners and helmets. It took a couple hours to take it down."

We told him we had free-climbed, and he was impressed. He wasn't even mad, just impressed. There were more push-ups involved, but when the black hats were dropping us for push-ups, they would drop us for twenty, and I guess in the army that was a big deal. But PJ cones do sets of fifty. In their perception, they were punishing us ultra hard.

"Give me twenty! Give me another twenty!" They didn't know that John and I could play the push-up game all day long. That was why they could never break us.

10

. . . .

Eating Ants

Despite the green feet stunt, I received my Airborne pin and packed my gear for a return to Lackland. Between schools, PJ trainees do most of their training at Lackland. On the flight back, I worried how the PJ cadre were going to respond to our prank. When I landed at the San Antonio airport, a blue air force van, driven by a cone, was waiting for me.

During the drive, I asked the driver if he'd heard anything about my Airborne prank.

"No," he said. "First I heard about it. Sounds awesome. I hope they don't shit-can you."

"Me too," I said, and the rest of the drive was gloomy.

The van delivered me straight into the line of fire; upon my return, I headed directly to the commandant's office.

I stepped to the threshold of the cadre offices. I knocked loudly three times and sounded off: "Airman Settle, reporting to commandant!"

I was greeted with, "Settle, bear crawl back to the cadre area!"

I bear crawled back, growling the whole way, *Rawr! Rawr!"*

When I reached the cadre, all were present, and one of them said, "Start knocking them out." I began, and as I counted I heard, "Now tell us the story of what happened, man, because that sounds awesome."

I shared the story while doing my push-ups. When I finished, they said, "Get up. That was a good one!" They were pretty stoked about our move with the flag, and before long I was tasked with unofficially doing some inspirational and motivational visual arts improvements on some equipment around the base.

In other words, I was encouraged to paint green feet on some retired fighter jets the base had on display. More planning went into this prank. Four of us moved out, late on a Friday night, to the entrance on our side of the base. The jets are part of a display attached to the area housing the students who want to become part of the Air Force Security Forces. The operation was to happen directly under their noses.

We split up, each with a handheld radio. Two stayed on lookout while the other two snuck over the fence with a ladder. We used the ladder to climb up on the wing of each jet, then walked along the top of the fuselage to the tail, under the bright lights that illuminated the aircraft display. It took both of us to hold the template, but we took turns spray painting the big green feet on the tail fins, strategically placed for everyone driving by to enjoy.

On Monday the grads formed up and jogged to the schoolhouse to report for morning PT. There were base security police cars, with security guys crawling all over.

One of the instructors trotted over to me and my coconspirators. "Quick," he said, "purge your rooms."

He didn't need to tell us twice.

We sprinted to our quarters, collected all the stencils and spray paint, and disposed of the evidence. The next thing we knew, the security guys were in the dorms. They shook down our whole building, top to bottom. They knew we did it. We knew they knew we did it. But none of us cracked and they couldn't prove it. Our cadre didn't smoke us for the extra attention, a slight nod of approval. The security police and the PJs had a rivalry that went back years.

Part of the opposition stemmed from some of the security detail wanting to be PJs, showing up to INDOC thinking they were hot shit, and then blowing the horn. The next thing they knew, they were cops, and they were disappointed and disgruntled. Some guys who don't make INDOC or the pipeline wind up saying things like "It wasn't my fault; the cadre picked on me."

Whatever the case, there was a mostly good-natured competition going on between the two groups. The wannabes and the trying-tos. They attempted to steal things from us all the time. We had a unit guidon flag that they would try to snatch. There was quite a bit of tomfoolery prior to our covert mission, but after spray painting the jets, we endured a week or two of the police really putting the pressure on the PJ trainees.

After Airborne, I hung around Lackland, working to stay in shape for my next big course, dive school. At this juncture in my life, I was as close to a professional athlete as I had ever been. The military paid me to work out most of the day. When I wasn't in the pool or gym, I studied the PJ handbook. INDOC was tough, but I knew dive school would be even more intense. I was waiting for a slot to open. Traditionally, PJ trainees attended the army's combat dive school in Key West, Florida. The army dive school has a limited number of slots per class per year, and between the growing number of PJs and the combat controllers in the air force, the wait could be months. Plus, army students receive higher priority, which naturally they should, since it is an army-run school. Luckily for me, the air force had recently started up its own school, and it looked like I would have a shot soon. Then one of the other courses for my pipeline opened up and off I went to Fairchild Air Force Base in Washington State, to endure a whole different level of abuse at the hands of the military: SERE school.

A quick little one-two on SERE. This is a classic military acronym. The military doesn't just love acronyms; the military lives and dies by acronyms. They have acronyms for the acronyms of acronyms. SERE stands for survival, evasion, resistance, and escape. This is the sequence of events soldiers are to attempt if they find themselves in a bad situation in a bad place. The first SERE I attended had been designed for aircrew and special members of the air force who are at a higher risk of capture by the enemy due to the nature of their jobs.

Essentially, SERE trains you for when you're in a helicopter and it stops working in a place where there are more bad guys than good guys. Drawing lessons from historic situations, the military has designed a sequence of actions you can take in order to survive with honor, a concept that shapes one of the slogans of SERE: "Return with honor."

One of the first things they teach you is how to *survive* the initial incident. You're given basic first aid and taught how to create splints with sticks and odds and ends from aircraft wreckage and parachute material. Improvised shelters and locating food and water in the wilderness are taught in the field.

They also teach you to use compasses, read maps, and understand *evasion* of the enemy. You're taught how to become invisible, to blend in with the earth, so you can reduce the chances of being detected while being pursued.

Then there is the *resistance* portion, which is where all the fun ends and you find yourself in the uncomfortable position of being detained. SERE will give you the basics of how to conduct yourself in a way that is honorable and falls within the United States military's Code of Conduct. You need to know how to conduct yourself, no matter what the enemy says or does. In theory, you could get captured by the bad guys, survive, but do the wrong thing and still get in trouble for your actions. There are things you don't tell the enemy and there are things you don't say about your country. The instructors showed us videos of interrogations, from very subtle to the openly violent. Each one was dissected and used to prepare us for our own individual interrogation opportunity.

Then there is *escape,* and that has to do with all sorts of tactics—how to get out of cells, to look for opportunity, to gather resources to flee, to plan for flight.

SERE turned out to be one of my favorite schools. A good portion of the first week was spent in the classroom, drilling down into the academic and theoretical concepts. The second week they sent us into the field to apply the academics, and that's when things really got fun.

On our way to the first field day, we loaded onto a bus with our issued ALICE rucks. All of us possessed exactly the same sleeping bag, socks, and even underwear. We were also issued maps and compasses. One of the first things we did when we got out of the bus was to break into groups. Each group had a SERE instructor to provide the basics of survival and evasion in the wilderness.

We headed into the mountains of the Colville National Forest. Once we arrived at our starting point, I felt immediately at home. We were surrounded by mountains and towering pine trees. Right off, the instructors began teaching us how to use a map and compass to identify where the hell we were. If you don't know where you're starting from, on a map, you're not going to be able to figure out where you need to go.

I enjoyed learning to triangulate mountain ranges and use terrain features to estimate distances. The SERE instructors displayed a deep knowledge of the landscape. They taught us all sorts of ways to improve the probability of correctly identifying the area where we were starting. They shared tips like how to gauge distances by identifying how tall the trees beside you are and their size relative to their distance from you. Lessons that would be handy if you actually crashed and needed to figure out your precise location without a GPS. Initially this is a guessing game, until you can positively identify where you are and then move to a second location and use the same system to see whether your coordinates line up. I enjoyed the hands-on application, and I loved being back in the woods. A familiar feeling crept up on me: *I'm getting paid to do something awesome and practical! Today it's learn how to survive. I'm on the clock right now, in the woods, about to play hide-and-seek!*

From the work with maps and compasses, we went on to the survival phase. First we had to build a shelter out of the available natural resources. I had just come from INDOC and Airborne, was in the best shape of my life. With muscle and endurance comes strength and testosterone. I felt pretty manly and pretty strong. Now, it's no secret that members of other branches of the military at times poke fun and look down upon folks in the air force. There are all sorts of derogatory names, like, say, "chair force." I cannot confirm or deny that I might have had a few chair warmers on my team. This romping around in the woods was brutal and horrible for a few of them. Their poor fitness levels and bad attitude made it easy for me to look good. The patrols they had us doing through the woods were fun. I felt like I was back home in Alaska, camping. The only thing we didn't have was a real tent, or much food. We would have to gather, scavenge, or kill to supplement our own meager meals.

After a few days of almost no food, we grew ravenous. The hunger pains hit with a stab to the gut and I'd wince a bit. Other guys bellyached about their bellyaches. We didn't have snacks. I was surviving on the chewing tobacco I had snuck in in my pocket. We were issued one MRE to last for our time on the field. We turned to eating worms and ants. I still like ants. They have a nice, surprising citrus taste when they pop, but make sure they don't bite you in the face. We ate anything we could find, but it wasn't really enough.

To forage enough calories is tough. We were in the Spokane area, and these weren't forests with fruits and vegetables on every tree and bush. After having survived INDOC, I was physically near my prime, but I was host to a body that liked being well fed. I had gone from consuming thousands of calories a day to taking in next to nothing, and my body wasn't happy. The hunger became intense. My stomach burned, gurgled, and rumbled. I started to get cranky. I didn't do as well as some of the other guys who didn't need as many calories, and that was when I would slip a pinch of tobacco. That worked; it took the edge off, just enough. I was still starving, but the nicotine held the hunger at bay and kept me going when I was tired.

As a kid in Alaska, I did a little bit of trapping and hunting with my grandparents on their homestead. I also spent time in the Boy Scouts. I had never snared before, but I had watched my grandparents. When the instructor pointed and said, "There is two feet of eighteen-gauge wire; go set a snare," I didn't need to be told twice. I wanted some real meat.

I didn't catch anything in my snare that night, but our instructor caught a rabbit. The next day we feasted on rabbit stew. I sampled every part of it. We had to share one rabbit among a group of eight. I ate a piece of the heart and shared the liver. I wasn't a fan of the strong, barely cooked flavor. But the grossest part of our meal? Easily the lungs. I cut off some rabbit lung, held it on the tip of my knife, and then stabbed it into my mouth. I started chewing. I can only describe what my teeth and jaw chomped on as a spongy, flavorless, mushy mass. The lungs crunched with a cartilage-like sound. I just kept chewing and chewing until I could swallow. I gagged a bit but hid the revulsion. Food was food, and I was hungry.

I loved SERE, though, romping around in the forests outside of Spokane. It was summer, and it was a great time of year to be out in those woods. The giant old growth reminded me a little of Endor, the Ewok planet in *Star Wars*, but without as much ground vegetation. Unlike so much of our Alaskan forest, this one was easy to walk around in. Giant trees towered over me, the ground was rocky, and the weather was warm. It was the sort of place where I just kind of wanted to lie down under a tree, take a nap, and relax. I didn't feel uncomfortable at all. Hungry, yes, but not uncomfortable.

All we really had to do, other than not eat and not think about food, was march. We navigated as we marched, the whole time. We had to keep moving. Reach an objective, do some navigation, then move to the next objective. There was a purpose to all of this, too. We needed to know precisely the time required to march a certain amount of distance in different conditions. They taught us pace counts, and we were learning to understand pace counts over different terrain. We would be asked if we could figure out how far we had gone during the past hour. Apparently, the best way to learn is through repetition, because we did pace counts over and over. With all the practice, I became decent at estimating the distance I could travel in a given time.

After days of learning how to survive in the woods, we reached a point where the instructors were ready for us to roam free. Thus began the evasion portion of SERE. We were broken into two-man teams and instructed to get from one location to a rally point. I don't remember the time they allowed for this, but I had spent plenty of time mountain running in my life, and it was only two or three miles. I knew my partner and I could sprint through the woods and get there faster than the cadre.

We tried, and my goofy logic got us caught. The instructors were already prepositioned, and I should have known. We were spotted by camouflaged SERE instructors acting in an enemy role, as the opposition force, or OPFOR. They blew the whistle and yelled at us, made us do fifty push-ups, told us what we did wrong, gave us a five-minute head start, and told us to get the hell out of there.

After getting busted that first time, I figured we had to do this the right way. We took their warning seriously, applied our training, and started using some of the tools they had taught us. We took leaves and branches and incorporated some natural camouflage into our clothing. We put on face paint and moved slowly, paying close attention to the sounds of the woods surrounding us.

Once I slowed down and opened my senses, the evasion portion became pretty incredible. My senses came to life and I felt alive and energized. My constant thoughts of food were gone. I'd been away from the woods and my running and skiing escapes in the wild, and suddenly I started reconnecting with the sounds of the forest.

I also recalled and tapped directly into an old talent of mine, something from my cross-country skiing days. This will sound strange, but I always liked to imagine lines cutting through the forest, and when I was a kid, I would chase those lines. It turned into a game, and I would try to follow the line through the woods, watching it bounce in front of me. I'd race toward that line, slicing silently through the forest, no trail required.

Listening with all my senses, I could hear and know what was going on around us.

We sat and waited. Someone moved below us, and someone else was talking in the distance. After a while, I turned to my partner and said, "Wait. Listen. Do you smell that?" Then I farted, wafted it toward him, and whispered, "Okay, let's move."

We'd move for about twenty minutes. We took slow, deliberate steps, staying quiet, trying not to allow a single branch to snap. We moved with stealth, slipping from cover to cover and steering clear of the trails. We crept through the lower bushes and avoided showing a profile. After a while we reached a broad, grassy opening. We paused in the bushes at the meadow's edge and pressed ourselves into the dirt.

"Should we cross or sneak around?" my partner asked.

Skirting the meadow would add at least mile or more. "Let's go for it," I said, thinking we could risk racing across.

He nodded. We began to rise to begin our run, and just as we were about to make our move to cross the hundred-yard opening, two other men broke out from the bushes nearby, at full sprint. We dropped back to the ground and watched. They made it halfway across, and all of a sudden five instructors popped out of the grass, screaming and blowing whistles. I'm sure that was a regular prank, and I'd bet those instructors wished they had paintball guns to blast those guys.

We took advantage of the situation of the two runners getting busted. The ruckus had attracted everyone's attention. They drew in the other instructors, so we stayed put. The other instructors ran right past us, and then, after about a minute of silence, we booked it around the rim of the action and were able to get in front of them. We reached the rally point ahead of the deadline—and the instructors.

Reaching the goal was almost anticlimactic, because once we reached our objective, all we could do was hang out, wait for everyone else, and be hungry.

In any event, the fun in the woods was about to end.

I don't want to spoil the surprise for anyone in the future who needs to take this class, but everybody ultimately gets caught in the end. When the majority of the class had gathered at the final rally point, these big, scraggly dressed guys appeared. They seemed friendly at first, but then they whipped out some AK-47s and started blasting the assault rifles into the air.

They yelled at us, "Identify yourself!"

In an instant, I thought hard and tried to recall my training. *Oh, wait a minute, there are rules here! They can't do this to us . . . or can they?* Almost immediately, the men with guns abused the rules relating to prisoners of war. We went from wrapping up a nice weekend in the woods to a shocking test of who remembered their lessons from class and who didn't.

The men were big, with flowing hair and long beards. They wore crazy clothes. A confusing garb—Mideastern but not at all Middle Eastern. These tough-looking, heavily armed men yelled and screamed at us. I know what you're thinking. You'd tell yourself, *This is all fake. All simulated. No big deal.* But these dudes were not people about whom you could just say, "Oh, they were actors. That's just an American pretending to be scary." No, these guys seemed like the real deal. This was loud. Violent. And real.

We were definitely being tested.

Our training taught us that you share only your name, rank, and service number. Limited bits of information. Remembering the code of conduct is all about "returning with honor." You don't want to get yourself killed over saying no, but you don't want to tell them too much, either. There were young Air Force Academy cadets and pilot-wannabes who were trying to be hard. As a PJ trainee, I was doing the opposite. Stay humble. I didn't want anyone to know I was a PJ trainee. I was trying to stay off their radar, trying to be invisible.

Some of the pilots were cocky and said dumb shit like "I'm a pilot! You can't talk to me like that."

"I can't?" might be the reply, and the pilot would receive a little physical correction. A slap or a shove up against a tree. "You think you can talk to me like that?" Then they might pull out a machete and . . . These men might have been kidding, but it sure as hell seemed as though they were really going to actually kill you. The enemy did a great job at giving the impression that you should be scared. This was not a game.

Of course, there were the cocky guys who would say, "I'm not going to give you my info!" Those guys garnered plenty of attention. Then they would get rattled. Right away, I noticed that the guys who gave their information weren't getting harassed, and I followed suit. I'm not the smartest monkey in the barrel, but I can pay attention and play along.

The bad guys dropped big black hoods on our heads and marched us on to a bus. They forced us to sit with our heads down, two people per seat. I knew we were in an old Blue Bird school bus because I could see through the material of the hood. I could make out colors and some shapes.

From the moment they started firing the guns to when they were loading us on the bus, I took the training seriously. I thought I'd be really cunning, so as the bus drove I started counting turns. After about an hour I lost track. Then I fell asleep. Not exactly heroic POW material.

I tried to stay focused on the training, but I was overcome with the urge to sleep. In hindsight, I can see it was the bus ride itself that reminded me of the seductive power of sleep. The ride was enough time to rest and be lulled into a sleepy stupor, seduced by the vibrations of the diesel engine. Then the brakes hissed, the bus lurched to a sudden stop, and I was jerked fully awake.

The bad guys, the OPFOR, were waiting for us outside the bus. It was similar to the first moments of basic training, when you come off the bus into the training terminal areas and there are these angry people yelling and screaming. We didn't have any of our personal gear, just the clothes we were wearing and the hoods on our heads. We were immediately formed up into a line, our hands on the shoulders of the person in front of us. I could vaguely make out my surroundings through a tiny pin-hole in my hood. We marched through a simple wooden doorway into a dimly lit corridor lined with doors facing each other across a concrete walkway. The first and most powerful sensory input was sound. Speakers emitted a nonrhythmic assortment of nearly musical sounds and incomplete news clips, blasted at ear-piercing levels.

We were thrown into individual plywood detention cells—a small box, not big enough to lie down. If you were a tall person, this would have been really horrible. The ceiling wasn't any higher than six feet, and I think if I stood up, the top of my head brushed the ceiling.

We had clearly entered the resistance phase of SERE training. They began to pull out the stops to teach us a thing or two about resisting the enemy. I was locked in a plywood cell. The cell had a cement floor, three plywood walls, and one plywood door. The captors furnished each cell with a coffee can to shit and piss in— what back home in Alaska we called a honey bucket. This was supposed to be degrading treatment, but by now you know enough about me to know I filled that sucker up right away. I would actually start to get worried about the fluid level in the can, toward the end of my confinement.

The door had two slats cut into it that were only accessible from the outside. The upper opening was about three by twelve inches; the OPFOR would flip this open to look inside. At the bottom of the door was a small flap that was bigger in size, so you could slide objects in or out.

They would peer in to yell at you, tell you to stand up and stay awake. Everyone was supposed to be standing at attention in their cell or the bad men would yell. I always quasi obeyed. I did a lot of leaning up against the wall, trying to sleep while standing and trying to listen for them coming down the hall. I could hear them yelling a barrage of caustic insults into cells near mine. I tried to gauge when they would slam open the upper peephole to check on me. I spent most of my time half sitting and half listening for the sound of someone approaching. My cell sat in the middle of the building, so I had a decent chance of them starting on the end and waking me up before they reached my cell. That was my gamble.

After what felt like days, I remember being deliriously tired and hungry. The only friendly outward source of input came from the man on my left side, an Air Force Academy graduate. He intended to become a fighter pilot. I had cut out from our text the little piece of paper with Morse code on it and stuffed that in my uniform. I started knocking on the wall, and the future pilot next to me knew Morse. We communicated back and forth. Over the non-stop noise, I strained to listen and feel for the taps from the other side. I learned who he was and his pilot goals, all through our raps on the wall. I had not memorized Morse, so my cheat sheet helped. I read the chart and knocked replies as we went along. I'd never held a conversation through Morse before. Our communication killed time and got us through the experience.

It wasn't like we were in a nice, peaceful environment, either. I haven't described it completely. The OPFOR wanted to make sure that we felt entirely at home, and to achieve this, they provided an interesting abundance of ambience. I told myself they wanted to make sure that we were all jamming to our own favorite tunes. All at the same time and at max volume. The sound blaring down at us was a weird combination of techno heavy metal, pop, rap, and news propaganda, all multilayered, one sound on top of the other, with no beat or synchronization. Blasted at full volume from a speaker outside each cell.

If you wanted to yell, no one would hear you. You couldn't even talk to the guy next to you. An attempted conversation might go like this: *"Hey man! My name is Jim! How are you doing?"*

"Sorry! I can't hear you over the death-techno-propaganda rap!"

The propaganda was insane. They had a recording looping back over on itself, saying bad things about the United States, over and over. This went on for quite a long time, but that was the point. They wanted to confuse us and throw us off our game so we wouldn't know if it was day or night. It worked.

I can't give away all the tricks and things they did, because everybody in the position of possibly becoming a POW someday should get tricked. There is a learning objective embedded in every single minute of the entire SERE experience. One example of eye-opening trickery came at mealtime. They formed us into lines and ushered us into a building. We were starved, and there came a point, when we were about to eat, that we had to sign for what we thought was our food choice: chicken or tuna. The whole time, they yelled and screamed at us to hurry into a small, dark room with hard seats on a wooden floor. I quickly signed, neglecting to read the fine print at the top of the page.

Then a man came thudding down the narrow walkway with a clipboard. When he reached the front of the room, he pivoted on his step, looked at us and yelled, "All right! Good job! You all agree to be communists, and you hate America."

The lesson here? Read the fine print. Know what you are signing.

Then there was the confined-space endurance training—as if our little cells weren't small enough. They took us into another building and pushed us into little wood cubes. Time for a little solitary confinement. They made us drop down into the box, in a squatting position, with our hands and knees around our feet. In this position, you could sit on your butt but couldn't put your feet out. Basically, they trap you in a horrible seated fetal position. Then they shove your head down and drop the lid on the wooden box.

Everyone around you is stuck in the same position, in total darkness, for an unknown amount of time. This is sensory deprivation mixed with claustrophobia, on top of the food and sleep deprivation. At first I found my hard little box incredibly uncomfortable, but one of the benefits of my years of cross-country training was my knack for mental visualization. That old training trick kicked into gear and I removed my mind from my body.

I had used this same technique at INDOC. Whenever my muscles or joints were killing me, whether in my bed at home or in the dorm at Lackland, I would lie down. I would try to shut down the system. The process is simple in theory and can be very effective. Pain is felt in the brain, and the brain has the power to feel, just as it has the power to shut off that feeling. The technique I used involved relaxing my toes and slowly working my way up my limbs to my core. I let each body part become weightless and visualized the pain leaving.

In a matter of minutes, I was free of the pain of my body being in such an impossible position. With the pain gone, I had a relaxing little cubby.

The giant bearded man acting as OPFOR threw a mini tantrum when they opened the lid and found me snoring. He pulled me out and made me stand against the wall. I tried stretching out, while my eyes adjusted to the light. Down the hall I could see John, my fellow trainee and friend from INDOC and Airborne, my partner in crime at Airborne with the green feet flag. John was being escorted out of the building. He wasn't wearing the POW garb they had us in. He wore an orange jumpsuit. A member of the OPFOR trailed behind him with a mop, swearing. "What a disgusting piece of shit."

As a student, I braced myself. An angry instructor is never a good sign. I worked on being invisible against the wall, but an instructor came up to me, saying, "Can you believe that? That guy pissed himself to get out of an interrogation. I bet you don't have the balls to do that, do you?"

"No, sir! Don't need to go pee, sir!" I lied.

Then it was my turn for interrogation. I can't give all the details, but I did terrible that first try. I definitely wasn't the tough guy being asked about the green feet flag hanging over Airborne. The training took a slight detour here, which was the nice thing about the SERE experience. Because this was training, if shit got bad, they could pause and say, "Remember the classroom stuff we talked about all last week? Let's give you a five-minute refresher." You'd get briefed on what you did wrong and how to approach the situation. Then the instructor would leave the room and the interrogator would come back in. It was set up so the interrogator never had to break character. He was always the big scary person. The instructor could come in and provide something a little more warm and receptive.

They pushed me into another little room, probably six feet by eight feet, with seven-foot ceilings. White walls. Doors on the long sides, opposing each other. There was a small table against one wall. On that table sat a camera, a bunch of paper, and two metal chairs. In the corner opposite that, on my side, was a metal folding chair. Sitting on that chair was a small piece of plywood with an American flag painted on it. The back of the room was nothing but a big cement wall.

I stood at attention as instructed and the interrogator began yelling at me. I can't divulge much more than this, but I will tell you that their tricks were brilliant. They totally fooled me. They had some clever moves up their sleeves. They had pranked a prankster, and I loved it. I laughed. Had it been a real prison camp, I would probably have received a beating or been killed. Here, I cracked up instead of cracking.

The interrogator yelled, "Training time-out!" He stomped out and the instructor came back in.

"Damn, son. They got you!" he said, shaking his head. He went over all my mistakes. Starting with a failure to take inventory of the items in the room, but mostly with me being so quick to follow their orders. They weren't happy with me breaking character, either. I had been able to maintain my composure, right up until they tricked me.

There was no doubt that they got me, but at least I didn't have to pee myself.

The interrogation phase seemed to last forever, but all shitty things must come to an end. After the interrogation and resistance phase, we were gathered into a group and moved into what would be more of a traditional POW camp setting.

There were armed guards, we had menial chores, and they had us sleeping in huts. This had the feel of a POW camp from the movies. Everyone was cold, tired, and hungry and was continually getting interrogated. If you caught a guard's attention or messed up somehow, correction came in the form of fifty-gallon barrels that were buried in the ground. Cold water awaited you in the barrel, and they would stick you in, close the big lid down, and spray more cold water over the top so that it rained down through the holes. Plenty of cold water. I got into trouble for making eye contact with a guard, at some point, and did a little stint in the barrel after he asked me, "You eyeballin' me, turd?!"

The highlight of the whole experience came through a series of barter exchanges. I worked my way up to a can of green beans. The folks in my hut shared a big, industrial-size can of green beans. Green beans for a future Green Foot. Those beans were the closest thing to a meal I'd had in a day or two, and they tasted divine. To this day, I find myself eating green beans and loving them for the joy they brought me in the camp.

Some students were really struggling with the interrogations and the captivity. The green beans had saved me. I figured we couldn't be here much longer, but I wasn't certain. Time had a way of messing with your head when you reached the mock prison camp. We had clearly moved toward the escape portion of the school, and although some of us were trying to work out a plan, it just seemed impossible. John, however, had the entire camp of students working together to get him all the supplies he needed to make a daring escape. John radiated focus and intensity. He was serious about getting the hell out of that camp.

The guards ordered the entire camp into formation for the very last moments of the POW training, and that is when good old John made his move. I remember seeing a brief orange flash tearing through the foliage, then I turned away to watch the instructors instead of him. I knew he was making his break and I didn't want my face to give him away.

The whole force of instructors stood spewing this rousing closing speech they had no doubt given to countless classes. The acting leader of the camp strutted back and forth in front of us. "Comrades," he began, in this thick quasi-Russian accent. "Very good of you to assimilate into our culture. We are very happy you prisoners of war have become our comrades . . ."

I knew John was escaping at that moment, and a huge grin threatened to split my face right in two. No one caught on at first, but word of the escape shot through the guards in whispers. The shift in their attitude and tone was amazing and hilarious to watch.

When word reached our new comrade's ears, he gave a disgusted, "What? Really? Shit!" Within seconds, all the guards broke character and sprinted toward the gate to catch the guy blazing away from the camp. There went John. Orange jumpsuit and all.

There couldn't have been a better way to end SERE. An actual escape attempt that caught the OPFOR off guard—and on the last day, too. Not long after they rounded John up, a bus came into the compound to take us back to the SERE student dormitory. We were free.

Back in my dorm room, happy to be free of my cell and my coffee can, I settled down on the comfortable toilet, showered away the

filth, ate, and then fell into bed to sleep. I didn't have to go anywhere for three days. I had a long weekend before another series
of classes to wrap up my initial series of SERE courses. I planned
on eating and sleeping the entire weekend. A bunch of guys headed
out to celebrate surviving SERE, but for once, not me. I needed a
deep-cycle recharge.

All told, I had the luxury of attending five SERE courses. Three
are required in the pipeline. One of these is worth a brief mention
for the lesson I learned. It was about survival in the water, in the
case of a downed aircraft. Essentially, what the class is about is getting people comfortable in the water and familiarizing the aircrew
with what to do inside the aircraft "in the unlikely event of a water
landing."

The training took place at an indoor pool facility built with an
impressive array of environmental controls: a wavemaker; a big
sprayer, hoses, and sprinklers for rain; flashing lights; and giant
fans to simulate gusting wind. And noise. Plenty of noise.

The main event works like this: You're seated in a giant metal
airframe, like a big metal container, and the entire structure is on
a long hydraulic arm. You're strapped in the seat of what feels like
it could be a smaller airplane or a helicopter, on a bench facing out
toward the wings of the aircraft. After you take your seats and
everyone buckles in, the skeleton arm lifts the aircraft high into the
air over the pool. The feeling is similar to sitting on a roller coaster
at night. You're lifted up, and then you hear the pins pop. *Clink!*
Clink! You hear a creaking sound of the metal arm and the mo-
mentum shifts. You can see nothing. For a fraction of a second you
are free, and then you feel your world starting to speed up. Then
the craft hits the water with a *boom* followed by a weird impact
shock. As the craft settles, there is a slow sinking sensation. It's an
odd feeling of weightlessness—not the full force of gravitation,
but not free fall, either. Water surges in and begins filling up the
cabin, coming in through cracks in the walls and floor.

My first thought, when water flowed between my toes, was

Whoa! This is cold. While I debated my different perceptions and interpretations of the concept of "cold," the water filled what would soon be our metal coffin if we didn't get out.

In the training leading up to the dunk training I was about to get, they taught us to first find where your buckle is and then grab some sort of reference point, so you know which way is up and which way is down in the aircraft. You need to locate the reference point with your hand so you can identify where the doors are and how to get the hell out of there, because when that thing hits the water it's lights out and you can't see anymore.

When the craft slams into the water, it doesn't just sit in one spot. That would be far too easy. Instead of sinking peacefully, the body of the aircraft spins upside down and does this fun little underwater dance. This is a team sport; there are a bunch of people inside the dunker, not just you. At this point, you can panic and fight to get out as quickly as you can, or you can be cool.

I had already gone through INDOC, and I'd practically grown gills by this point. I sat back and relaxed and let the panicked people get through. There were folks who weren't proficient swimmers, and they were scared as hell and having a difficult time being upside down, under water, and in a sinking plane.

Rescue divers stood by in the pool the whole time, always ready and watching. I remember coming up one time and hearing the rescue diver yelling at someone, "Don't you ever grab at me! Don't ever grab at the diver!" The guy being yelled at had panicked; he wanted air and to reach the surface so badly that he began clawing frantically at the rescue diver.

For me, the first scenario was fun and informative, and I felt relaxed and comfortable. When we hit the water, I just sat there, like they had instructed us to, and waited for the aircraft to settle. Dark. I'm upside down and under water. I located my reference point, and my buckle, and I kept that reference point firmly grasped. Once I was ready to escape, I unbuckled with one hand while the other hand kept me oriented. I maintained positive control from one hand grip to another, and then to the next, hand over hand until I found the exit. Then I pushed out through the door and swam to the surface.

It sounds so simple, but when there are other people in that cramped space, men and women who can't swim well and are panicked, a level of chaos ensues, naturally adding to the challenge. I spent most of the time keeping my space protected. I had been through enough abuse at INDOC that I had gained a sixth sense for when a foot or fist was coming my direction. As the airframe made impact and began to sink, I relaxed, took a big breath of air, and waited for all the nastiness to settle. Who cared if I was the last one out of the bird?

The instructors picked up on my casual attitude. After I had crawled out of the pool, I was told something along the lines of "Okay, clearly you have the hang of this, Settle. So, this time, you need to be the first one out of the bird."

This upped the stakes considerably. On the next training iteration, I had to be the guy who opened the door. I felt the pressure of being the one with all the people behind me panicking and wanting out now. Things get a little more difficult when you're not the one in the back just chilling out.

We hit the water and I waited in position, doing what I needed to do in a flash. But these guys behind me were fighting for their own lives. The whole damn group was on my ass. If it had been just me, by myself, I would have done it slow and right. But with the frightened folks at my back? I felt the pressure. I struggled a bit to get the door open and get out through the hatch. I'm admitting now that this took me longer than I had anticipated. In my mind, I thought I was the cool guy with all the water training and could get that door open and get out way faster than these slow-asses. Not so. I rushed and screwed up trying to get that door open and get us out. Lesson learned. Ego put in check.

A little humility in the water was a good way to end the course there in Spokane. My graduation from SERE came with a little treat, as I jogged alongside the airfield one morning. There on the tarmac sat Air Force One. Or Two. It didn't matter. Seeing that enormous white jet with the presidential seal instilled in me a sense of pride. I stopped and watched as they refueled and someone I imagine was the pilot did his inspection walk beneath one of the expansive wings.

I wasn't a PJ yet, but I was on my way. For once in my life, I knew I was doing what I was meant to do. When I resumed my morning run, my stride was a bit longer and faster.

11

. . . .

Strike Two

For a while, I hung around Lackland, awaiting an opening at one of the schools. The break in my orders was long enough that they decided to call me back home to Alaska to continue some of the other training I needed. This training was the in-house Alaska cone stuff. I had just begun the first part of some SERE training, a survival upgrade training on being interrogated, which I was proving adept at after the green feet stunt at Airborne.

Life back in Alaska as an official cone, in the pipeline, came with a small degree of respect from the PJs in the unit but no fewer push-ups. Cone life meant waking up early and hitting the pool by 5:30. The other cones and I would get in a couple hours of pool time before having to report to the section by nine o'clock. This was to stay in shape for dive school while awaiting that call for an opening, and to train the next generation of cones behind me in the pipeline.

I'd returned to an empty house. The time away in the pipeline cost me my first serious relationship. Despite the heartbreak, I was enjoying my time home, newly single, hiking and skiing up a storm. But my time back in Alaska wouldn't last long.

I was supposed to know when I would be headed to dive school, and I thought I did. The training scheduler in charge of my unit informed me that the first class at the new air force school had started, but they didn't have any spots for me. "Sorry, Jimmy," he said. "Maybe in the next class they'll get you a spot."

This news was fine with me. I was enjoying being home in Alaska. I started the survival course at the section, and on the middle of the first day of training, the unit training scheduler came in and said, "Jimmy, you ready to go to dive school?"

"Hooyah, Sergeant! Sure am!" I said, lying.

"Great," he replied. "Your plane is in two hours."

"Oh! Okay! Cool!" I laughed. But it wasn't funny.

This was another bit of PJ training in action. Be ready for anything.

Luckily, I was a single guy at that time and it took nothing for me to get ready to fly out. So before I really got to enjoy being home, I was off again. I wasn't exactly depressed, because the destination, Panama City, Florida, had a reputation that appealed to me. Early reconnaissance from other cones informed me this was where all the beautiful college coeds in the country would frequent to escape the stresses of college life.

On the first day of dive school we got a loose inspection, and then, right off, we were hit with a tough PT test. They were making sure everyone was up to the physical standards for dive school, and that opening-day test was similar to the eight-week standard evaluation at INDOC. I needed to do a minimum of fifty-two push-ups, sixty-two sit-ups, and fifteen forward-grip pull-ups in a minute for each event, and a five-mile run in under forty minutes.

They considered this a baseline. People who took the PAST and passed but didn't become PJs sometimes like to fool themselves by saying, "Oh yeah? Well I *could* be a PJ." But the PAST is just an entryway into the program, and that's not even a fraction of what it takes to graduate. You have to train to a higher standard than the PAST, and that standard becomes the base level of fitness. All this work in the PJ pipeline is never a onetime training event.

A cone in the PJ pipeline doesn't ever say, "I'm going to do this marathon one time in my life and never do another one again." Rather, a cone says, "I'm going to be a marathon runner for the rest of my life." This is the kind of never-quit mind-set that must be maintained, right along with the body.

Heading into the PT test, I was a little nervous at first, mostly because of—again—those damn pull-ups. But the big thing that set this PT evaluation apart from others I'd been through was that the swim test would be in open water. I had only swum in open water one other time in my entire life. And it wasn't for any great distance.

Before the PT test, the cadre issued everyone their gear. I was assigned a little two-foot by two-foot shelving unit area with a chain-link partition between my cage and the cage next to me. In the dive school area, the dive gear was stored in an area with chain-link walls, to ensure airflow for drying gear. This was the first time in my career that I got to actually experience my own cage. Later, as a PJ, I would get a real cage. The PJ cage is full of some of the coolest gear on the planet. My area at dive school wasn't all that different; it contained some pretty sophisticated dive equipment. I'd been issued a depth gauge, stopwatch, dive boards, and an assortment of other gear that I didn't even know how to use.

The water in Panama City was warm, easily twice as warm as what I was used to in Alaska, but unlike our pristine Alaskan waters, this stuff was brown. Think mocha with a lot of milk in it. You couldn't see through the thick, silty mess. When you're under water, your visibility is, at best, five to ten feet. Because of this, everybody swims in two-man "buddy teams." You're tethered to each other by a rope with a carabiner on each end. We called that rope a Budweiser line, referring to the Budweiser horses that pulled the wagon with all the beer.

The first event was a run. First thing in the morning. No problem, just a race through the nice, tall, old-growth woods. My favorite kind of running. But then the sun rose and the heat hit, hard.
Oh, no, I thought. *This place is going to suck!* The air felt heavy and
thick. It was 99 percent humidity, with the mercury in the mid-
eighties and getting warmer. And the sun had only just risen. I'd
never run in heat like what I was about to face. Alaskans melt in
heat like that.

Enough daylight streamed through the canopy to reveal where
I needed to run, illuminating the ground with long shafts of light. I
remember enjoying that run, but I really began to worry. *Wow. It's
this early and it's already this hot and humid? I've never run in a place
like this. This could be interesting. Damn, this could be bad!*

The heat would turn out to be one of the biggest challenges I
faced in the pipeline. Heat and humidity is something no Alaskan
kid is accustomed to.

I barely survived the blazing hot run through the woods, and
next came the sit-ups, the push-ups, and the pull-ups. No more pull-
up failure for me. I had other things to worry about.

They sent us to our cages. I admired my fins and all this other
gear, and so naturally the PT instructor yelled, "Get that stuff on,
and let's start playing!"

We loaded up into two big Boston Whalers. The class split, half
in each boat. The boats took us out about a thousand meters from
shore. Our objective was to swim back to the pier.

I wore the required three layers. First came underwear. On top
of that I wore a very thin, almost spandex-like suit to protect my
skin from whatever stinging creatures swam around in the ocean.
Then, on top of that, my battle dress uniform. I would be swimming
with fins, a snorkel, and a mask.

We'd been instructed to jump from the boat, one by one, when
we reached the dump-off point. At my turn, I bailed. Once I reached
the surface, I gave the guy on the boat the *Okay* with my hand and

said, as instructed, "I'm okay, Dive Supe!" And then he gave me the *Okay* back.

When he yelled *"Go!"* I started swimming for the pier way off in the distance, thinking, *All of this for the eval?* I began finning and freestyle at the same time.

Unlike my grandmother, I had never swum in big waves before. The experience, that first time, was unsettling and scary. I crested one wave and thought, *Everything is just fine. It's just like I'm in a pool.* But I wasn't in a pool. My face would be back down in the water for a few more strokes and then I'd come back up to see and make sure I was still pointed in the right direction, and I'd be in the trough of a big wave. *Holy shit! I can't see anything. Am I even pointed the right way? The wrong way? What way am I going?*

The power of waves is humbling. So much force and energy. One moment I was up high, then down, then being thrust forward. The ocean was such a new experience, and at first I was scared, I'll admit it. My emotions surged with each rise and fall. I finned hard and lifted myself atop the crest of one wave like I was flying. I spotted the pier. I was on target and making good progress. I started to enjoy myself. Then I'd be down in a trough and unsure where I was or if I had made any progress forward. Each wave reminded me of a combination of flying and the floating feeling that comes with skiing on perfect snow. I think I associate everything that doesn't jostle my bones and joints with flying and skiing. Once I associated that feeling with a balance between flying and skiing in a snowstorm in white-out conditions, I put my face in the water and kicked with all I had. I'd come up every now and then to make sure I was pointed in the right direction, but then I let go of my fear of missing the pier and began relying on my internal GPS.

I really had to learn to trust myself on that first swim in open water. One thing I remember very clearly from that day is finning, finning, and more finning. I'd put my head down and fin for what felt like five minutes, then I'd pop my head up to see if I was still pointed in the right direction, thinking, *It doesn't look like I made it anywhere. The waves are pushing me away.*

My second big lesson about open water was about current. The current does one thing, while the waves do another. The current pulled at me, causing me to drift off target, and those frequent checks became important. It turned into a hard fight. In dive school they teach you that a combat diver is ineffective in water over three knots.

That first day, I felt ineffective as hell.

Later we tried to plan our water objective work during the tide changes, at slack tide. From that day forward, I really began to appreciate the power of the tide. Tide and current are incredible forces that were new to me. I grew up alongside the ocean, but we never swim. It's too cold, too dangerous. Other than rivers and creeks, which I had never really considered swimming spots, the concept of current was always sort of academic. I think, in some ways, I was afraid of big water on some instinctual level, perhaps stemming from my family's tragedy at Skilak Lake. For example, when I saw signs on any the beach that said, "Watch out for the rip current," I would think, *Rip current? That sounds terrible!* There wasn't any way I was getting in water with a warning sign.

Combat dive school would change that. The mentality of the instructors was simple, despite the current or waves: "You're getting in the water here, boys, right now. And you gotta get to that point over there in a half hour. *Go!*"

It only took a few open water swims for me to start to appreciate what it really takes to be a proficient swimmer in the ocean. I reached the pier that first day and passed the test, but all the way, it felt like I'd been swimming in a water treadmill set on high.

They ranked everybody in class based on our swim scores. I don't remember how many people were in my class, but I do remember I was number twenty-three. There are some fast swimmers in the world, but I'm not one of them.

The next day, after the evals, they sent us right to the pool. Here, we started doing the pool assessment. This included a fifty-meter underwater swim and many of the "ditch and don" exercises that we practiced at INDOC, where you remove and stow your gear under water and then put it all back on, often in pitch-black conditions. This portion in the pool was basically a rehash of the finals at INDOC. The instructors were making sure that we could still perform those same tasks at that same standard.

They issued us real scuba tanks, and before long we were swimming around in combat dive gear. Whenever we got into trouble—over whatever wild hair had wriggled up the instructors' asses—they made us wear these horrible scuba tanks filled with sand. Clearly, there is no air in a tank filled with sand, and you can imagine how heavy and difficult even just a few strokes are, with a heavy tank on your back.

Dive school quickly became a hellfest. Each new day made the one before it seem easy.

We were regularly having our balls smoked off in the pool or on the beach. They would have us wear fins and flooded dive masks while lying in the surf in our BDUs, the waves washing over us. We did flutter kicks and push-ups in the sand while the instructors screamed obscenities at us.

That was one of a very few times when I almost thought my body would quit, sprawled out in the white water and nearly drowning. I couldn't see anything with my mask full of sandy water, and my mouth was full of salt and sand. David Schumacher, Schu, a friend from my INDOC class, saved me by saying, "Holy fuck, dude! This is way harder than INDOC! I don't know about this." He was right, but that one little line focused me and brought me around. I wasn't going to let them get me there on the beach with a little water and sand.

The pool was pretty much torture, but manageable torture. They signed you off on being able to scuba. You learn pretty much what you'd get in a normal civilian dive course, but it's an intensive, all-day, five-day course in the pool. The instructors are doing everything they can, the entire time, to get rid of you: buddy breathing, full underwater harassment, and insane drills with your gear.

The grand finale, the moment you're building up to the entire time, is a version of buddy breathing, but you're by yourself. They call it "one-man comp"—"comp" being short for competency, or perhaps "completely out of your mind." For this exam, you're in the pool, wearing your scuba tanks and breathing through your regulator. You wear a weight belt to keep you on the bottom of the pool, and fins on your feet. Your dive mask has black duct tape all over the glass. You can see nothing.

When my time came for one-man comp, I sat on the bottom of the pool, surrounded by total darkness. I tried to be calm. I took long, slow, deep breaths. Nobody really knows what is going to happen during the one-man comp—it's all very hush-hush—and as a cone, up in Alaska, I didn't have access to scuba tanks anyway, so I couldn't exactly train for what was about to happen. Not that that anyone would have let us in the first place.

First, I got clobbered in the solar plexus with a cannonball. An actual pirate's iron cannonball, I'm fairly certain. The impact launched me through the water. I tumbled. The instructor lunged off the side wall and tackled me with his shoulder. He drove me, causing me to spin. I didn't know up from down. I tried to protect my regulator by keeping a hand clamped on it. One hand on my regulator. One on the tanks. Just as they told us to do. The hand on the tanks was to keep the tank bottles from coming up and hitting me on the back of the head. I kept getting tossed and turned and tumbled, and all the while, the regulator was stripped from my mouth again and again. I'd put it back, and they would tear it from my mouth yet again. All I could do was put it back in. Finally, they snatched it away and the damn thing disappeared. Now my oxygen source was gone. I reached back to where the hose for the regulator came out of the scuba tank manifold, right behind my head, searching for the origin of the hose.

You are taught to memorize where all these hoses come out, and which ones are which, so you can reach behind your head, feel the appropriate hose, and then trace it out to your mouth. That's how you find your regulator. This skill is especially important in blackout conditions. I did this a couple times, and then they took the regulator away again and tied a few simple knots in the line, twisting it up with the other hoses. I attempted to untie the knots behind my head while holding my breath. This whole time, they continued to pummel me, tossing me around in a washing machine of confusion.

The torture kept going and going, escalating until I couldn't undo the knot that the instructor had tied in the back of my tanks. I'd been warned this might happen, so at this point I had to ditch my tanks.

They had taught us a special sequence, in preparation for such an emergency.

I moved to my knees. With one hand behind my back, I held on to the manifold of the scuba tanks and, with the other hand, unbuckled my weight belt. I grabbed the tanks and pulled. The world was still all blacked out. I couldn't see what was going on, and I was doing all this by muscle memory and feel. I hoisted the tanks over my head and laid them down in front of me. Then I took off my weight belt and draped it over the top of the tanks—otherwise, the buoyancy would cause the tanks to float away.

The whole time, my lungs screamed for air.

I followed the other instructions. I stashed my fins under the tanks. I worked as quickly as I could, because I knew they would allow a quick cheat, a breath off the regulator. But first I had to untangle it. By this point, I'm sure I had probably gone without air for close to a minute or longer. My lungs were guppying, my diaphragm in spasm, trying to kick-start my lungs as my brain said, "Something is wrong. Let's get this show started and put those lungs to work!"

I'm underwater, lungs in contraction, and my consciousness is now in a battle with itself, saying, "No, we don't want to start

breathing right now. This is not the place to do that sort of thing."
I knew I didn't have much time left before I would either have to
pop to the surface or finally meet the wizard. I traced the regulator lines, found the knot, and got the system working.

That first lifesaving breath was nearly orgasmic.

I took that breath of relief. I could calm down for a second. Then
I made my final moves of the test. I took my mask off and hooked
it underneath the pile of gear. My eyes adjusted to the light, and a
quick glance told me I had my gear in the right order. Then I held
my fist high over my head and made the slow ascent to the surface,
blowing bubbles out the whole time so that I didn't come up too
fast and hurt myself.

I broke the surface, took a deep breath, and began to tread water
while the instructors inspected my gear. They swam down, making
sure I had put everything in the right order, and in the right way,
because there is a military standard to the whole process. They gave
me the all-clear sign. But it wasn't over.

I had put everything together right. I took a deep breath, dove
back down, and donned the fins, tank, regulator, and mask.

I made sure all the straps were right and swam for the surface.
I had completed the worst part of combat dive school. The event
was all but over. The rest of the course would be more hands-on,
less about abuse and more about learning the ropes of combat
diving. I felt a great sense of relief at having survived.

All I had to do was reach the side of the pool, get out, and get
inspected to make sure I had put everything back together properly, without twists or loose straps. I was almost there.

And, in that relief and sense of euphoria, I screwed up. Bad.
Really bad.

As I climbed out of the pool, my mask slipped from my hand.

I watched it slowly sink toward the bottom of the pool.

Just like that, I failed dive school.

I only dropped a piece of equipment at the end of the test, but
the bottom line is I failed. They had all the men who failed swim

to one corner of the pool to wait. I wasn't the first one there, and a handful of other people soon joined me. One of the people who failed was our class leader, Major Goodman. His name was spot on. He was as good a man as you could get. To me, he personified para-rescue. Physically a stud, the fastest runner on the course, and one of the fastest swimmers. Despite his age, probably early forties, he was on top of all the physical training scores.

When I reached him in the corner, treading water with the other failures, I said, "Man. Talk about going from hero to zero. Just like that."

Major Goodman said, "I went from the *top* of the class to I'm not even going to be able to graduate *from* class."

And just like that, Major Goodman put things into perspective for me.

"We'll make it the next class," I said, trying to be positive, but keenly aware I'd just hit strike two.

A few hours later, I was on a plane bound for Alaska, boiling with frustration. I was frustrated because I didn't feel that I could just go home and train to be any more ready than I was. The event I failed was not an event I could practice. I was frustrated with my-self because I think I'm a slow learner sometimes, and I often need to learn things twice before I can get it. I'd already been given a second chance, once. I didn't know what would happen when I got back to base. *I didn't quit. I worked hard. Does that matter?*

My answer came as soon as I got back to the Alaska unit and met with my boss, Chief Skip Kula. He said, "You know everyone gets three strikes. You get three attempts at the pipeline, Jimmy. However that plays out, you get three strikes." I already had one against me, with the pull-up failure at INDOC. Now my second, at dive school. One more, and the PJ dream wasn't happening.

The failure weighed on me. I didn't like the feeling that I was letting my Alaska team down. I also didn't want to bring any un-wanted extra attention upon myself. The Alaska unit had given me so much liberty to train on my own, so that I could do what I thought was the right thing. They had started cutting cones a little bit more slack. So I didn't want to let my brothers down or make them get any negative attention because of me.

I won't lie. I was bummed. Back in Alaska, back in cone life. All I could do was wait for another opening, and work. Naturally, I caught serious hell from the PJs for being recycled again, and I got smoked all the time, but there was really nothing I could do to get better at the event I had failed, without a scuba tank, a deep pool, and people willing to harass me to the point of drowning. Logistically, that was not going to happen. I had one option: fall back on my old habits of visualization. I had to prepare for my second shot at dive school mentally, by pretending.

Several times a day I would hold my breath, pretend to be working knots, and go over the entire underwater sequence in my mind. It was like one of those visualization moments from high school running, where I just started rehearsing each move, each step, and instead of visualizing the failure I had experienced, I was always visualizing ways to succeed. I saw that line through the trees, the way of getting past the failure. I worked past the frustration and regret of failing and became determined not to get stuck in the loop of failure that keeps people from reaching their dreams. You can learn *from* failure and succeed, or you can learn *how* to fail and never succeed.

12

. . . .

Yo-Yo and the Shark

The first combat dive class I attended at the Air Force Combat Diver School occurred early in the school's history—ours was only the second or third class from its inception. The instructors were intense and the standards were challenging. Training occurred in a building with several dive schools from other branches of the military. There were navy, marine, and explosive ordnance disposal divers, all in the same building and all working in the same pool. My guess is that the air force instructors had something to prove. Nearly all of the training events, that first time around, were unnecessarily hostile and difficult.

My second shot at dive school, with a new class, was almost like a poolside vacation by comparison. We got punished, and we got yelled at, but I could tell something was dramatically different. The punishment and physical exertion were more directed, geared in an instructional manner, as opposed to the almost vicious demeanor the previous classes had to deal with.

The instructors didn't seem to be trying to prove anything. They behaved more professionally and the atmosphere was way less harassing. I landed in a solid class. We weren't a bunch of fuckups;

we were all wired tight, mature and motivated. The instructors seemed to have a new level of respect for the men in the course, and we, in turn, held a similar respect for them.

The dive course begins with open water in the snorkel phase, then the pool with the scuba tanks, and then open water with scuba tanks. From there, you move to the deep dive. Then you do the same process all over again with a "closed circuit"—the ninja style of scuba diving. This is a complex rebreather system in which you have two hoses coming in, one on either side of your mouth. I think it's the coolest way to scuba dive. It's silent and stealthy.

During normal scuba diving, loud bubbles erupt next to your head when you exhale. But with the closed-circuit rebreather system there are no bubbles at all. This is some serious James Bond stuff. Using this apparatus, we could sneak up both on fish and on each other. Before dive school, I didn't even know such technology existed, and here I was, using it to swim up on unsuspecting sea creatures.

The problem with a closed-circuit system, however, is that you can't go deeper than twenty feet.

I received a nice little surprise during the transition into closed-circuit diving. The instructors assigned me a new swim buddy. I couldn't believe my fortune. "Jimmy!" There at his cage stood a muscle-bound bundle of energy and inspiration, my most motivational instructor from INDOC: Yo-Yo.

His operator name is Yo-Yo, and I've left it at that. It is best I not say too much about him. He's a chief now, but at the time he was headed to the 24th Special Tactics Squadron, the big-dog team of pararescue. These are some of the most elite PJs, doing "special tactics" around the globe. The 24th is based on the East Coast, and they do all the cool-guy missions, the ones no one can talk about. Yo-Yo got picked up for the 24th, but he wasn't closed-circuit qualified. He had joined our class to get that box checked on his overly impressive résumé.

Yo-Yo started his career as a boxer and as a cop in the air force.

He worked his way up to become a PJ. With him at my side, the course turned into fun, and because of who he was, he had a little leeway. More than once he goofed during dive prep. His mistakes often led to laughter rather than push-ups or flutter kicks.

One of his mistakes had us all laughing. Part of the closed-circuit system requires you to charge your lines with bottles of highly compressed pure oxygen. Great care needs to be taken while bleeding down the line. This required the instructors to come around and check us after each step in the process.

An instructor would say, "Step 1. Everybody get step 1?" And they would walk around and check us. "Step 2. Everybody got step 2?" Same process. And then this ear-piercing *"Ee-e-e!"* erupted. Imagine the sound a balloon makes when you squeeze the end while letting the air out, amplified with a thousand speakers. It was the type of loud that hurts. The instructors freaked out and made ready to bring serious pain for the mistake. They stomped toward us, ready to rip someone apart, ready to make us all do push-ups. The whole class stood there, holding our gear, petrified in fear, buttholes puckered. All of us were thinking, *Please, God, not another dive session smokefest.*

And then one of the instructors says, "Oh, it's Yo-Yo? All right. Well, carry on guys, carry on."

As our closed-circuit training progressed, we moved from daytime diving to nighttime diving. This wasn't simple vacation diving—scoot your butt off the boat, fall down in the water, float to the bottom of the ocean, and then swim your way back up. We practiced navigational diving. We dove with dive boards, which are buoyantly neutral and look similar to a kickboard a kid might use in the pool. The black-painted board has handles on the sides. On it, we wrote notes with a grease pencil. Attached to the top of the board were a depth gauge and a stopwatch, and in the middle was a compass.

The boats would drop us far out from the pier. We could barely see the target, or they'd give us a heading based on a GPS and say something like "All right, guys, your objective is two kilometers east at this heading." We would write the coordinates on our dive board and jump into the black water. We were not allowed to go above ten feet or below twenty feet. So, not only did we need to reach a certain point at a given time but also we needed to maintain an awareness of our depth and our overall heading. When swimming in the dark at night, you want to make sure you aren't drifting too far to the left or the right, and you have to keep track of how long you've been swimming. If you don't, you'll run into trouble.

Sometimes they would have us do "dogleg training," where we would swim a couple kilometers under water into a harbor, and then into our training harbor. We swam under the boats in order to reach a specified point, all the while doing these crazy doglegs, meaning we would swim on a heading for a specified amount of time and then change and swim on another heading.

They built us up to the point where we knew exactly how far we could swim under water in a given time. If we had to cover a thousand meters, we knew the time it would take to reach a location, given the water current and the gear we carried. And, as I would learn in the PJ world, once you become proficient at a task in the light, you become even better at that same task in the dark. They built our skill set up until eventually we were doing everything at night.

Even with all our advanced technology, the military still relies on inexpensive and simple items, too. Take, for instance, the simple glow stick, those silly six-inch plastic tubes filled with magical glowing liquid that mesmerize little kids at Halloween. Night work requires light, and for night dives we were issued glow sticks. To use, you crush the glow stick but don't take it out of the wrapper. Instead, you cut the wrapper slightly and then slide the entire stick into a narrow slot built into the dive board. The stick casts a soft green glow over depth gauge, note board, and compass. The compass also glows in the dark.

For me, the coolest thing about swimming at night was the

microscopic plankton. They glow when disturbed, turning into beautiful glow-in-the-dark streaks. Sometimes, when I was bored while swimming along, I would wave my hand in front of my face to see this color eruption. The closest comparison I can make would be to swimming through the aurora borealis in Alaska, if that were possible. The little phosphorescent creatures exploded into a vibrant green band of northern lights. One wave of my hand could light up the world around me in vivid colors.

Beyond that, night conditions in the water weren't always the stuff dreams are made of. One particular night, we faced some dark and murky water. I felt pretty unsettled. This wasn't too different from swimming in the pool with my mask blacked out—except that the sharks here weren't angry instructors but actual sharks. Yo-Yo led the way, so I figured if we ran into trouble he would do what Yo-Yo did best. Nothing bad could happen with him in the lead. On the Budweiser line, we made a decent two-man team.

If you're the second guy, as I was that night, you have two jobs. First, you're in charge of the floating buoy. This float is attached to you and trails up to the surface so boats know there are divers below. Your job is to make sure you're pulling the buoy. Your other job is to not slow the guy with the navigation board. To keep from doing this, you kick extra hard, so he doesn't have to pull the buoy. You want him focusing on the board. You put all your faith in him. This is like buddy breathing, but instead of relying on your partner for air, you need him to be navigating like a salmon headed home. The good part of trailing is that you don't have to pay attention. It's a trade-off: you pull the buoy one day, and then the next day you navigate.

Yo-Yo had point, while I finned and pulled. We swam fast through the complete blackness. I couldn't see anything, and I momentarily found myself daydreaming, in la-la land. All I could actually see was the Budweiser line connecting the two of us, but with all the sediment in the water, I could barely make out the rope just inches from my face. I needed to watch for a drift to the left or right. I wasn't really paying attention to anything but the rope, and then, all of a sudden, I felt the familiar movement of strong current, inches from my face. I sensed a hard hit coming at me. A blast of water pushed with force, the sort of pressure created when Sergeant Pack slammed the water around me in the pool at INDOC. Suddenly, Yo-Yo's fins were fanning my face as he kicked hard.

It doesn't take much to imagine how strong the legs of a PJ accepted into the 24th might be. Now take that same PJ and add some actual fear. Something in front of him had caused him to change course. He kicked with fury.

The side of a fin blasted me in the face, and my mask started leaking water. *What the hell is going on?* Before I had a chance to think, or to react to the shot to my head or the leaking mask, something slammed against me.

Something enormous, powerful, and with distinctly rough, sandpaper-like skin bumped me. Hard. Something about the water we were in changed, too. The atmosphere became charged and dangerous. I can't describe it any more clearly than that.

If there hadn't been a true test of the success of my heart surgery to that point, it happened that night in the ocean with Yo-Yo. If I didn't have that closed-circuit system in my mouth at the time, my heart might have jumped right out through my throat.

I didn't grow up with big creatures jolting me in the water, and I don't know about Yo-Yo's experience, but we both decided— without talking to each other—that it was time to head straight to the surface.

We both popped up, like two scared seals.

Yo-Yo asked, "Are you okay, man?"

I took a deep breath. "Yeah," I said. "What the fuck was that?"

"I don't know. Was that . . ." He paused. "Was that a fucking shark?"

"I don't know," I said. And I didn't. I didn't know and I didn't want to know.

"Maybe a manatee?" he said, more as a suggestive statement than a question.

"Yeah," I said, understanding what he was saying. "Let's go with manatee."

"All right."

We both took another deep breath of the night air and tried to relax. We still had to reach our objective. We had no choice. Back underwater we dove. Down toward whatever creature lurked beneath.

We were absolutely breaking protocol by surfacing. But, for a moment, we were in real trouble. I have no doubt. I was as terrified as I've ever been. I can't speak for Yo-Yo. At the time, I imagined he had probably never been scared in his life, and he surely wasn't scared that night. For all I knew, he probably frightened the shark. I thought of Yo-Yo as the Chuck Norris of pararescue. Later, I would learn that Yo-Yo didn't need the shark to frighten him. He was afraid of the water itself.

Speaking of action stars . . . Toward the end of the course, *combat* enters into the training, and we executed full combat gear beach assaults. The kind of mock attacks that Chuck Norris himself would be proud of. What we were doing looked and felt like we were coming right out of the latest blockbuster thriller. I don't want to give away any of our special training secrets, but the way we performed those assaults left me thinking, *This is how you do it. This is the real deal. This is what "special operations" means.*

What I appreciated most were my teammates. These were people who were taking everything deadly serious. These simulated battles weren't a game we played with friends. This wasn't like any of the times before, when I'd been pretending to do stuff for training exercises. The combat dive training felt real and raw. The instructors were out there hunting for us, and we had to get our whole team out of the water undetected.

For example, they might give us a navigational objective to

reach on land, but to get there we would go under water for a kilo-meter or two, at night. We had to be invisible and get the entire team onto the beach and into the jungle.

These were intense combat training scenarios, and I loved them. I'd never done anything similar. I'd advanced way beyond having my ass handed to me on the pull-up bar. We carried train-ing weapons—we called them "rubber duckies." They looked the same as an M4, and they weighed the same, but they lacked mov-ing parts and bullets. It was a solid piece of rubber-coated steel, and you could drop it, throw it, or roll it around in the sand. We used rubber duckies for everything. That's what we jumped with, and that's what we carried when we dove.

I was a young bachelor at the time, so my favorite exercises were the midday beach assaults. I won't deny feeling pretty cool as one of the tough-looking dudes who magically appeared from the depths of the ocean, strode up the beach in all this camouflage, ninja-like combat gear, and surprised a beach full of bikini-clad coeds relax-ing on their spring break.

I happened to hit this second shot at dive school right at spring break. When we weren't in the water and didn't have our faces in the books, we did our fair share of partying. The instructors knew where to go for fun, and because we were a good class, worked hard, and didn't do anything stupid, they had lightened up a little bit as far as the intensity of their harassment. Saturday nights were about the only time we could let loose. And we did. The rest of the time was spent studying, recovering from the rigors of the course, and getting ready for the week.

The six-week Air Force Combat Diver School was as tough aca-demically as it was physically. We studied an array of dive academ-ics, from medicine to physics. Dive medicine is crucial, because as a PJ you're studying to be a paramedic, too. We had to understand pressure and its effects on the human body. We needed to make sure we didn't hurt ourselves, and we needed to know how to treat people with diving-related symptoms.

For example, coming up to the surface too quickly can be a real problem. There are several different reasons, and we had to understand what all those reasons were and how to identify them if someone was showing symptoms. Then we needed to know what to do if a patient presented those symptoms. If a diver slurs his speech and his pupils look goofy, for instance, he might be having a brain aneurism because he came up to the surface too fast holding his breath. You have to get him into a dive chamber and drop him down as fast as you can, to get that air out of his system.

A diver has to surface from the bottom slowly enough to release the nitrogen from his bloodstream. When we're walking around on earth, there's a certain amount of nitrogen in the air, but only a small amount actually makes it into the bloodstream, through the permeability of the system and the alveoli sacs in the lungs. But when you go underwater and you're breathing scuba tank air, everything is different. Scuba air isn't pure oxygen, as you might think. It's actually the regular air you're breathing right now. The scuba tank guy fills the scuba tanks from the air right next to his house. The pressure in the tank is where the magic happens.

To fill a scuba bottle, the tank must be submerged in a barrel of water. Because you're compressing all that air into the bottle, you're creating a lot of heat. The chamber of water absorbs the heat. It also doesn't hurt to have the bottle inside a special case. Scuba bottles are mini bombs, and they can and do frequently explode, killing bystanders with shrapnel.

What this all means is that when you're scuba diving you're breathing normal air, but it's all compressed by a certain number of atmospheres of pressure, depending on how far beneath the surface you travel. The deeper you go, the more restriction. The big bubble molecules turn into little bubble molecules. The holes in the alveoli, the "colander" of your lung sac, don't change size, but the bubbles—the "pasta," if you will—have changed size because of the pressure. Now more of the pasta noodles can get through that colander. Nitrogen molecules are being compressed small enough to fit through the holes of the alveoli sacs and to enter the bloodstream. This is actually okay; it's not going to hurt you unless you come up faster than the nitrogen can escape your bloodstream. Once nitrogen becomes trapped in your bloodstream, though, and starts to collect in places like your joints and your spine, you're in trouble. Your spine starts turning, *bending,* and you've got "the bends."

The bends are one thing, but the other big problem is that, if you do a real nasty job on yourself, you could potentially form a bubble big enough to find its way to your brain, heart, or lungs. This gets nasty in quick fashion. That's why we studied and learned the decompression tables and decompression stops.

Deep underwater, you have to know how long you can be under before you enter decompression stop status. If you go down only twenty feet, you can pretty much stay underwater all night long— until a shark bumps you. But if you dip down to one hundred feet, a clock starts ticking. If you stay past twenty-two minutes, you have to start incorporating decompression stops, which means that instead of coming up from the bottom at the same rate as bubbles, which is normal, you have to come up about ten feet or so and hang out for fifteen minutes. Then you come up another ten feet or so and hang out for another fifteen minutes. This process can take up to an hour and sometimes requires supplemental support, with people bringing extra air tanks down to you. All of this is to give your body enough time to let those nitrogen molecules come back across the membranes. In civilian recreational diving, this is a big deal. In combat and rescue diving, the stakes rise significantly. Knowledge of dive physics and human physiology become even more essential, because you're talking about the lives of others.

We spent a solid four hours a day in the classroom, nearly every day, with tough exams every week. Not only were we learning about diving and its effects on the body but also we had to learn to identify dangers lurking in the water, such as the creepy living things that sting and bite, and about currents and tides, boats, submarines, navigation, and emergency protocols.

When graduation from the course arrived, I felt a huge sense of relief, and even a little pride. To be combat dive qualified was empowering, and I was proud to have that box checked off on my route through the pipeline. As far as the military goes, combat diver qualification is not something you see every day. I was lucky. Not very many people get to rock that pin or patch, which shows a diver with a superhero-looking mask and rebreather unit. Crossed dive knives below make it a divers' version of the pirates' skull and crossbones.

There was no patch or pin for the two strikes I also had earned in the pipeline, but I knew the truth. One more mistake, one more failure of an objective or a class, and the pipeline would spit me out to join the rest of the eighty-some percent who don't earn the beret. I still had a ways to go, and the hardest academic courses were in front of me. I knew I had it in me to make it, but I didn't anticipate that what was coming in my next course could spell the end of my dream.

13

....

Free Fall

The next tier of the pipeline for me was free fall. This school is based in Fort Bragg, North Carolina, at the John F. Kennedy Special Warfare Center and School. Your first week at free fall school is spent learning how to pack free fall parachutes, and then you are introduced to one of mankind's craziest inventions, the wind tunnel. If ever you want to be locked in a round padded room, it's at the Fort Bragg wind tunnel. The room has a heavy green padded barrier surrounding a sixteen-foot-diameter hole covered in heavy green webbing. Monster turbines blow up through the opening with enough force to slam you off your feet.

In the wind tunnel you learn how to fly. It gives you a place to practice learning how to be stable in the air. The movies make flying through the air look easy. You just jump out and *bam!* Anyone and everyone in the movies can instantly fly belly-down to the earth, flat and happy. Not so in real life. Flying takes work and strength. To stay in a flat, horizontal position is tough because of all the different inputs, from your feet, your hands, your head, your elbows, your knees, your hips, and then from all the gear strapped to your body. Each and every little movement needs to be adjusted and accounted for. Free falling is a dancing game, where you fight to stay in the correct position, with your belly facing down toward the earth. Once you learn to merely hold yourself stable in the air, then comes the fun stuff, like rolling over, doing flips, sliding left, right, forward, or backwards, and accelerating and decelerating. The best part of learning to fly in the wind tunnel is that you can simulate an extended free fall—instead of taking countless jumps out of an airplane to get the same amount of free fall time—and you won't die if you screw up.

After that first week in the tunnel and getting the rudiments of free fall under my belt, I moved on to Yuma, Arizona, to complete the course. There's a whole lot of nothing outside of Yuma, but it's a great place to jump out of airplanes. This was my introduction to the desert, to red mountains, sand, and constant sunshine, but not my last experience of it.

The first jump of free fall school was a ramp jump from a C-130. Talk about exciting. I wasn't the first guy out this time, but that didn't matter. We were significantly higher than any of our jumps at Airborne. The air temperature felt significantly different from the blazing heat on the ground. A chill hit me when they dropped that ramp for the first time, and the cabin pressure changed. The wind began to rip inside the aircraft. I'm sure we were jumping from around twelve thousand feet the first time, but it looked like a million feet to the ground.

Oh, baby, this is real! I'm about to skydive.

I watched the red desert passing so far down below us. I looked around and glanced at the other students to see whether they were as excited as me. Some looked like they were. A few others looked pale. For that first jump, we were launching with a two to one ratio, meaning two instructors for every one jumper. The two instructors were there to keep you from dying or killing someone else. One would fly directly in front of your face, giving you hand signals, perhaps directing you to straighten your legs out or relax your arms. The other instructor was behind you to help you control your body. They knew most of us would be terrible on that first jump, tumbling and sliding. And they were right. We were all over the place, one big, hot mess in the sky. Essentially, to keep students from colliding with one another, resulting in mass casualties, there's an instructor to babysit.

And hell yes, that first time flying was incredible.

Prior to the first jump, we went through the movements of the entire pull sequence, to the point that I could do it without even thinking. During this pull sequence training, you're looking at the altimeter and pretending to watch the needle drop, and then you go through the steps of deploying your chute. But on the ground there was no time pressure, because the earth isn't racing up to greet you. The time wasn't an issue at all. But when you jump out of an airplane, the clock is ticking away faster than you can even imagine. Scientists recently proved that time moves faster for someone on top of Denali than for the guys having beers back in Talkeetna, and if there is any place you can feel this, it's when you bail out the back of an airplane.

On that first jump, I looked at my altimeter and thought, *The hands on this damn thing are moving so fast I can't even make out my altitude.* The wind blasted my face with such force that if I opened my mouth my cheeks would inflate. If I hadn't had goggles on it would have been impossible to see at all—the eyes become instantly watery and blurry from the rush of air. I would learn this the hard way, on more than one jump, when my goggles flipped up on me.

From the moment you jump from the plane, you're trying to adjust your gear and get your goggles clamped down. But that screws up your flight because your arms aren't where they're supposed to be, so then you're spinning or sliding. "Sliding" is a term that skydivers use to describe somebody moving horizontally across the sky, instead of just straight up and down. The fall arc of someone sliding would look like a slope instead of like a straight line down on top of the target. You don't want to slide. If the jumpmaster puts you out the door on a certain spot, he's doing it for a reason. If you go sliding around, you're off the target—and the farther off target you are, the longer your hike out of the desert with your heavy chute and gear.

When my turn came, I stood looking out the back of the airplane. One instructor was directly in front of me, at the edge of the ramp, his back to the world. He was looking into the airplane, over my shoulder, at the jumpmaster behind me. Then the jumpmaster behind me yelled, "Go!"

The guy behind me had his hand on my shoulder. When this instructor said go, I had been told, "Run as fast as you can off the back." It was only a step, but he said, "Don't hesitate; just go. You run and do a belly flop."

One step. Two steps. The first instructor fell away. In that instant I thought, *Whoa, that's weird!* Then, before I even realized what was happening, I was yelling, "Whoa-a-a-ah!" and following him down.

The whole world changed as I tumbled, naturally, and because I was a rookie, I had the profound opportunity to see the bottom of the airplane as it flew away. Then, for half a second, I thought, *Oh my God. I did it!* I turned my body and flipped back over. *Oh! There's the earth! Oh God!* I attempted an adjustment and *Whoops! There's the sky, again!*

Eventually, the world stabilized beneath me, probably due to the rear instructor grabbing me and lending a little assistance. Then the main instructor magically appeared in my field of vision. He began to give me hand signals to relax, straighten my legs, and relax my arms.

To mean "straighten the legs," they give you the peace sign. The instructor got in my face and threw the peace sign. It's not the movies, so you can't talk while skydiving. There are no deep conversations in the sky. The sound of wind rushing through your ears is beyond deafening. Communication is solely through hand signals. The one big intervention I received that first time was the peace sign: "Straighten your legs! Straighten your legs!"

One of the big issues, with new jumpers especially, is backsliding—

sliding backwards—and that happens because the legs aren't straight enough. They're bent up, with heels kicking the butt. Staying stable in the sky is hard. You have to actively engage your muscles in order to keep your appendages where they need to be. The resistance of the wind is powerful, and right out of the gate you can feel how your flight changes with even the slightest movement of a hand. If one hand is even palmed a little bit differently than the other, it will cause your body to rotate. The instructors teach you how to slide intentionally, and this way you can correct and counterslide if you begin to slip. This knowledge becomes especially vital when jumping with gear; the equipment can take you for a wild ride. The more crap you have strapped to your body, the more effort is required to control the flight surfaces, and you've got to know how to counteract. Many times, for instance, you're going to be trying to free fall straight down on a target, but the equipment will be pulling hard to the left, and this leaves you trying with all your might to force yourself to slide right.

Once I stabilized on my first free fall, I got a good glance at my altimeter. I was shocked that my pullout was seconds away, and a bit of disappointment hit me. *I barely had time to enjoy free falling!* I took a moment to take in the sensation. *I'm flying. I'm really flying! This is the best thing ever.* That moment I took to enjoy my first free fall really was magical. I checked my wrist again and it was time. My moment of appreciation over. Without thought, I made my pull. Whoosh!

The crush of deceleration as the parachute opens is jarring as hell. They call it "opening shock" for a reason. You decelerate from more than a hundred miles an hour to a very comfortable drop speed of fourteen miles per hour. The initial shock when that chute opens and fills with air squashes you, sucking the wind right out of your chest. I appreciated eventually learning to pack the chute so it didn't destroy me when it opened. There's a right way and a wrong way to pack a parachute. Even so, adjusting to the opening shock was a bit brutal those first couple of days.

I landed my first free fall, quickly packed the chute, and then scrambled toward the drop zone for the pickup for the next jump. We did three or four jumps that first day.

I was in love. After that first jump, I wanted more. Free fall was a shot of adrenaline, beauty, and magic. Dreams and visions of flying are great, but they've got nothing on the real thing. I relished the anticipation that came with standing on the ramp, staring down at the earth, and then launching myself out toward her. Free fall, to me, was what life was all about, and in those minutes of soaring through the sky, life couldn't get any better.

But not everybody caught on quickly, and my PJ friends in the course with me decided we needed more practice at night. We didn't have a plane or a wind tunnel at our disposal, so we did the next best thing. We broke into the pool on base and practiced jumping off the high dive. We worked on our airplane exits and practiced being stable in the air as we jumped off the ramp. When you leave the aircraft, you have to stick your exit. If your body is too loose and floppy, you'll end up tumbling through the air; if you're too stiff, the force of the air will treat you like a sheet of plywood in a hurricane and flip you over and over. You have to find the happy medium where you are a cross between Gumby and that sheet of plywood.

This is was what we were practicing in the pool. To the untrained eye—or a security guard—we would have appeared to be some buffoons doing belly flops off the high dive. In typical PJ fashion, we were guys breaking in to a government military facility, but only for the purpose of getting extra training. Clearly, the training we did all day wasn't enough, and we wanted more—and we found it. We didn't get busted, but we were pretty paranoid the entire time.

The first few days of jumps at free fall were what we call "Hollywood" jumps. These were slick, meaning no military equipment. We wore only a helmet and a parachute. We worked up from

Hollywood to jumping with equipment. The gear jumps began with a rucksack. Each man's ruck weighed the same, forty to fifty pounds. Inside the ruck, we carried the most sophisticated military training technology ever: a giant sandbag. Next came the combat jump, where we added a weapon. The next step up was the O_2 jump. Here, we had the ruck, the weapon, oxygen tanks, and an oxygen mask strapped to our helmets.

This is the action hero setup. The gear is pretty neat, but with the new gear comes added difficulty. Instead of paying attention only to your altitude, you've got your hands full. Now you're flying through the sky with a hose in your face, some limits to your vision, and additional concerns, like oxygen or explosive tanks strapped to your back. You look like a *Star Wars* stormtrooper.

The next level was the night jump series, where we did the same sequence, but at night. The whole course built up to the final for the class, successful completion of two night-combat-O_2 jumps.

The grand finale of free fall school is a full-locker night jump—jumping at night with everything in your locker: weapon, rucksack, and O_2 bottles. This is exciting, but it also means you have more things to pay attention to, which makes it infinitely more dangerous as well.

On the sequence of night jumps, I felt cool and confident about my situation. I was two jumps away from getting my free fall patch and one step further through the pipeline. All jocked up, in formation, I awaited our chalk's chance to jump. Beside me sat my buddy Schumacher. They had us on the floor with parachutes on our backs, rucksacks in our laps, and oxygen masks hanging from our helmets, fighter pilot style. I looked side to side and admired what I saw around me. Like nearly every other boy in America, I grew up admiring the gear and gadgets on toy action figures, and here I sat, with men dressed in gear that looked just as cool. We were minutes from jumping out of an airplane at night, in our first full-locker jump. I doubt anyone was more excited than I was.

The plane climbed to altitude, and then the ramp opened to this yawning blackness. There were no reference points. I couldn't see the horizon, could only make out a few lights far off in the distance. A cluster of houses, a gas station, or a UFO? They were too far off to tell.

The little illumination in the cabin came from the jumpmaster's lights and our ChemLights. We each wore a green ChemLight on back and a red one on front. There was just enough illumination to recheck all our buckles and straps in the pale glow. I eased up closer to the door. The jumpmaster pinched his fingers one inch apart and hollered, "Thirty seconds!"

At that signal, a wave of goose bumps rushed over my skin. Behind that came little jolts of electricity that started at my stomach and raced out to the periphery, all the way out to my fingertips. My whole body started to come alive with anticipation. I took long, deep breaths, as I would do before the start of a big race. The cargo bay smelled of airplane exhaust and the stink of sweaty men, their digestive systems releasing gas as we hit altitude.

The jumpmaster gave the sign for "ten seconds." We moved to the edge of the ramp. At this point, if I had any second thoughts, the chances of backing out were gone. I was committed now. The voices in my head were dueling: *Are you crazy? This is insane. Jumping out of airplanes is one thing. Doing it at night? You're a lunatic. This is the best thing ever. Oh, baby. Oh, shit, here we go!*

The little red light that hooks to the door turned green and I watched the guys in front of me vanish. I would be the second guy out of the airplane, with one instructor. He stood in front of me as that first pair disappeared into the blackness. I stepped up, and my instructor disappeared. Then, without thinking, I dove right out after him.

That jump into the void was a really weird sensation, like following someone into a giant rabbit hole. I shouted out, *"Wahoo! This is awesome!,"* which I'm sure I probably yelled on every single jump at free fall school. My night free fall and parachute opening was awesome. Everything was going according to plan. Right up until my feet hit the ground.

One of the dangers in all jumping, and one of the things you're never supposed to do when coming in for a landing, is to reach your foot out. They teach you, over and over, *Don't reach. Hold your position and allow the ground to come up to you.* Rookies won't listen, and in anticipation, fear, or stupidity, they will reach for the ground. This is an easy way to strain an ankle, sprain a knee, or worse. Ideally you want to have your feet, ankles, and knees together, all working as one unit, so you don't jerk or twist them up.

Don't reach.

I pulled off the entire free fall sequence. I was solid. I had this jumping thing in the bag. Below, I could see the drop zone, marked with some lights. I was trying to fly toward it but found myself a little farther downwind than I wanted. Then I made my first mistake: I misread the wind. Instead of heading into the wind, I approached my landing with it. Not smart.

A little backstory on the parachute is in order here. The parachute, as you fall, turns vertical energy into horizontal energy, converting your fall into a horizontal ground speed of nineteen to twenty miles per hour. That night, gusts of wind were just about hitting the threshold at which the jumpmasters considered canceling the night jump. Since it was dark, I didn't have a great read on where the ground was, plus I made the rookie mistake of misinterpreting the direction of the wind in the night. I had turned around and run with the wind, so my canopy speed of nineteen miles per hour was amplified by the wind gusts. I saw the ground at the very last second, and my brain responded, *Shit! Land! That's way faster than it should be! Shit! Shit!*

The ground raced up to greet me. That's when I made my next rookie mistake. I was coming in hot and crabbing sideways, and I did the first thing that came to me. I reached. *Wham!* I hit hard with my right foot and crumpled into it. Lightning ripped through my

leg; pain sliced up my shin and across the outside of my calf, shooting all the way up my right leg to my knee. All of this came a fraction of a second before my knee felt like it hit a land mine.

I screamed, then writhed in pain on the desert floor, a mess of
gear, man, and words that didn't even exist in the English language
in the seconds prior to my foot hitting the hard-packed earth and
rocks. One of my fellow jumpers ran over and asked the obvious
question you ask any man writhing around the desert floor, swearing in pain. "Are you all right?"

"I. Think. So." I responded through gritted teeth and grunts,
between stabs of agony. I held my knee and tried to relax. I stared
up at the sky and watched the ChemLights of the other guys coming in to land. There I was, the night before the last jump, almost
done with free fall school, one of the easier and more enjoyable
schools, and also one of the hardest for regular people in the military to get into.

My mind raced. First I thought, *Shit. Third strike. I am going to
fail.*

Then I told myself, *I'm not going to let that happen.*

And that was about the time when the endorphins and adrenaline started to kick in.

I forced myself to stand. I tried taking a step, but I really couldn't
bear weight. I bundled up all my gear, and that night, because of
the wind, we were really spread out. The distance between jumpers
had been so great that the cadre came zipping around in these
little ATVs we called Gators, a little six-wheel side-by-side with an
open pickup truck–like bed in the back. The Gator could fit four
guys in the back with our chutes. When it pulled up to grab me, I
piled in the back. The appearance of the Gator gave me a slight reprieve, and on the bumpy ride back I tried to ignore the pain and
come up with a plan. I wasn't sure if I was going to tell the medic or
the doc. I didn't want to get disqualified, especially being so close to
completing.

That first night, I iced my knee and took a handful of ibuprofen.

I went over my options with my cone teammates, but I didn't talk to the cadre about my knee. I wasn't sure if I was going to be able to complete the next jump, but I was going to give it a shot. I couldn't really put weight on my right leg, but I wasn't going to quit. I had a limp I couldn't hide, and I had no idea how I would pull off another free fall.

That final jump was a night jump. We showed up in the afternoon, and with a whole lot of help from my pipeline brothers I was able to put all my gear together and get jocked up. Then to the waiting point, and that inevitable limp on to the airplane.

By this time, my instructor had noticed the hitch in my gait.

"You all right, Settle?" he asked.

I gave him the *Okay* sign, and as enthusiastic a "Hooyah" as I could muster. I wasn't one hundred percent confident I would get a refire at free fall. I didn't want to find out and I wasn't going to ask. If they did give me a medical pass and allowed me to take the course again, it would mean months of waiting, akin to a giant stopper jammed right in the pipeline, slowing any and all movement toward my maroon beret.

The cones helped me by carrying my gear to the jumpmaster station next to the airplane. This saved me from having to waddle so far. The near-pants-pissing delayed parachute inspections of the army were a thing of the past. If anything, the military is efficient when it comes to free fall school. We inspected planeside.

The full load on my knee would have been roughly three hundred pounds, between body weight, chute, and gear. The cones not only carried my gear out to the plane but also walked tightly behind and beside me, each using a bit of his might on the sly, hands on the back of my ruck, attempting to lift me skyward as I hobbled aboard the aircraft. My left leg muscles bore the majority of the weight, and the fibers began to quiver and send unpleasant electric threats of impending and crippling leg-shocking cramps. Meanwhile, my right leg dangled along for the ride, sending its own crude warnings and alarms of pain radiating up my leg each time my boot hit the ground. I'd been in so much torment earlier that day, I couldn't eat dinner. I couldn't eat anything. I only wanted to get the day over with as soon as possible.

The exact moment I had both feet into the plane and could sit, a loud "Thank God" shot out of my mouth. I nodded an appreciative thanks to the men around me. I could finally sit and relax. Twenty more steps and I'd be done with free fall, one way or the other.

Soon we got the signal that we were on approach to the drop zone. I found the strength to stand. I rechecked my equipment, then checked the guy in front of me and tapped him on the shoulder to let him know his gear looked okay. Someone did the same behind me. The light lit up red, the ramp began its slow drop, and then the one-minute call went out. Everybody shuffled forward, packing in tight. At thirty seconds, we closed tighter, and at ten, everyone was amped and I could feel the tension, the excitement, and so I was counting every second. One leg throbbed because it bore all three hundred pounds, and something was dreadfully wrong with the other. I'd never wanted out of a plane as bad as I did at that moment. I wanted only to be in free fall so I could get the weight off of my leg and get that free shot of pain-relieving adrenaline.

Green light. Go.

That was probably one of my best exits ever, because as I jumped out of the aircraft, I was totally and absolutely relaxed, as opposed to being rigid and instantly tumbling. This was full combat load. I had a ruck hanging on my belly, my weapon, and a mask on my face. The moment I went into free fall, all those needles, knives, and broken glass bothering my leg? Gone! None of it mattered anymore. All those troubles with my knee, and all the weight of the world, evaporated. All that mattered in that moment was the beauty of the black earth below and the starry night sky above. That, and the altimeter.

Once I passed through the opening altitude, and that opening sequence, everything was fine. Because of the hard lesson the day before, I knew which way to fly—into the wind—and I read the ground signs. I made my approach, and when I was about one foot from the ground, you better believe I didn't reach. If anything, I pulled my legs right up inside my colon. I tucked both legs and I hit the ground like a sack of wet shit. I let the ruck take the impact, and I just balled up and *splat!*

That landing was a yard sale of expensive military equipment flying everywhere. This time there was no screaming or swearing. I was just happy I didn't hurt my leg any more. I rolled to my knees and tried to stand, but I couldn't. I did the only thing I could think of doing. I rolled over on my back, facing up at the sky, and packed my chute up. With my typical luck, I was just close enough to the drop zone that they weren't going to come get me but far enough away that, on a normal day, it would be a good five-minute walk. The distance was a little heartbreaking. If only I'd landed on the V, I wouldn't have to walk. I bagged up the chute.

In the darkness I could see a figure approaching. I hoped it might be someone benevolent. Before he reached me, I heard his voice. "You in one piece, Jimmy?"

Good old Schumacher. I couldn't have asked for anyone better to appear out of the blackness, and I didn't even have to beg for his help. Schu lifted me to my feet and helped carry my parachute and ruck while I limped alongside him, back to the drop zone.

"We did it, Schu!" I said. "We did it!"

14

....

Emergency Medicine

Three weeks later, back in Alaska, they figured out the problem. When I hit the ground that night, I ruptured the fascia and soft tissue around the muscle groups in my leg. The trauma created a form of compartment syndrome, straining and stressing the tendons.

I owe my recovery to our flight doctor on the Alaska pararescue team. He figured out what was wrong with my leg and gave me an excellent course of therapy. He put me in a high-tech Bledsoe boot for the next six months, with an additional six solid months of rehab. Without him figuring out the problem, my PJ dream would have been over.

I had to stay home in Alaska for those six months, instead of dropping into my slot in Albuquerque, New Mexico, to begin the medical training to become a PJ. The knee set me back, but that was fine. I scooted around the Alaska unit on crutches with the boot, which made an easy target for the PJs to find and smoke. They would drop me constantly for push-ups and flutter kicks. Flutter kicks were the worst, with that damn heavy boot on my leg. I still had to wear the workout gear of a cone, with no pockets, so I made some cool modifications to my crutches. I took a plastic water scoop and, using duct tape, Alaska-fashioned a holder under the middle handle of the crutches. That was where I carried my keys, wallet, and phone. To this day, I'm surprised my invention hasn't caught on commercially.

During my recovery, when I wasn't trying to be stealthy on my crutches around the PJs, I watched them put the screws to a new batch of toads pushing their way up around the section, their eyes set on becoming cones. One of those young men was Aaron Parcha, a wiry eighteen-year-old kid with an anything-goes attitude and the determination of a hungry wolverine, a characteristic that seems to be common among those with a goal of coming out the other side of the pipeline.

He was preparing to head off to INDOC, so I gave him some sage advice that would be key to him getting his beret. I had picked up the line myself along the way, perhaps from Yo-Yo, Major Adrian, or Maddamma. According to Aaron, I was driving him from or to a smoke session up in the mountains and offering my own pointers and tricks that I'd gathered in the pipeline. He took my advice to heart, and when he got to INDOC he placed in his mask a piece of white medical tape with "PARCHA" written on it, facing through the glass, as instructed, for identification purposes. On the back side of the tape, the side only he could see when he was wearing his mask, he wrote the two words of wisdom I had shared with him. He said that, during the worst of those diving sessions in the pool, with Mount Pack and the other sharks eating him alive, he would look up toward his forehead and use my phrase to keep him calm and centered.

Later, during Hell Night or one of the many other times the cadre took everyone's shit and threw it in the pool, one of the instructors grabbed his mask from the deck, read the inside, and laughed.

The cadre yelled out, "Who the fuck is 'Be Cool'?"

Aaron raised his hand.

The cadre whipped the mask out into the middle of the pool. "Don't just sit there! Go get it, Be Cool!"

Before long, I was back to running at one hundred percent and was off to Albuquerque. The next iteration of training on the pipeline was the medical phase. The course structure requires you to pass through the first portion before you can move on, and much like INDOC and the Air Force Combat Diver School, a filtering process ensures that only the best will move along.

The EMT course fed into the paramedic school. All through the pipeline, the majority of attention and focus is on the body and the spirit. Not in the New Age guru way but in the no-nonsense, military way. How much can your mind, body, and spirit handle? When are you going to break? The pipeline tests your physical and emotional endurance. Then you come rolling in to the medical side and you can put those bulging muscles on a shelf. All the strength and might in the world doesn't mean shit anymore. The time has arrived to use that muscle between your ears.

Some struggled with the adjustment to academics. There is no crawl, walk, run phase when it comes to learning medicine. This is a flat-out sprint, from sunup to sundown. The air force takes a normal EMT course, normally a six-month program, and crams all the same information into four weeks. *Four weeks.* The final exam isn't in the pool or at the pull-up bar; instead, you sit for the national exam. Pass, and you move on to the paramedic phase. Fail, and it's another strike.

The paramedic phase takes a standard two-year course and crunches it into six months. After that six months of academics, you do a six-week intensive practical.

The first day, we formed up and jogged in as a unit. The schoolhouse was set up just like the one at INDOC, with pull-up bars outside. When we arrived at the school for the morning, we all completed a required set of pull-ups and entered. At the time, the school was connected to the rest of the pararescue trainee areas, the instructors' gyms, and the medical supply area. The class was being proctored by real-world firefighters and paramedics. They were brilliant instructors; most of them were out of Eastern New Mexico University's Roswell campus. One of the instructors, Tom Cremeens, would become a lifelong friend. Tom taught me medicine and how to be a medic. He seemed to know everything about emergency medicine and could always answer my questions. I felt like I could ask him anything without feeling silly. Tom explained things in a way that a knuckle-dragging PJ student like myself could understand.

When we hit our desks for that first class, they issued us our textbooks. I felt small behind the tall stack of slaughtered trees sitting in front of me. These were thick books, the kind you could cut the middle out of and hide a small child inside. I'd done my short stints at college and the naval academy, and I'd seen some fat textbooks, but these were monsters. Who needed sandbags in your ruck? They could have just issued giant textbooks.

The instructor that morning said, "We're going to get through these books this month, so you guys cancel your plans for the weekend. You are going to be studying."

Our education came through a fire hose. The course was hard, fast, and tough, but incredible. I learned more in those few weeks than I had in all my previous schooling, and I excelled in that sort of learning environment. School hours were from dawn until dusk. Then, at night, we studied. In class they had us practicing plenty of hands-on skills. We learned how to assess patients, take pulses, and grasp the basics of emergency medicine.

I passed the EMT test and it was on to the big leagues, the paramedic portion. EMT basic is Robin to the paramedic Batman. The learning curve was about to go vertical.

Paramedic school jumped right into all the sexy lifesaving procedures. Stuff like IVs, airways, and pushing meds. I became as excited about the medical lifesaving part of my future job as the free fall part.

Many of the procedures required us to practice on dummies, and some of those dummies were my fellow cones. We practiced on one another all the time for training purposes. We needed to be adept at IV starts, and going through this part of the training really gave me an appreciation, later on in life, whenever I received an IV from nurses or medics. I learned to appreciate somebody who is good making the needle stab. You really don't want someone fishing around in your arm for vein, poking you with a needle like you're some kind of human sewing machine.

We were all brand-new at giving IVs, and none of us knew what the hell we were doing. Our competitive nature came out when practicing on each other. No one wants to miss a vein, and so we're all trying and trying, stabbing in and out of each other's arms like amateur serial killers. We were all completely black and blue from that training phase. My arms looked like I was a heroin addict, but in that short time, I became adept at giving IVs. Later, I would learn this is a valuable tool to have when it comes to battlefield or emergency medicine. If you're not good at placing an IV under great lighting in a stable environment, you're going to struggle when the lights go off and the helicopter is bouncing through turbulence over the mountains.

An IV access point allows for some serious medical miracles. I had no idea at the time, but I would use those classroom skills in Afghanistan, where I gave a wounded soldier an IV in the dark of a rumbling HH-60, delivering some lifesaving Hextend when he was bleeding out. Hextend is a medicine that you put in the veins, but it doesn't fill the veins in the same way that saline does. Instead, it fills up veins by pulling the water out of what are called the "third spaces." These are the spaces between your intestines, between your guts and muscles. The goal of pushing Hextend is to deliver moisture into the veins and keep the blood pressure stable.

If someone's blood tank is leaking, the blood level will drop to the point that there isn't enough blood in the system to create pressure for oxygen and carbon dioxide exchange at the capillary level.

I share all of this because the ability to keep people from bleeding out is directly related to the mission of a PJ, and even to the origin of paramedic medicine. There is a whole cascade of events that happen when you start to suffer blood loss. One of the big takeaways from the Vietnam War, as far as first responder medicine is concerned, came from initiating IVs when trauma patients were bleeding out. IVs administered in the field save lives.

Paramedic school meant long, hard days of sitting at a desk, intense hands-on simulations, and hard brain days. My personal habits had to change to reflect the intensity of the intellectual demands placed upon me. Earlier in the pipeline, with the exertion mostly all based on fitness-level work, I kept my diet very controlled as far as what and when I ate and drank. At other courses, I could get smoked at any time, so, for example, I wouldn't want to have coffee erupting from my belly when I was forced to do hundreds of push-ups. The paramedic instructors might make us "pay the man after school," as they would say when they were going to smoke us, but during the day we remained in intense academic mode. This meant that I could enjoy the finer things in life. A big mug of coffee. Sitting in a chair. I enjoyed using my brain for a change, and I loved thinking about what it might be like on the other side of the pipeline.

A couple other key lessons for me came at paramedic school. One was how to perform an endotracheal intubation. This is done when an unconscious person possesses an extremely compromised airway. You establish an airway that is protected, and you can breathe for the patient by hooking him up to a machine or using a bag.

The procedure isn't easy, and it takes practice. Essentially, you take a tube and stick it down the person's throat. We had a special tool called a laryngoscope. The instrument looks like the metallic business end of a scythe. You hold the device like a *hang loose* sign, scoop it in, lift the tongue out of the way, visualize the vocal cords, which look almost like two snake fangs, and then pass the instrument and the tube by the vocal cords so the balloon tip at the end of the tube is clear of the cords. Then you inflate the little balloon and remove the syringe and the tool. This is also handy if someone has taken a bullet or shrapnel to the face. There are a lot of situations where you could find yourself intubating somebody.

I would also learn that, in dire situations, a person might have to skip the endotracheal intubation altogether and go straight for the throat. Literally. They taught us how to administer a field cricothyroidotomy, or cric. PJs learn to perform crics, a surgically placed airway through the cricothyroid membrane, between the thyroid cartilage and the cricoid ring. A tracheotomy is when you place the airway lower, between the tracheal rings, and this is a procedure normally reserved for the hospital.

That seemed crazy to me, cutting into a man's windpipe. Never once, even with my wild proclivity for imagination and visualization, would I have guessed that one day I would perform this operation in the back of a helicopter while hovering over a battlefield.

Other crazy procedures we practiced on one another were inserting an NPA tube, the nasopharyngeal airway, also known as a trumpet, and nasogastric, or NG, tubes. Some will find this a bit disgusting, but we had to learn, and what better way than to try it out on a buddy? The NG tube insertion meant taking a clear, flexible tube lubricated with a water-based lubricant, such as K-Y Jelly, and then shoving the tube in through the sinuses and down the back of the throat. This is fun because you're looking at your friend's face, slipping this in, and he's turning purple. And you're feeding this tube down his throat, and before long, you've fed this thing right down into his belly.

Needless to say, this is a really uncomfortable process, but at paramedic school, getting an NG tube inserted, and inserting one, is a rite of passage. You have to be able to do it. I received a nasty bloody nose out of the deal, which was a pretty common occurrence. The instructors, seasoned medical professionals that they were, had a solution to end the bloodbath. They handed us tampons. For the rest of the day, half a dozen of us were walking around with tampons shoved up our nostrils.

We'd just completed the NP/NG section of the course, and then it was time to learn about urethral catheters. The instructor teaching the section gathered us around a table, the tube in his hands. He glanced around at us and said, "All right guys, now for the urethral catheter. I need a volunteer to lay down on the table."

I remember thinking, *Oh, shit! No way! Not that, too?*

We had been stabbing and sticking each other all over. I know for a fact all of us were in a state of disbelief and disgusted shock. The pipeline had already asked so much of us, and now this.

Then, one kid's hand shot up.

The instructor gave him a strange look, shrugged, and said, "Okay. Drop your pants, up on the table."

I couldn't believe it. The kid starts to pull down his pants and the instructor says, "No! Don't! Shit! I'm just kidding! Pull your pants back up!"

What came next I can only describe as "awkward as hell." The kid said, "Ah, man!"

To this day, I'm not sure if he was just putting on an Oscar-worthy performance or he actually wanted to be the guinea pig who got a tube inserted into his penis in front of everyone. The instructors were trying to have fun, but they picked the wrong guy. As it turned out, they had a real weirdo on their hands, and it wouldn't be long before that guy washed out.

Much to our relief, we learned how to insert catheters on fake rubber penises and vaginas. Jokes flew, but the instructors were quick to bring us back on point. They stressed that, as medics, we needed to be able to administer a catheter in the field, especially if the patient is a burn victim. You need to be able to track the fluid being processed through the kidneys versus the fluids dripping off the patient's body. The skin acts as the primary moisture retention barrier, and a large-scale burn oozes fluids. A patient with a bad second-degree burn or badly charred flesh will become dehydrated very quickly. You can dump fluids into them and the fluids will pour right back out of their flesh, because the skin is missing. Knowledge about burns and how to treat them is an integral part of paramedic training. There is a special technique to administering fluids—how much to give over a given period of time—and how to dress the wounds.

This isn't a first aid book, and there won't be a test at the end, so I don't want to go too far into detail, but dressing wounds and providing long-term care in the field is one of the primary roles of a PJ. They trained us to provide care and to stabilize patients over an extended period of time, either independently or with very minimal support and guidance. This philosophy of medical care originated with the first real pararescue mission, in August 1943, in the uncharted jungle between Burma and China. Twenty-one Americans jumped from an ailing C-46 as one engine failed and then the other caught fire. The group included some American leadership, press, and military personnel, and all but one survived the jump. They had broken legs, a broken ankle, fractured ribs, and other serious injuries.

There were no roads, they were surrounded by Japanese patrols, and the US military had no way to rescue them. The only feasible option was to fly in, parachute down, render aid, and then lead the walk out through a forest known to be the domain of tribal headhunters.

A flight surgeon, Lieutenant Colonel Don Flickinger, and two combat surgical technicians, Sergeant Richard S. Passey and Corporal William MacKenzie were the men who parachuted in for what everyone was certain was a suicide mission.

The story has become a part of PJ lore, and the version I was told went something like this: As they circled above, watching the signal panels from the survivors below, the doctor turned to the two enlisted guys and said, "The only way to save them is for me to jump down there, patch them up, and walk them out. Do not come. I'm giving you a direct order. Stay in this plane."

Of course, they replied, "Yes, sir!" He jumped out and into the jungle below.

The sergeant then turned to the corporal and said, "As the highest-ranking person on board, I'm telling you to stay." Then he jumped out. The third guy, with no one else to stop him, bailed out after his buddies.

So these three guys, over the course of a month, with the help of some Naga tribesmen—the very group they feared would chop off their heads—evaded the Japanese, treated and stabilized the victims, and kept them moving the whole time. This was the first time such a rescue, with medical personnel parachuting out to the field, had ever been accomplished. This seed, planted during World War II, grew into the tree of pararescue.

That's the origin of why we jump. Sometimes pilots will put their airplanes or their passengers in precarious spots, and a PJ has to jump in to render aid. Much of the medical curriculum in the pipeline is also taught with interesting anecdotes and bits and pieces of history related to the field. Those lessons stuck with me and gave the heavy academic material we suffered through some military and historical context.

As you might guess, I excelled when we hit the cardiology portion of the course. I had some personal experience there, and I loved getting into the science of how the muscles of the heart function. I gained a whole new understanding of my own heart failure, and I nerded out on the technology. I often thought about that crazy mesh shirt and heart monitor the navy made me wear. I'd gone from being a heart patient to being someone who could place leads on a person's chest and read the feedback like a map.

The heart monitor provides a window into the heart, which in turn enables you to know what is wrong and how to treat it most specifically. But what it can't pick up are the emotional parts of life. The pipeline would send me through a gauntlet of emotions. Relationships came and went. Time and again I suffered severe heartbreak. There were crazy bouts of girl chasing, which led to a marriage and a son. Then another sort of heartbreak hit, and hit hard. It came while I was running, no less.

Deep into the first paramedic course, in formation with my class, running with a heavy ruck on my back, I tripped and fell. As I toppled forward, I made one of those classic Jimmy Settle mistakes. You might see a theme emerging here. I reached. I stuck my arm out to catch myself and *pop!* Just like that. *Pop!* Then shooting pains. I had dislocated my left shoulder, right out the back side. In medical terms, this is called a posterior shoulder dislocation. They somehow got the arm back in its socket, but I couldn't do pull-ups or raise my arms above my head. For a good part of the paramedic class, I didn't have to do pull-ups, but that didn't keep me from trying. I entered physical therapy, but the therapy wasn't working. An MRI revealed a superior labrum anterior to posterior tear, a SLAP tear. In the shoulder there's a small cup, and the cartilage inside my cup had been torn up and looked chunky. The surgeon had to go in arthroscopically to fix it. The first night after the procedure, I wanted to go back to the hospital, because the nerve block wore off and it felt like he was still performing surgery on me, but with a much duller knife.

My surgery came right after the academic portion of the first paramedic course, and my class went on without me to do their clinical rotation in Tucson. The cadre rolled me back into the next class. I had two months to recover from the surgery before I had to step up and do paramedic work. I had to be able to come up fast and hard. I jumped into my new physical therapy with serious aggression. I had no other option. It had already taken a couple weeks of babying my arm after the surgery until I could finally wipe my own ass. The rehab and pain from the operation was, in a word, brutal.

After weeks of intense physical therapy, hours upon hours each day, I was finally able to raise my hand above my head. After about a month, I could do a dead hang off the pull-up bar and began to do muscle engagement. From there, they worked me up to being able to do pull-ups again so that I could pass the physical assessment and be signed off to go to the paramedic rotation. The entire situation was touch and go for me. At any moment, the military could have decided enough was enough, but luckily my unit didn't ask for an explanation or give me an ounce of static. They figured the shoulder injury was just that, an injury. Like a family, my unit encouraged me and I felt supported throughout the process. There was always someone, like Chris Robertson back in Alaska, ready to help me and to tell me I could make it.

The material I learned was challenging, but I passed my tests and I kept advancing. Soon it was time to head off for the paramedic practical in Camden, New Jersey, and Philadelphia.

I was stationed at Medic 25, in a lower-income area of the Philadelphia suburbs, and on the first day I was that white guy in a rental car, lost and driving around and looking for the place. I had never been in such an economically depressed and gang-ravaged neighborhood. It felt like I'd driven straight into a scene from *The Wire*. It might surprise people that the city of Anchorage has its own fair share of gang violence and poverty, but even the roughest places in our community looked like Mr. Rogers' neighborhood compared to this. The whole place was scary and sad. My first thought, when I couldn't find the station, was *Holy shit! Should I be in this area? Can I even stop my car here?*

I drove past burned and boarded-up houses. Stripped cars sat on cement blocks. Trash and debris littered the streets. People stood on every street corner, and sometimes in the middle of the street. It felt like people were everywhere, but no one appeared to be doing anything but hanging out. They were just watching and talking.

And they were clearly looking at me like *Who* the fuck *is this white boy?*

Much to my relief, I finally found the station. I parked the rental car, wondering if I would ever see it again, then headed inside to introduce myself and begin my rotation. I'm sure my skin appeared a bit extra pale, out of pure excitement and fear about what I'd be doing.

Clinical rotations take the classroom theory and dummy training and thrust it straight into real-world, life-and-death emergencies. You are assigned an experienced paramedic, a preceptor, to watch over you and make sure you don't do anything silly. The preceptor also grades your performance. My preceptor was Larry Bloomfield. I called him Big L because he was the size of an ambulance. He spoke in a low, rumbly voice and was quick to point out how white I am, but was he ever a good guy and a great teacher. He had fun watching me take on challenging patients, and he knew I was there to learn. Nothing was going to stop Big L from making sure the guy from Alaska received as complete and full an experience as possible before he let me out into the world.

Big L schooled me on the hard streets of Camden and Philly. Philly would take this naive kid from Anchorage a long, long way from his comfort zone.

The first time I had to handle a body was with Big L. "You about to see the real shit, Jimmy," he said.

We rolled in on a lady who had a heart attack during the night and was found by her daughter the next morning. This woman made Big L look small. She pushed four hundred pounds. To make matters worse, she had slid off her bed and into the gap between the mattress and the wall, a two-foot opening. Somehow, her body had become wedged in tight. I won't ever forget her skin. Not quite cold, but moist and slippery. If there was a pulse, it was faint.

She lived on the second floor of a run-down brownstone. The buildings in that area are the skinny, tall kind, built one right beside the other. The narrow staircase was too small and narrow to fit our litter, and using the wheels was not an option. Instead, we carried her on a canvas stretcher, with the help of a half dozen firefighters.

All of us were straining hard, and all the while Big L had me trying to do CPR, even while we were on the stairs. I'm adding my
weight to the woman's weight, and these tough firefighters are
doing all they can to get her down the stairwell.

We finally got her into the ambulance, and Big L shouted, "In-
tubate her ass, Jimmy!"

"Her ass?" I said, pretending not to know what he was saying.

He laughed. "Go on," he said.

I set to work, and I dropped the tube into her right away. Big L
was still getting us prepped to roll and didn't realize I already had
the tube in place.

"Holy cow," Big L said. "You already got it in?"

"Yeah!" I said, probably a bit too proud.

"Good job!" he said. "Don't just sit there! Keep going!"

That was my first live intubation, and from there it would be
one crazy thing to the next with Big L. Nailing that first intubation proved to be a key experience for me. Having a chance to use
my classroom skills right away on a human being gave me a little
confidence.

The urgency that comes with medical trauma in real life is something you just can't replicate in the classroom. This is where the
true value of ride-alongs comes into play. You have to get out there
in the real world and experience the bile and blood, the stench, the
screams, the groans. In the classroom, the instructors can try to apply stressors with time constraints and noise, but it just isn't going
to hit you the same as it does when a real person's life lands in your
trembling hands.

Every time we went on a call, we found ourselves immersed in
urban blight. I thought I'd grown up fairly poor, but this was
poverty on levels that I'd been isolated from and didn't even know
exists in our country. We entered more than one place where the
walls crawled with flies, spiders, and cockroaches. My rotation also
gave me a new understanding of stench. Horrible smells of feces
and vomit, with a weird mixture of some inexplicable sweetness,

became commonplace. I came from a place known for fresh air. Even our oldest homes in Alaska aren't really that old—maybe the 1950s, at the earliest. Philly was different. The place possessed an aged smell of mold, rot, and death. Some homes that we entered contained generations of filth, and I felt a sense of sadness that I hadn't expected.

Doing those paramedic rotations, I constantly heard echoes of my grandmother's voice in my ear, reminding me of my need to be empathetic and understanding of those around me. I got to see things, parts of humanity and parts of our society, whose existence I had only registered in the most vague and academic way. Before I came to Philly, it was all stuff that happened somewhere else in the world. But when I was there, I would catch myself thinking, *Shit. This is real.*

They chose to send us to Philly and Camden for that exact purpose. The shit is real there, and it comes in the form of a high volume of trauma. Shootings, stabbings, head wounds, car wrecks, you name it. The first person I ever saw who'd been shot was a teenage kid. The bullet had traveled from the bottom of his foot through the top, which meant one thing to me: the bullet had caught him midstride, as he was running away from the gunman. The bullet hole appeared as a small wound, a through-and-through as paramedics call it. Luckily for him, it didn't hit any bones, but the entrance and exit of the bullet ruined his shoe. One little black sphere in the sole and one large, bloody exit hole in the top.

I responded to several knife wounds. There was one dude with long slice marks all over his arms and hands. Another guy had been intentionally stabbed with a dirty hypodermic needle. Some of the people we picked up smelled worse than many of the homes we visited. One of the things you don't think about when you see an ambulance is that many calls aren't necessarily emergencies. A good portion of the calls are to attend to mentally unstable people, often referred to as frequent fliers. These are people with serious mental illness, who lack basic personal hygiene and haven't bathed in months, perhaps years. The smell, at times, could be overwhelming. They were people I was afraid to even touch at first. But I learned that, no matter what, you've got to glove up and do your job.

At the time, many people in the area were doing some rough drugs. "Wet" was big; it's formaldehyde-soaked marijuana, which produces a horrible stench. Those on meth also had this awful cat urine and rotten egg smell. Learning to get past that smell barrier was important for me, because once I was over it, I could provide care to anyone. Down the road, when I got to Afghanistan and had to deal with the awful smells that come with battle, I was ready for it, after all I dealt with in Philly and Camden.

The paramedic rotation taught me something else that would become important, namely, how to compartmentalize situations so my patient doesn't know what I'm thinking, so they don't even notice I have a reaction to how they look or smell, or to the severity of their condition. You don't want people feeling bad. You don't want someone who is hurting and needs help to see your reaction. It doesn't help anything. I learned to set my personal hang-ups aside, to put compassion forward, and to try to view every individual as someone. My mission was not to judge them for what they've been doing in their life but to be there to help them in that instant. I signed up to help, so I had to put my issues and beliefs away.

On top of the ambulance rotations, I also did clinical rotations in different departments of the local hospital. Much of my training came in the emergency room, where I really sharpened my trauma skills. I did patient assessments, IVs, intubations. I hooked up and interpreted twelve-lead ECGs and did my fair share of triage. All the while, I worked closely with doctors, nurses, and anesthesiologists. I was quick to learn from all these professionals, and I picked their brains any time I could. When I went into the field on my own, I wanted as many tools to work with as I could get. I saw my work with these experts as my chance to use their personal experiences to help guide my decisions.

I delivered two babies in the obstetrics clinic. I also witnessed an emergency cesarean section, which at the time seemed to me a barbaric procedure. The necessity of the operation was clear, but there was something about that particular experience, seeing a mother cut open, that I found disturbing. I knew then that I wasn't an OB guy.

The first time I delivered a baby, I reported to the OB as I normally would, and there were two or three women in various stages of labor. This was intentional, and it allowed me, in one twelve-hour shift, to examine the various stages of labor on different people. Getting to see so many stages of birth accelerated the learning curve. I didn't have to wait through the birthing stages with one person; I could catch the highlights of each part of the process with different mothers.

Witnessing an experience like childbirth teaches a guy in the PJ pipeline about real pain and how to be humble in the most delicate of positions. You're no longer the cool guy in the action figure gear. You're a dude in scrubs trying not to blush as you learn how to measure the opening of the mother's cervix, using your fingertips. I'll never forget my first cervix check, a cute young woman—with her partner, of course. They were my age at the time, late twenties. Can you say awkward? I might as well have told them, "Hello, I'm a paramedic student and I really have no idea what I'm about to do, but the procedure will require me to reach into places I've never been before. Don't mind me while I feel around. Just talk among yourselves."

To be fair, it wasn't like I just barged into her room and started probing her. The female doctor attending her turned to me and said, "Jim, I want you to come over here and tell me how far dilated you think this patient is." I'd heard such terms used on medical dramas and had read about it in our textbooks, but up until that point I had never really considered exactly what "cervix dilation" means.

I hesitated.

"Well, get in there," the doc said. "Tell me how far along she is."

Really? I'm really going to do this? I'm looking at this young couple, they're looking at me, and I'm thinking *This is weird*, and I know they are thinking *This is weird*, but we're all pretending we're cool with the situation. I would go on to deliver their child, but that moment stuck with me more than delivering the baby did. I'd been jumping out of planes and working out obsessively, all with the end goal of becoming a PJ. I'd never quite visualized or prepared myself for this awkward moment.

Witnessing birth and participating in that miraculous and often scary and traumatic process would come in handy later, when my son was born. He had an emergency birth, because he had a nuchal wrap—his umbilical cord was twisted around his neck and began to affect the blood flow to his brain. They had to pull him out quick, and because of my training they said, "You can come in. Go ahead and glove up."

My son arrived purple. The color and look on his face scared me. I'd seen numerous kids delivered in Philly, and I knew a baby wasn't supposed to come into the world looking like an eggplant. I knew how deliveries were supposed to go, and when things didn't progress the right way at first, I felt a fear I hadn't known before. That fear hit hard, the moment I saw his purple skin. But, within seconds, he started screaming and pinked up. Once that happened, I could take my paramedic hat off, shed those concerns, and focus on being the proud dad.

The training I received during my paramedic rotation with Big L and the other professionals on the East Coast gave me confidence in my medical skills. I learned some valuable lessons, and I learned not to hesitate or question my actions, because I knew exactly what to do. When I deployed to Afghanistan, that experience of dealing with the nonstop trauma in Philly helped me find the strength and confidence required when treating soldiers in the field.

———

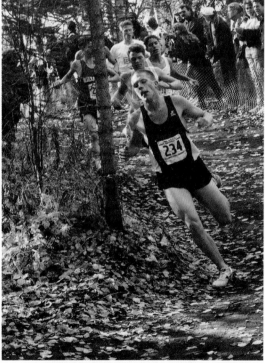

TOP LEFT: Christmas 1985, my first set of BDU's. still wearing the same outfit twenty years later. *Photo courtesy of author's family*

ABOVE: I don't know what is sweeter, the headband, T-shirt, or the ride? *Photo courtesy of author's family*

LEFT: Racing towards victory at the 1995 Cross-Country Running Championships. *Photo courtesy of author's family*

LEFT: First taste of victory on my way to a state championship. *Photo courtesy of author's family*

BOTTOM: The glorious taste of victory! *Photo courtesy of M. Scott Moon*

Entering the pool, Sergeant! INDOC, Day One. *Photo courtesy of Pararescue IDOC team 003-06 Archive*

INDOC teamwork bell. *Photo courtesy of Pararescue IDOC team 003-06 Archive*

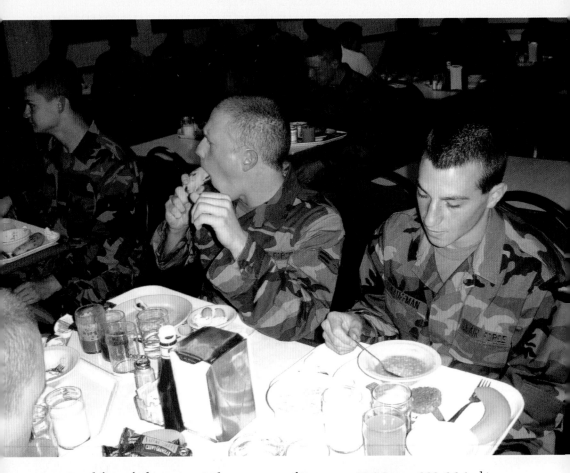

TOP: Breakfast of Champions! *Photo courtesy of Pararescue IDOC team 003-06 Archive*

BOTTOM: Schumacher and I sport the blue ascots awarded to the cones who have survived Hell Night. *Photo courtesy of Pararescue IDOC team 003-06 Archive*

The graduating class of INDOC 003-06, Hoo Yah Ballz Three!! *Photo courtesy of Pararescue IDOC team 003-06 Archive*

Fine looking paintjob on those fighter jets. *Photo courtesy of the author*

TOP: Matanuska Glacier, 2007, a last glimpse of home on my way from Alaska to the PJ apprenticeship course in Albuquerque. *Photo courtesy of the author*

LEFT BOTTOM: Roots of the 212th. Spenard, Alaska, 2008. *Photo courtesy of the United States Air Force*

RIGHT BOTTOM: Hoist training in Kachemak Bay, Alaska. *Photo courtesy of Nick Gibson*

ABOVE: Backcountry Workhorse, traversing across snowfields and crevasses on White Elk Glacier, Alaska while training for technical alpine rescue. *Photo courtesy of Chris Robertson*

BELOW: High Alpine and Glacier Rescue training, serious business. *Photo courtesy of Chris Robertson*

ABOVE: The "Prophet" Chris Robertson and I on my first day in Afghanistan. His half-joking prediction came true, "If anyone's gonna get shot, it's you Jimmy." *Photo courtesy of the 83rd ERQS PJ team archives*

BELOW: A sample of the rescue equipment PJ's keep handy. We were prepared for anything from Timmy down a well, to collapsed structures, burning armored vehicles, underwater ops, and much more. *Photo courtesy of the 83rd ERQS PJ team archives*

RIGHT: Just a small selection of weapons Pararescueman are prepared to use. *Photo courtesy of the 83rd ERQS PJ team archives*

BELOW: Our glorious chariot, the Pedro Bus. *Photo courtesy of the 83rd ERQS PJ team archives*

LEFT: An assortment of last-minute items on your way out of the door for a mission. *Photo courtesy of the 83rd ERQS PJ team archives*

TOP RIGHT: Patching up an injured soldier in the back of Pedro. *Photo courtesy of Brandon Stuemke*

BOTTOM RIGHT: Capitalism flourishes, ev in the most austere environments. *Photo courtesy of the 83rd ERQS PJ team archives*

BELOW: Parcha and I on our way to work, Afghanistan. *Photo courtesy of the 83rd ERQS PJ team archives*

ABOVE: First 9-line for Operation Bulldog Bite II, I was shot twenty minutes later. *Photo courtesy of Brandon Stuemke*

TOP LEFT: Hoisting a patient out of a combat zone. *Photo courtesy of Nick Gibson*

BOTTOM LEFT: Pedros 83 and 84, five-minute launch posture. A short flight from the battlefields of Bulldog Bite. *Photo courtesy of the 83rd ERQS PJ team archives*

RIGHT: Time to go to work. *Photo courtesy of the 83rd ERQS PJ team archives*

ABOVE LEFT: The night after I was injured, I autographed the bullet hole that hurt me, but didn't kill me. *Photo courtesy of the 83rd ERQS PJ team archives*

ABOVE RIGHT: Shortly after injury, luck to be alive. *Photo courtesy of Brandon Stuemke*

BELOW: Author receiving The Purple Heart from 176 commander Brigadier General Chuck Foster. *Photo courtesy of Alaskan Air National Guard, John Callahan*

academic challenge of my life, and I made it. I hadn't earned th
maroon beret of a PJ yet, but I was a bit further down the pipeline
And now, after nearly two years in the process, I was a paramedic
I had the card to prove it.

Rear-Left, Ted, Leo, Matt, Roger, Aaron, Doug, Koa. Front-Left, Author, Brandon.
Photo courtesy of the 83rd ERQS PJ team archives

Danger! Flying cats. The Settle Crew, Shannon, James, and I surrounded by our furry posse. *Photo courtesy of Fern Ohayon*

After Philly, it was time to dive back into the books. The pipeline would end for me if I didn't pass the National Registry of Emergency Medical Technicians paramedic exam, an odd, organic test unlike anything I'd ever taken before. You sit down at a computer and the text asks you questions. If you get it right, you get a more challenging question or move on to the next subject. If you're wrong, then the questions start exploring that particular area of knowledge until you either fail or pass. Rather than being a test where you know you have two hundred questions, this exam could possibly ask you a question about everything you've been taught during the entire course.

Everything rides on this test, so no stress, right? I suspect the number has changed since I took the test, but at the time, the minimum number of questions you could be asked was one hundred and fifty. If you were asked fewer than two hundred questions, you did good—or you did really bad. You didn't know. I was at around one hundred seventy-five questions when my computer shut down. For a second, I thought the damn system had failed. Then something popped up on the screen that said I had completed the exam.

The waiting game began. Results arrive in the mail, and for a week, all of us were unsure and on edge. Fellow trainees and friends would attempt to be encouraging and say things like "You're smart. You got it." But I honestly didn't know. The test had gone by way too quickly. It wasn't like the pull-up test or buddy breathing. All I could do was wait and see.

The day the letter came, I stood turning it over and over in my hands. So much depended on the results. I was standing at the door of the airplane again, looking out at the dark sky beneath me. I could stand or I could jump.

I ripped open the letter. I had passed. Inside I found my national registry card.

It was one of the first feel-good moments in a long while, ever since I had survived INDOC and Air Force Combat Diver School. The paramedic portion of the course had been the most grueling

15

. . . .

Dirt Medicine

After paramedic certification came a wave of relief. I could finally move on to the next step, the big step, the final step before becoming a PJ. This is the pararescue journeyman course, the twenty-four-week Pararescue Recovery Specialist Course. This is basically "PJ school," located at Kirtland Air Force Base in Albuquerque, New Mexico.

PJ school was where we took all the training and skills we had learned in the various courses of the pipeline and put it all together through intense practice. The course takes all the individual components from all the other courses, combines everything together into a nice package, wraps it with a ribbon, then hands you a loaded M4 and Med-Ruck.

In addition to what we already knew, we added weapons, battle tactics, mountaineering, rope work, high- and low-angle rescue, and countless other rescue techniques. At this point in the game, the instructors began to treat us more like students, as opposed to trying to filter us out of the pipeline. The constant filtering part of the process had ended. Now that we had made it that far, they were going to help us advance our skills to an entirely different level. They were going to treat us like men, as long as we didn't fuck up.

It didn't take us very long to fuck up.

The good times lasted for about two weeks, until a teammate had a little too much fun one night. On his way home, he realized he'd had too much to drink, so he pulled his car over and locked his keys in the trunk. His line of thinking was that he couldn't get into trouble if he didn't have the keys in the ignition or in his pocket. He awoke to flashing lights and a field sobriety test, which he failed. The policeman asked where the keys were.

"In the trunk," he replied. "I didn't think I'd get in trouble if they were there."

"No," responded the policeman. "They are in the car with you, and you're in possession of them." That was it.

The PJ trainee program has a strict zero-tolerance policy with regard to driving under the influence. One and done is the rule, and this poor guy was out. One night of celebrating cost him everything. His fuckup gave the instructors the impression that we, as a team, were not looking out for one another and were maybe a little too wild. This led them to the conclusion that our class needed to have the hammer dropped on us. We lost a teammate and we lost our weekend liberties. We also earned the privilege of reinforcing our team's love for one another by utilizing that alternative training device, the log.

We all thought we had moved beyond packing around a log. Not so. So close to the end, and here was the damn log again. The instructors took it upon themselves to remind us constantly that we were one of the worst teams they had ever seen.

The log, however, gained us notoriety and respect around the base. Not many teams were forced to carry the big stick everywhere they went—and I do mean everywhere. We would even pack that thing into the on-base convenience store when we were picking up refreshments or energy bars before or after class.

People would ask, "Are you guys crazy? What are doing? What's the deal with the log?"

We might tell them we were PJ trainees, or we would mess with them. I often responded, "We're building a log cabin here on base."

The log, of course, was part of PJ training, to help us build teamwork. By the end, some of the guys were really starting to get jaded, bitter, and angry. Every time we thought we were done, someone else would screw up and we would find ourselves beneath it again. We'd been doing this for years now, and the actions of a couple people kept bringing the log back into our lives like an obsessed ex-girlfriend. This was one of those times when a peer elimination system, like the Rangers or SEALS have, might have made things a bit different for us, but there is no peer elimination method in para-rescue.

One of our first classes was instruction on ropes. We learned the ropes, literally. Knots for all purposes, with a focus on climbing and harness rigging. We practiced mountaineering and setting up rescue systems. High angle is a situation in which somebody falls down into a ravine, so you set up a rope system and rappel down the cliff face. You stabilize the patient and get him attached to ropes so the people up top can bring you up, using the system you've established.

We practiced all the different pulley-type systems to use a mechanical advantage for human weight and gear. I loved this stuff. I'd never done anything similar. I learned to create a system that enabled me to easily lift a two-hundred-pound guy up out of a crevasse or a hole on my own. This training took place in the mountains, and if there was anything in life I missed while in the pipeline, it was mountains. All that time inside, or trapped on a military base . . . I felt as though I had become less of an outdoorsman.

My entire life I was active outside, nearly every day, and while I was still active every day, I wasn't out in the wilderness maintaining a connection with nature. Not in the way my soul felt it needed to, at least. Once we moved into the mountain phase, I felt whole again. No matter how hard we were working, I found myself enjoying and appreciating the natural world around me.

The orienteering phase took our knowledge of ropes and mountain work and merged all of it together. We learned how to move around on mountains, reading maps—not just referencing terrain features, like we did in SERE, but actually triangulating by using a compass and taking headings, all while doing pace counts. That knowledge about pace counts, from SERE, came in handy, and we built upon that skill by using beads or picking up rocks to keep track. This was the outdoor training from SERE but taken to the next level. The skills suddenly felt more useful, and we were all becoming much more comfortable with the application of that knowledge.

I enjoyed that training in the high mountains of New Mexico's summer. Due to the heat, we worked mostly in the evening, and much of our training occurred at night. As operators, we had to become adept at nighttime navigation. Once again, everything we learned to do in the daylight, we had to learn to do better at night. I like to kid around with my son, now, that I was a nighttime warrior. You're only half as good at something if you can only do it during the day. Later on, I would appreciate everything I learned about missions during the witching hour, because nighttime would become my preferred time to operate when my deployment came.

Next came the weapons phase, and combat. We learned hand-to-hand combat and became proficient with all sorts of weaponry, from knives and pistols to M4s. We learned how to strip our weapons and zero them out. Then came the shooting drills. We spent days and days on the firing range. We would shoot all day long. Hundreds and hundreds of rounds. First M4, then nine millimeter. During that period, I had the best job on the planet. I was getting paid to deliver lead from one end of the firing range to the other.

Then, just when I thought the course couldn't get any better, it did. We advanced to the moving-and-shooting course. This is where you're walking through an obstacle course with pneumatic targets that pop up for you to shoot. *Bang. Plink!* An instructor walks behind you, holding your shoulder. He's keeping track of your hits, and he keeps you from stopping. He controls your speed. This was another first for me. I had no experience walking and shooting. Walking and shooting was, of course, far more challenging than shooting while standing or sitting, but I got the hang of it.

I'm not really an awesome shot. I have to get that out there up front. Shooting is probably one of my weakest areas, in fact. But on weapons day, the day of the final, after everybody had passed their test, we had a shooting contest.

Pneumatic targets were set up on the range. They were similar to the old biathlon targets that I had seen at Kincaid Park as I was growing up. You shot at a white metal plate, and the target area popped out and turned black if you hit it. We were using nine-millimeter pistols, and there were three sets of targets, five targets on each set. Man on man. Two guys. Head to head. A single-elimination tournament. Fifteen shots. A shooting race. First one to knock them all down, with one magazine, wins.

As I've admitted, I'm no Annie Oakley. But somehow I managed to tie in the first round. We had a rematch after everyone else went head to head, and I won the rematch. Then I won the second round, but this time by a narrow margin. In the final round, it was just me against one other really amazing shooter for the title. Too bad for him, I had reached some kind of shooting Zen state.

I won the pistol contest. I knew I didn't have a chance against all those crack shots, so I didn't put any pressure on myself. Then came the prize. I would be shooting against the commandant. The whole time against my peers, I was actually feeling pretty good and gaining confidence, until this announcement came. I would be shooting against C-Lo, the man who would later go on to become chief of the 24th, the PJ squadron Yo-Yo had joined. C-Lo was, by definition, a badass. He was tough, highly intelligent, and a motivating force. And I had to go up against him. I never once thought I would be facing down one of my favorite instructors.

The show must have been fun to watch. I was so nervous, I'm sure my pistol shook like in one of those movie scenes where the guy with the gun can't bring himself to pull the trigger. When the time came and they gave the signal, I sprayed and prayed. It was probably pretty comical. I dumped my whole magazine. *Pow! Pow! Pow!* I attempted to hit the targets before C-Lo could. The competitive part of me wanted to win, but another part of me knew that the only way I could possibly win was to get lucky, because this guy would kill me. Then there was a third part of me that was saying, *Don't beat him! Do not beat this guy! This is not a good thing. This is not one of those times.*

I blasted away, and the entertainment in my loss must have been quality, because my classmates doubled over laughing.

Next came the aircrew and jumping portion of the training. PJs are delivered to rescue sites via aircraft. This requires intimate knowledge of all sorts of flying machines. We received a crash course in crashes. We learned basics of flight and how to turn off a plane in an emergency, as well as the location of simple essentials: crash axes, extinguishers, and oxygen masks. They taught us how to be a part of the aircrew, how to be a troubleshooter while in flight, and how to help the aircrew if something does go wrong. Logistically, the PJ can't just be a bystander during flights, fights, and rescues, he needs to be an active participant.

After we learned all we could about different aircraft, we started jumping out of them again. PJ school takes free fall jumping and applies it to pararescue scenarios. This involves jumping out of the plane loaded with your weaponry, oxygen tank, mask, and serious medical gear.

We began with a series of dry land jumps and then flew to Florida for the water phase. This was the first time I got to work with helicopters in the water. I had worked with helicopters in some of the other training, but it was always on land. Jumping out of a hovering helicopter and splashing down into warm ocean is as good as it gets. I occasionally worried about jumping right down into the mouth of a shark, but by this point we had so much gear on that a shark would have to really work to eat me.

We followed up the helicopter water work with night jumps from the C-130. It was high-altitude free fall parachuting right into the ocean. As with so many firsts in my life, my first night jump into the ocean wasn't without trouble.

Gloves seem to be a recurring theme in my pararescue life. The first time I jumped into the water at night, I wore neoprene gloves that were so thick I couldn't feel the rip cord. I thought I was going to die. I passed through my opening sequence. I traced my lines. I couldn't get the rip cord. I tried again. Still nothing. I struggled three times to find the damn rip cord, and I fell right through the opening altitude. The material on my hands was so thick I couldn't even feel the parachute. I had no dexterity at all.

I swear I could hear my heart beating over the roar of the wind. Finally, I looked down and was able to see the rip cord. I grabbed it and pulled hard. The chute opened just in time, but I had nose-dived enough to get a big pendulum swing. For a moment, before I found that cord, I was scared shitless. Missing the rip cord was something I had never even considered as an option during free fall. I didn't panic, but the situation definitely felt intense and had me pretty focused. Once the chute opened I was fine, but the mishap shook me up.

The very next morning I went straight to the store on base and bought myself some baseball batting gloves. They were the only black gloves I could find. Ultra thin, with a great grip. They worked perfectly for parachuting in warm weather. The scare forced me to make positive changes, and I learned yet another lesson: I would always test out new gear, especially gloves. At least, that's what I told myself at the time.

On that same training session, during that same week of jumps, I learned a little lesson about jumping into the ocean in windy conditions. One night, there was enough of a breeze that, upon landing, my chute didn't hit the water and collapse. Instead, the damn thing stayed inflated. I didn't know it, but I was about to invent a new sport: underwater parasailing. I felt helpless for a second or two as the full force of the wind filled my chute and towed me beneath the water. I only had to survive; then I could begin signing up Florida tourists for the fun.

For water work, we jumped with snorkels, and I guess this PJ "Nantucket sleigh ride" is why. I was under water with the water rushing around me. Now and again I got snatched up to the surface for a moment, then just as quickly got dunked under again. This was all the fun of buddy breathing but without the buddy. My training paid off, though, because I was able to remain calm. I knew I had a good solid minute of breath to work the problem, unless I got knocked out. I remained calm and traced my lines up to the shoulder harness buckle, where the chute attaches to the body harness. I popped off the cover plate, grabbed the metal wire, and released one of the shoulder straps to jettison the parachute. The chute flailed away in the breeze and fell to the ocean.

I treaded water for a minute or two to catch my breath, and then began packing it up. Even though you've had a crazy day and felt like you almost drowned, you pretend nothing happened. The training continues. The mission keeps going.

I packed up the chute and waited for the boat to come get me, thankful that it was dark and no one witnessed the show.

The winds on the water that night were a little higher than anticipated, so we were scattered all over the ocean. One of the men picking me up said, in a slow Southern drawl, "Hope we don't leave none you out here for the sharks! Y'all splashed down all over the place." I could only sit in the boat, shiver, and hope he was joking about leaving anyone behind.

When we were donning our gear at five P.M. for a nine P.M. jump, we dressed for Florida warm. By the time jumped and were picked up by the boats, the ambient air temperature had dropped significantly. Once you got picked up, the wait wasn't over, either, because you had to help the other guys climb into the vessel. When you hit the water, you had to pull your chute in as well as you could and contain the mess, and after you got picked up you helped to pull the other guys' chutes into the boat. It was a hell of a chore to do it without getting all the lines and stuff caught up in the motor. The pickup process could take more than an hour, and the gear you were wearing earlier and sweating in was now cold and wet.

Whether I was bobbing in the water or in the boat, I tried to ignore the cold and instead absorb and enjoy what was happening around me. Staring up from the ocean and watching friends jump from a C-130 at night isn't something you get to do every day, and certainly not while decked out in the latest stealth combat apparel. I'd watch the sky for little green glow sticks and listen for the *fah-whump* sound of parachutes popping. I watched overhead for small, dark, moving patches. Searched the night sky and looked for the darkest spots; these were my friends, blocking the starlight.

While in Florida, I had the rare opportunity to witness a shuttle launch at night. We were fifty miles from the site, but the sound and sight of the rockets made an impression. We could see the light from where we were, similar to a big firework shot, except the sound came in a thunderous wave that vibrated houses all around us. That giant fireball ascending into the night sky gave me pause to think that, as a PJ, the protection of astronauts would be part of my job.

When the shuttle launched, I was out on the town with Schu and Dan Murray, already a PJ. Dan was the one who got us to where we would see the launch. He knew the liftoff time because his team sat on alert for the launch. Whenever there is a space shuttle launch, or a space launch anywhere around the globe with Americans on board, you can be assured there are PJs stationed throughout the entire world to respond to any possible emergency. If the shuttle had had an accident that night, these guys were the 911 for the astronauts. It was cool stuff.

When you're a PJ, these covert operations missions can take you all over the world. I can't really tell you anything more than that, but you can earn the beret yourself and find out. I never got to do one of these missions, but my friends did, and I heard plenty of stories about traveling the planet and hanging out in exotic locations for shuttle missions or other politically sensitive operations. This sounds extravagant, but the logic behind having PJ stations abroad makes sense. Can you imagine what would happen if a shuttle or a rocket with American astronauts went down somewhere and the bad guys got to them before we did? We can't let that happen. PJs are ready to make sure it doesn't.

Dan filled us in on what his crew did when they sat shuttle alert. Many of the techniques and equipment used today for water rescues were developed as a part of the shuttle recovery program. For example, we practiced the rigging alternate method Zodiac, or RAMZ, while in Florida, and I performed countless RAMZ jumps back in Alaska. Basically, you take a deflated Zodiac raft, roll it up with a scuba bottle and engine, and bundle it all up in a nice tight package. Then you attach a parachute on top of the bundle and push it out the back of a C-130. The RAMZ is a static line jump, tethered to the airplane, so once the raft falls and hits the end of the static line, the chute opens itself.

What we learned to do is to jump out after it and chase it, Superman style. The game is to land right on top of the package as soon as it hits the water. The parachute is supposed to detach when it hits the water, but it doesn't always work that way, and sometimes that RAMZ begins scooting across the surface, an unmanned parasail. If you're wearing any kind of gear and you need to chase down something that is being dragged through the water by the wind, you'll never win. And if that RAMZ is your primary form of transportation once you hit the water, you better hope to hell you land on top of that thing.

When you swim up to the package, you locate the "God ring," a twelve-inch-diameter ring where all the webbing that bundles up the raft comes to a point. You take your knife and cut the God ring and the whole bundle falls apart. You're in the water, and the entire package is rolling and turning, and the wind is blowing, and there are waves, and it's probably cold. You locate the scuba bottle, turn it on, and inflate the Zodiac. If all goes well, it will inflate right up. Then you find the motor, put the motor on the transom, hook up the fuel, give a few pulls, and away you go.

That's what it says in the manual, but I've never had it go that smoothly. Not once. I've done a dozen jumps with the RAMZ and, at best, there is a lot of pulling and a good amount of swearing. The motors tend to get water in them upon splashdown. Sometimes you're pulling for half an hour, trying to work the water through, while someone else is pumping the fuel ball. Another guy might be working on pulling and replacing the engine plugs. I learned to hate the RAMZ. I'm not sure I would trust one to get me to the astronauts in time.

I was relieved when the water training ended. I had certainly had my share of fun during the phase, and I learned volumes, but I didn't enjoy being dunked and dragged around under water, and the whole open ocean thing in general still had me uneasy. I tried to assure myself that it would just take a while for me to get really comfortable doing water work at sea.

The second to last phase was what they called PJ medicine, or what the instructors called dirt medicine. Dirt medicine is essentially learning how to use all your medical skills without any of the resources. This isn't just how to think outside the box; this is how to think *around* the box and then use the box to save lives. PJs need to be innovative, divergent thinkers. Each situation will be dynamic, and no two will be the same. In essence, we were taught to ask, *How do I solve this problem, following these principles, with only what is around me?* Much of this training was, as you might imagine, in the dirt, out in the field.

We learned tactical medicine at this time, too. Shooting and medicine. Tactical medicine has a whole different list of priorities from traditional paramedic medicine. In paramedic medicine, the first thing you are taught is to survey and see whether a scene is safe, and if the scene is not safe, to get yourself safe and wait for the scene to be safe. In tactical PJ medicine, it's not a matter of whether the scene is safe—it often isn't—but knowing which direction the danger is coming from and then getting to work. Get things between you and the danger. This applies to bad guys with guns but also to avalanches, bad weather, or the very helicopter coming to rescue you. The rotor wash alone can be destructive and can cause severe injury. It's the PJ's job to be the protective dog between the wounded pup and the threat. That's how I liked to visualize myself. I didn't like the word *sheepdog*, but I definitely liked to think of myself as the dog trying to protect his flock by fighting whatever threats are present. If one of my pack gets hurt, I'm going in with teeth bared to do whatever it takes. My pack wasn't necessarily my team, or even the military; it was the world. People who needed help. I wanted to help everybody. That's why I became a PJ. I wanted to help people. This was the part of the course where everything was really coming together for me.

This was the first time I had a chance to do live tissue training. We learned to complete many of the more advanced tactical medical procedures on something other than a mannequin. I'm fairly certain that is about all I can divulge, because the training is controversial. What I can say is that the live tissue training was the best medical training I ever received. Period. I learned so much in such a short amount of time by having my hands on living tissue rather than mannequins.

Later on, when real combat hit and the lives of real soldiers were in my hands, I was five hundred times more confident because of the live tissue training than I would have been without it. This was phenomenal preparation. Live tissue training makes sense, at least to me. The first patient on whom you do a procedure shouldn't be a human who can only hope you paid attention in class.

After dirt medicine, we dove into the final piece of the pipeline, the part where we had full-blown tactical combat scenarios and missions. Here, we worked as a group, a squad of ten, with mission plans. Full-on night work every evening. One night we would hike to isolated victims in the mountains, in full combat gear, and then stabilize and transport them to a rally point. The whole time, we worked off maps and radios. The entire final portion, to me, was beyond a dream.

As I approached the final week, I started to realize how other-worldly and phenomenal my entire experience in the pipeline had been. I never wanted to quit, period. The entire pipeline had been such a life-altering event, and every school seemed more incredible than the last. Each school in the pipeline, even as a stand-alone course, was something that anyone would be lucky to have under his or her belt, and here I was, this kid from Alaska, getting a shotgun blast of the most awesome medical and military courses in the world. And, not only did I not have to pay, but someone was *paying me* to learn! I gained this brotherhood of friends and family, and I had more fun than I ever imagined possible. It sounds unbelievable, but I truly awoke excited and ready to go, every day. Other than getting tired of having to do push-ups all the time, I genuinely had fun in the pipeline.

Don't get me wrong. It certainly wasn't easy street. We weren't just going home at the end of the day and eating doughnuts; we were earning it. These were long, hard days, and long nights spent studying, but when we reached that final phase of training, and we were right there at the end, we were, for the first time ever, allowed to grub out. We let our facial hair grow, we wore modified uniforms, and we began to be treated as future operators—albeit inexperienced, baby operators.

The final portion of the course was set up so that we had a central location for resupply and sleep. It was an old, abandoned warehouse. We slept in shifts, and there was a guy on watch, the CQ. We treated our sleeping area as we would if we were in a war zone. Someone constantly manned the computer, waiting for an e-mail or phone call, a 9-line—the military term for a medevac request. Nights were cold. Almost Alaska cold.

When our first night mission launched, we all geared up and climbed into the bed of a six pax. We drove a few miles and jumped out. The vehicle played the role of our mock chopper. We hiked through the mountains around the outskirts of Albuquerque, in the dark, using night vision goggles and maps. We found and identified the injured individual, used the code words, then stabilized and began transporting the patient out.

That pack out was hell. The night before, it had poured down rain. The ground froze to a depth of six inches, and then it snowed. Then, the next day's scorching sun came out and melted the top inch of snow. The dirt around there doesn't handle moisture well. The earth turns into slime. Heavy, sticky, viscous, boot-grabbing mud. There were four of us, carrying one man on the litter, and it was one of the hardest things I've ever done in my life. Men were tapping out left and right. Usually you don't tap out; it's like a badge of honor that you wait for someone to get so sick of seeing you struggle that they jump in and help. That's the mind-set. PJs don't want to be spectators; they want to be in on the action, even if the going is tough. And this was tough. Each step was sticky and slow, like trying to hike through caramel. The litter pushed us from behind, because the three other guys moved forward and weren't as stuck, and guys would suddenly trip and fall. Several times we almost dropped the dude.

We started with a shoulder carry, up high, but eventually we went to a low hanging carry. The night became a nightmare. Our rifles banged against our knees, and we were trying with all the force left in our legs to make it through this mucky stickiness. We blew our timeline by hours, and the instructors were at first visibly disappointed. For a moment, they didn't seem to know what to say or do. But then the dude who had been along for the free ride, our fake patient, said, "No, it's disgusting out there. They did all they could. Go have a look."

Not quite ready to take the man's word for it, the instructors hopped in the truck and drove down the road. They didn't make far before they had the truck buried to its axles.

PJ school culminated in an intense six-night examination period, the FTX, final training exercise, where they threw everything at us. On one of the nights we experienced a simulated mass casualty event. A dozen injured people were scattered over a wide swath of desert. We used night vision and radios and raced around searching for them. Once we found a patient, we would colocate and triage them and then call for transport. For the mass casualty event, we radioed the helicopters, the HH-60s. The pilots were in training, too, and we called them in using the scripts we had memorized. We had practiced these calls back and forth in the classroom, but this was the first time I made the support calls over the air and had someone on the other end respond. The call was followed by the air-chopping sound of the copter on its way. Within minutes, the chopper hovered overhead, creating a tornado of rocks and sand in the rotor wash. The hoist cable dropped toward me, and this was the first time the realization hit home, full force: *I'm almost a real PJ! This is what it is like. This is unbelievable!*

What actually was unbelievable was my level of naïveté. I still had training wheels upon training wheels at that point, and as real as the scenario felt, down the road I learned that it didn't come close to the real deal. It would take a war for me to understand what it felt like to be a real PJ. Add blood, bullets, and fear, and you're getting close.

They hoisted me and I felt the exhilaration of twirling up the cable to the aircraft. That was the first time I worked on a training patient in a helicopter. I was excited as a third grader to be in the helicopter. For as long as I could remember, I had loved helicopters, and their ability to hover and maneuver in high mountain regions added to it. I think some of my fascination with choppers came from the fact that there are so many places in Alaska where the terrain can only be accessed by air. I had spent my life dreaming of helicopter trips into the mountains to ski and camp.

I had only been in five or six Pave Hawks to this point, and although I was focused on my fake patient, I did geek out a bit. I'm sure someone on the ground could have spotted my white teeth in the darkness, I was smiling so wide. I did my best to put my excitement on hold as we came in for our landing at the mock hospital. We pulled out the patient, thinking we were done, and rolled right into an ambush. The moment the helicopter lifted off, the bad guys attacked. We carried the patient to safety, returned fire, and I called in our location for an air strike. The helicopter swooped in low and fast, making a couple passes, simulating the strike, and then I passed the radio off and someone else called in another strike.

Gunfire blazed back and forth between our position, behind a barrier, and the enemy's. We all shot blanks, but the sound and muzzle blasts created some serious intensity. Gunfire pointed in your general direction, fake or otherwise, gets the heart pumping a bit harder than usual. No one was really going to get hurt, but that didn't matter. At the time, the attack seemed real enough. The element of surprise enhanced the authenticity. None of us expected an ambush as we landed at what we considered the end of the mission and a safe location. I learned another one of those valuable lessons the pipeline reinforced time and time again: danger is always present in the job, so never let your guard down.

Then, on the final night, the 9-line sounded at around four in the morning, catching everyone in deep slumber. A couple of us tried to stay awake, because we knew a call would be coming. I made it until two A.M., then hit my cot. I found it was easier to stay awake than to be ripped from sleep, but after a while I couldn't keep my eyes open anymore. We were already so exhausted from the cadre messing with our sleep schedule. Most of our operating came at night. We weren't used to those graveyard shifts, and these 9-lines would often drop after midnight. We would do the training mission and then, after, we would complete a debrief. The next thing you know, it's six or seven in the morning and you're saying to yourself, *Crap, I've got to get some sleep!*

They dropped that 9-line on us at four in the morning and we scrambled. We grabbed extra gear, extra litters, and loaded up in the back of the truck. They raced us up to the mountain on a winding, bumpy gravel road until the truck couldn't go any farther. They told us to get out and instructed us to hike the rest of the way to the top. Snow covered the road. We began our march, in a tight formation, up the steep switchbacks. Instantly, I found myself comparing the entire situation to the Arctic Valley Road. I recalled that day, before life as a cone, and thought about those men I started the difficult journey with that morning. Koa. Maddamma. Zach Kline. Major Adrian. I swallowed hard when my thoughts fell on Major Adrian.

The black night sky began to lighten in the east, but the morning air had a bite and we all had plumes of steam rising from us. We wore heavy rucks, our weapons, and each had a hand on an empty litter.

We all knew this was the very last exercise, but we had no idea what was coming. The whole march up the mountain, the instructors hovered all around us, popping questions at us. They quizzed us on tactical and medical knowledge left and right.

This patient has third-degree burns on both arms from the hand to the shoulder, and the front of his legs, how much fluid are you going to give him in the first eight hours? What is your goal for the patient's urine output per hour? How do you monitor urine output if his penis has been blown off? If his arms begin to show signs of compartment syndrome because his flesh is too crispy to stretch with the swelling and is called eschar, where would you cut to perform an escharotomy? The patient who was responsive and in pain received a dose of morphine and is now unresponsive, how do you differentiate between a TBI and an opioid overdose? The helicopter is coming and can only take two patients; who do you triage to go first and why?

They grilled us like that the entire way.

The top of the mountain came into sight. Sweat poured from us and froze as frost on our brows. All of us were short of breath. Daylight began to break over the mountains. An hour had passed, and we'd been hiking at a steady clip. We crested the top and our collective hearts sank. We must have all had the same look on our faces, like a pack of sad, sweaty puppy dogs.

There, standing in a big group, with stern looks on their faces, stood all the instructors.

I know for certain we all thought the exact same thing: *Oh shit! No. God no. We've got to carry all these guys down the mountain? Oh, no!*

I mentioned one of the most grueling elements of the pipeline, a drill that arose again and again. It's a test of endurance that you must be able to complete as a PJ. The buddy carry. The only way we'd get all these men down the mountain would be to buddy carry them. Sling these giant, muscle-bound men over your back, with your pack on, and carry them down the mountain.

I'm sure, like everyone else, I was doing the math in my head. *This is impossible.*

They lined us up in formation. We stood waiting for the command to fall. Whatever it was they were about to bring, it would be tough. We knew that in our bones. We had to be ready for anything.

We weren't.

C-Lo paced in front of us and then stopped. He faced us, and then dropped another ambush on us. "Congratulations, men!" he said. "You have completed pararescue training! You are now cleared to graduate."

That was it. A blessing from C-Lo and we were done. Our grand finale to the top of the mountain at sunrise. We all stood there for a moment, dumbfounded. It took a few seconds for the shock of the surprise to set in, and then the celebrating began. We jumped in the air. High-fived. Tackled each other. We were exhausted, but the excitement overrode all that.

We flew down that mountain to the trucks, super fast. We were all freezing cold, but excited, and chattering like teenage girls on the school bus. Back at our mock base, we set to tearing it down and packing up our stuff. I was busy with all that when the class instructor pulled me and two other gentlemen aside, saying, "You men have been selected to interview for the commandant's award. You need to get cleaned up and be in C-Lo's office in an hour."

We were in the field but we needed to be presentable. I had to scramble to get my uniform prepped and ready. I hadn't shaved or showered in weeks. I was exhausted and delirious, and also a bit giddy with excitement. *I did it! And I'm being considered for the commandant's award? Me? No way . . .*

I couldn't believe any of it.

My nerves got the best of me in the interview. I was overthinking, nervous and jittery. With C-Lo doing the questioning, I should have been comfortable, because he was one of the coolest guys around, but I was off my game. I'm sure I came across as some red-faced boy on his first date. After about twenty minutes, C-Lo dismissed me with, "It's been really great working with you, Jimmy. Good luck in your career."

My career. Those two words were magic to me. *I have a career now!* The concept was almost too overwhelming for my tired mind to completely comprehend. I needed to eat a decent meal and, more than anything, I wanted crawl into a real bed and sleep. I was exhausted to the point of delirium, but I had one more major task. Two, if you asked my friends.

Graduation was that night. My *career* required me to don my new maroon beret. My friends, family, and fellow PJs and cones would insist upon celebrating.

My brother real brother, Chris, and my PJ brother Chris Robertson, Bobby, Schnell, along with "Be Cool" cone Aaron Parcha, other PJs from my unit, including the chief and the commander, made the trip from Alaska. They held our graduation in a hotel ballroom. High ceilings, chandeliers, the whole works. The scene presented an atmosphere of elegance, in stark contrast to our camp situation for the weeks prior.

There was a stage at one end of the room, tables in the middle, and along one wall, where all the fun was happening, the bar. Every graduate had his own eight-top table for guests and friends, and if you had empty seats, there were plenty of other folks who wanted to sit with the new graduates. The huge room quickly filled with important people and those pretending to be important. The mayor, a general, and half a dozen other politicians. The room had a fair share of brass, some with stars on their uniforms and others with stars in their eyes.

Before the ceremony, I mingled. Chris Robertson and Bobby Schnell began feeding me shots. Chris threw an arm around my neck and half strangled me in a huge hug.

"Congratulations, Jimmy!" he said. "Welcome to the team! I *knew* you could do it."

Chris really did know. He knew all along. From that first day when he came into the shoe store and filled me with this pararescue dream, with a new life goal, a direction, and a purpose.

I had my beret tucked into my waistband, like the rest of my classmates. The cadre had given us our berets a week before the FTX. The irony is that what they hand you isn't anything you'd ever want to be caught dead wearing. You're issued a big, fuzzy, maroon-colored Pépé the Artist–style beret with a comically large dome. One glance and you know something isn't right. No self-respecting man would wear such a monstrosity.

The hat needs to be shaved, shaped, and made to be worn sexy-like. This takes a bit of effort and a Bic razor. First you shave the hat, running the razor across the outside surface to smooth off all the fuzzy fur. Then, to form the beret, you soak the felt thoroughly and put the wet hat on your head. With water dripping down your face, you shape it, pulling the top flap over your ear. The beret should sit with the flash above the left eyebrow, the front flap up and almost covering your right eye and then wrapping around the back of your head. This is perhaps the sexiest piece of military-issued equipment, and it was rumored that if the maroon beret was worn just right, women's underwear could lose all elasticity and fall right off.

We all spent time playing with our berets in the bathroom. The shaping and wearing of these special hats wasn't in any of the pipeline curriculum. We figured the hats out on our own, with a little help from searching online.

After the mingling time came the ceremony. There were a bunch of speeches, then the graduates were seated on stage in front of the ballroom. They began to announce the awards.

I wound up not getting the commandant's award, but that wasn't any surprise. The real shock came when they announced the Arthur N. Black award for esprit de corps. They present this award to the PJ graduate who demonstrates overall superior esprit de corps, motivation, and teamwork.

The award is named in honor of Air Force Cross recipient and pararescueman Airman Third Class Arthur N. Black. On September 20, 1965, an HH-43B went down near the Vietnamese city of Tân An, and North Vietnamese troops captured all four personnel aboard. They held Airman Black as a prisoner of war until February 1973. Black became the first enlisted Air Force Cross recipient of the Vietnam War and received a battlefield promotion to second lieutenant for his esprit de corps, motivation, and teamwork while a POW.

Arthur N. Black embodies the PJ value of *never quit*. Of his nearly eight years as a prisoner, he said, "There are many lessons that we all learned during our captivity, but the most important lesson for every countryman to learn and remember is that no matter how difficult, hopeless, or futile the situation might appear, a strong faith in God and country will somehow, in time, resolve that situation."

When the words came through the speakers, they took a moment to register with my brain. The emcee leaned down into the microphone and said, "Now, for esprit de corps, the Arthur N. Black award goes to Airman James Settle."

I couldn't believe what I was hearing. It didn't even make sense. The crowd erupted in cheers.

The guy next to me elbowed my ribs.

"Go on, Jimmy! That's you!"

I stood. My legs felt a bit wobbly. I made my way across the stage, grinning wide, and accepted the beautiful black plaque. I did a grin-and-grip with C-Lo for the cameras. Everyone was smiling, clapping, and cheering.

I returned to my spot, still a bit shocked. My face burned red from the attention—and perhaps from a few of the shots I'd had before getting onstage. This award meant more to me than just a nice little plaque; this was recognition from my peers. It meant I was the guy the other men would want to be shot down with and survive nearly a decade of captivity alongside. Me. The guy telling jokes, laughing, and *always* playing pranks.

We wore our blues and our fancy black jump boots, buffed so shiny they reflected the crystals from the chandeliers overhead. The command from the emcee blared over the speakers: "Graduates. Have a seat. And blouse your boots." That order meant we were to take our pant legs up and, using the special blouse strap inside, clip them, exposing those beautiful black jump boots. There I was, in fancy dress uniform, cool shiny black jump boots, and then the emcee gave the order, "Class of 2008, stand at attention!"

We jumped to our feet. All of us stood a little taller.

"Class of 2008, don your berets!" We whipped out our berets and slipped them on.

The emcee finished the ceremony with, "I'm proud to introduce to you the graduating class of 2008. They are now PJs!"

The ballroom explodes with cheers and whistles. We file down off the stage, and in the first round of handshakes everyone is coining us—slipping military coins into our hands. Officers and other operators have these unique silver dollar–size coins, which are the equivalent of a high five or your grandfather's "Good job, son." Usually, the coins are given as congratulations from a high-ranking officer or high-ranking enlisted person. The person gifting you the coin palms it in his hand while offering a handshake, and you respond with a prompt, "Thank you, sir."

My pockets quickly filled with coins.

And guess who shows up in line? The coolest man ever, my shark-wrestling partner, Yo-Yo. He flew from the 24th out on the East Coast to come see the graduating class. I gave him a big old hug. "Man, I knew you would make it," he said. Then he added, in his own way, "You're one motivated dude."

The spirits continued to soar, as well as flow, for the duration of the night. PJs have a reputation for not being afraid, and perhaps the philosophy transfers not being afraid to have fun, either. There is a special energy and a zest for life the profession seems to attract, and most of the guys I know with a maroon beret are the best kind of guys you'll ever meet. I learned that it takes a special breed to come out the other side of the pipeline in one piece, and when someone new joins the rank, that entry into the fold is cause enough for some serious celebration.

And celebrate we did. I'd survived the pipeline. I had only five days to pack my belongings and drive the 3,600 miles back to Alaska, where I would begin my career as a PJ. I couldn't get home fast enough.

16

· · · · · · · · ·

Alaska PJ No. 72

Finally home, I became Alaska PJ no. 72, a full-fledged member of the Anchorage-based Alaska Air National Guard's 176th Wing.

The military has played an interesting role throughout Alaskan history, in terms of war, rescue, and building vital state infrastructure. The Army Air Force's 10th Emergency Boat Rescue Squadron operated in Alaska from the 1940s, using airplanes, boats, and dog teams. They distinguished themselves in the battles of World War II in Alaskan waters. In the 1990s, when the Air National Guard squadron took over rescues operations in Alaska, the new unit was named the 210th to honor the 10th Rescue outfit, becoming the "second" Tenth Rescue Squadron. I came into the unit after the 210th was already subdivided to reflect the specialization of key components of the unit. The simplest way to delineate these is that the 210th was for the HH-60G Pave Hawk helicopters, the 211th was for the fixed-wing HC-130s, and the 212th was reserved for PJ, CRO, and SERE specialists. Combined, the three units create the backbone for our rescue missions in Alaska and beyond.

My number, seventy-two, meant that seventy-one PJs had the distinction of serving Alaska before me. I couldn't believe my luck, to be back home with such an incredible job—literally a dream come true. I hit the ground not just running but flying, more than a hundred miles per hour with nearly every training and mission.

Back at the section in Spenard, I was shown to my cage. The cages sat on a concrete floor in a room with a twenty-foot ceiling supported by steel I-beam rafters. Bright parking lot lights created long shadows and only added to the Batcave feeling. Most of the people who had been around for any period of time installed supplemental lighting in their cages. The cage essentially turns into your home away from home. The eight-by-eight cage is basically the PJ locker room, office, and, for some, sleeping area, all at once.

The main component in your cage is your alert rack, a cart where you store all your alert gear. You might have up to ten gear bags, depending on what mission you're trying to be ready for. When sitting on alert, you keep everything in gear bags preloaded on a cart, so that when a search or rescue call comes in you can roll out the door at a moment's notice.

I inherited my cage from the outgoing chief, Skip Kula, a man whose rescue stories were legendary. Skip had been a PJ for nearly three decades, and he left behind great cage lights and some cool items, like old pararescue manuals and gear. I liked to think the cage still had some of the superpowers that had kept Skip safe all those years.

The first order of business was to acquire the gear I needed to operate, and to get my cage in order. I installed curtain rods so I could hang everything—jackets, dry suit, mountaineering gear, and all the specialized clothing you need for the variety of terrain and weather found in Alaska. I mounted speakers so I could listen to music. I turned that wire cage into my little home, and it was also my mini office when at work. The old section had few assigned offices, so our personal files and books remained in our cages. When there was anything resembling downtime, that is where I would hang out, drink coffee, and read—mostly studying PJ manuals. But there never really was downtime. If you thought you were bored, you were wrong. There was always something to read or study—that is, if you weren't prepping for training or taking care of your gear. Specialized gear requires special care and maintenance.

The cage area was located inside what we called "the bay," the garage where the two alert trucks were parked. This was an enormous warehouse, with doorways leading off the perimeter walls of the bay area into the armory, supply, and parachute rooms. All our mission-related service areas were attached to the room, like a big organ.

My unit basically took the pipeline training that I had just completed and redid it all. This was Alaska orientation. Upgrade training, they called it. Due to the terrain, the weather, and some unusual living and working conditions, Alaska can be a dangerous place. There isn't a single rescue unit in the entire Department of Defense busier than the 212th Rescue Squadron (212th RQS). The 11th Rescue Coordination Center, the brains behind the brawn of the unit, took over coordinating the rescues and searches for a host of Alaskan agencies, and since 1994, it has staged more than five thousand missions and saved the lives of well over two thousand people.

When people require rescue in Alaska, which is often, the situation facing the person or people needing help is often dangerous. To be a PJ in Alaska, you want to make sure that you are proficient at operating in all the wild scenarios Alaska might throw at you, from wicked weather to bear attacks. You don't want to hurt yourself or anyone else when you drop in for a rescue. There was a long menu of required Alaska upgrade training.

A large portion of the training deals with rescues in inclement weather or hazardous conditions, such as snow, ice, or glacial silt. Another significant piece of the training revolved around using our specialized parachute. Then there is all the other team stuff, like mud rescue, earthquake rescue, glacier rescue, and Arctic sea ice rescue.

The mud rescue gear is really unique, designed for the mudflats all around Anchorage and Cook Inlet. This mud is treacherous. Tidal deposits of silt, sand, and muck from the outwash of the surrounding glaciers pose a serious threat to people who attempt to walk on them. It appears at first glance to be a nice long stretch of beach, but that muck acts like quicksand and will suck you right in. You're stuck, or you're playing around, having fun and laughing at your stranded boot, and then you realize the tide is coming in, and coming in fast. You will drown if you don't get out.

Several people have died this way, and their deaths or rescues have become local lore. Rumors abound of someone being torn in half by a last-minute attempt to use a chopper to pull the victim from the ruthless grip of the mud. In July 1988, Adeana Dickison and her husband were mining at Ingram Creek when their Jeep became mired in the mud. As they attempted to free the vehicle, Adeana's leg became immovable. Her husband tried to free her, but couldn't. He went for help. By the time emergency crews arrived, the tide had risen to her chest and she had little time left. She pleaded with them to do something, but they simply could not get her leg free as the water rose. With her final breaths, she was begging them to save her. The trooper on the scene gave her a tube to breathe through as the water rushed over her head, but hypothermia had already taken hold and she couldn't keep her hands on the hose for long.

Dickison's horrific death prompted rescue agencies, including our unit, to be better prepared for emergencies on the mudflats. Part of my upgrade training dealt with learning the system we had set up. This included building a working platform with plywood and using these funky, snowshoe-like shoes for walking on the mud. We had a specialized backpack, similar to a five-gallon metal cauldron, that we could use to pressurize the water around stranded limbs, using the pressurized water to break the suction.

At the same time, I began working with the helicopters and C-130 crews and learning those aircrafts. Every day, I was learning new stuff; then I would go home and hit the books. When I came back as a new PJ, I was more intimidated and scared than I had been as a cone. As a cone, it is okay to screw up. You're new and you don't know anything. But as a beret-toting PJ, if you are going to be the dude, you've got to know what the hell you are doing. The margin of error is that there is no margin for error.

I put in long days. I was usually the first one there and I would stay late, working. But it paid off, and I got the upgrade training done. The kinds of things I got to do for "work" and training in the Alaskan wilderness are things that people pay ridiculous amounts of money to try just once. I loved all the winter training. This really brought home to me how fortunate I was to be able to train outdoors and to work in preparation to save lives in my own state.

They flew us into the mountains for avalanche rescue training. We'd go into the wilderness on backcountry skis, ATVs, or snow machines. My favorite sort of delivery to the wilderness was, of course, by helicopter. There was nothing like taking off from Anchorage and racing toward impossibly difficult and remote terrain. That sea of mountains I spoke of seeing from the top of Arctic Valley? The pilots could deliver us far into the remote reaches of the Chugach range and deploy us to practice our winter skills. In the name of practice and training, I'd get dropped off on glaciers or mountaintops to ski.

This sounds like fun, and it was, but the Alaska wilderness was our educational proving ground. The very places where we trained could become the site of a downed aircraft or a lost hiker. Alaska is amazing, but she also gobbles up her fair share of victims. If we were going to rescue people all across the state, we had to know how to handle ourselves in all sorts of sticky situations.

Crevasse rescue work was some of my favorite training. That first May as a PJ, I was dropped at the Denali base camp for some glacial crevasse rescue and mountaineering training. There is nothing like dropping down into the blue-black depths of a glacier. I couldn't believe my luck, getting to spend time at the base camp.

PJs have been involved in some daring rescues on our highest peak, and on others, over the years. All of us had to be ready to jump or hoist in to rescue climbers anywhere on the mountain.

Another training involved a fun but intense glacial traverse in which a group of us were dropped off by helicopter deep in the Chugach Mountains to camp and then ski out. That trip involved some gnarly ice climbing and mountain traversing, and it included what I considered to be my first crevasse rescue. One of the guys lost control of the sled he was pulling. It tipped, and the tragedy of the day occurred. A small cask of wine fell out and slid down the ice, disappearing into a crevasse. Everyone looked at me, the new guy. Someone had to rescue the wine. They roped me up and down I rappelled, a couple hundred feet into a deep glacial fissure, to rescue our libations.

Being a PJ in Alaska is about operating in the various physical states of water—vapor, liquid, and solid—and all of it is cold. Right after my boots hit the ground, we began the water jumps. Alaskan waters tend to be too cold for the standard wetsuit, so I learned how to parachute in a dry suit. The dry suit is just that: a layer of protection designed to keep the water away from your body, exposing only your hands and face to the elements. I learned how to parachute wearing a dry suit as well as how to dive with a dry suit. Both require different techniques from what I learned in the pipeline.

Alaskan weather conditions pose additional challenges not taught in the pipeline. Naturally, I learned some lessons the hard way, and one lesson was a bit shocking. It turns out that when you're playing with the helicopter and preparing to hoist out, especially in dry air, static electricity can build up on the bird. The static will discharge through the cable when it grounds out against the earth. The first time I grabbed the cable, in winter's bitter cold, a strong pulse of electricity surged, knocking me back a step. I let go of the cable. When I grabbed it again, I took another big jolt. I was with a fairly strict, no-nonsense PJ, and when I dropped the cable the second or third time, he snatched the hook, said, "Don't be a pussy," and then handed it off to me.

One of the Alaska upgrade training checklist items was parachuting and diving in the dead of winter. And then doing it again, at night, in the cold. Not just below zero, but where anything above twenty below sounds tropical. Frigid winds. Ice. And most of all, snow. Hard-packed snow. Powdery light snow. Fun snow-angel-making snow. Butt-puckering, avalanche-prone snow.

Snow adds an interesting twist to working with everything. Snow and specialized tools and gear create issues and hazardous scenarios. Drop something precious and it is gone forever. The snow eats tools, carabiners, weapons, and people. Drop something into deep powder and you can kiss it good-bye.

Then there is landing your parachute in the snow. Skydiving in Alaska in the winter is mildly nerve-racking because you have to layer up your clothes to a point where you look like a sumo wrestler. Not only is the weather cold on the ground but also, on an altitude jump in Alaska in winter, you're talking about temperatures that can be forty to fifty below. Add the wind speed of free fall and the temperature drops to somewhere around absolute zero Kelvin.

One morning, before a training event, I found myself considering the glove situation for one of those frigid deep-snow jumps. I debated having a hand that might become frozen and unusable versus having a glove that might be too thick to feel the parachute's opening ball. One of the parachutes the Alaska PJs jump with is an awesome piece of equipment. The MC1-Delta SOV3 was our standard unit parachute. This is a bottom-pull parachute, more like a civilian rig than the type of parachute I trained with at free fall school. Those have a rip cord handle that you trace and pull at the shoulder; the SOV has a pillow or golf ball that you reach back for, as if to scratch your butt crack. You pull the ball out and throw it to the side, looking out over the same shoulder to make sure the little drogue parachute catches the wind. The drogue deploys your chute. For half a second you see a miniature parachute flying next to you, and then it takes off and—*whoosh!*—you get whipped through that opening shock sequence and you're snatched from flying face toward the earth to sitting comfortably in the sky, floating your way home.

We constantly trained for a parachute failure opening sequence. We would practice reaching back and pulling the drogue chute. If you can't grab it, the first thing you do is reach back and try again. If it's not there, you're hosed. You enter what I would call an *Oh shit* sequence. If you don't get the drogue, then you come to the conclusion that you'll have to cut away the main chute and pull the reserve chute. You deploy the reserve by pulling the two handles on your harness chest, located at your shoulders, where a set of backpack straps would be. One handle is red, for the cutaway; the other is green, for the emergency reserve parachute.

Fortunately, I never had to deploy my reserve, which was a blessing, but if that event ever occurred and I was unable to open the reserve, there was an automatic assist device built into the parachute. It's a small computer attached to the emergency reserve parachute, and it tracks your altitude and your speed. If for some reason you drop through the preset parameters, it fires your reserves by engaging a small explosive on the retaining cord of the emergency reserve parachute. One small *pop* and the emergency reserve parachute deploys on its own. If a parachutist happens to get knocked unconscious, the parachute will open automatically for him. This is called "riding the reserve." I've only heard of it happening to one guy. He took a bit of ribbing from our friends, but he survived. It's a thing of pride not to ride your reserve, but it beats the alternative.

My concern with this particular jump had to do with the cold and with my struggles on that jump in Florida. Would my glove be too thick to open the parachute? That early struggle to deploy my chute had become a stressor whenever I jumped. I started constantly practicing. I learned my lesson in PJ school, and I knew to practice, and any time I had new gloves, I would rehearse over and over.

Eventually, I figured out a compromise. I wore a heavy glove on my left hand and a slightly thinner glove on my right. I wanted to maintain the dexterity I needed to do my job. Dexterity versus warmth was the same debate I would find myself struggling with during winter water work with Roger, later on.

I learned that, once you figure out how to dress appropriately, winter jumps aren't all that bad. They are cold, but not bad. One of my most memorable winter jumps occurred on the back side of Mount Susitna, a mountain I had grown up seeing on the horizon north of Anchorage almost every day of my childhood.

We climbed into the C-130 and left out of Kulis. We flew across Cook Inlet and directly over Mount Susitna, also known as Sleeping Lady because, from Anchorage, it appears to be the profile of a woman at rest on her back, rising above a tidal flat and a dense spruce and birch forest. The mountain has always had a special place in my family, because this is where they sprinkled the ashes from my aunt recovered in the lake tragedy.

The land on the north side of the mountain is an expanse of frozen meadows and marshes, sparsely treed with willow, Alaska's version of bamboo stalks. Out there, they can grow six to eight feet tall.

The plane banked. Then the ramp dropped and my adrenaline spiked. At fifteen thousand feet, we were well above the surrounding mountaintops. We had turned south, back toward Anchorage, so out the back we looked due north. Denali rose another five thousand feet, off in the distance. We received the *Go* sign and I shuffled to the door in my heavy mountaineering boots. These have metal eyelets that you hook your laces through, and earlier I had slapped duct tape over all the eyelets to keep the parachute from tangling with my boots. I looked down at my big silvery boots and had this funny thought: *All this high-tech gear I could never afford, and I'm relying on duct tape?*

With that, I jumped out into free fall. All the weight on my shoulders and my lower back, all the compression of all the straps, disappeared. I was weightless, the pressure gone. I could breathe and relax and take in the stunning beauty around me.

I flew through the air, but my mask and goggles were not quite dialed in perfectly. Cold air leaked in, blasting my eyes. They began to tear up, and I blinked away the freezing droplets. I watched my altimeter through half-closed eyes that burned with the biting cold. Ice crystals formed at the edges where the tears gathered. When I hit my low opening zone, I reached back and pulled the ball on my chute. *Poof!*

I glided toward endless whiteness below. Sleeping Lady rested in front of me.

There I was, finally a PJ, and this was the first time in my life I could see this mountain up close. She slept, covered in white, facing up at me, and down around her neck somewhere rested the ashes of my aunt.

The beauty of this mountain and my connection to it so entranced me that I may have forgotten to pay attention to what I was doing for a fraction of a second, and this little lapse took me off the drop zone. Four of us were jumping and expected to land on the snow-packed V the crew had established on the ground as the drop zone. Off by about a hundred meters, I flew toward untracked snow and brush. I stuck like a lawn dart, right up to my waist. *Boom!* The world erupted in a blast of powder. Then the parachute floated down and became entangled in the willows all around me. These trees are not a problem when you're walking; you can stroll right through them. But when your chute lands in them, it's a different story.

My parachute, fouled in the willows, billowed over my head, knocking snow from the branches onto me. Then the chute dropped down over my helmet. I couldn't see where everybody was. I waited for the parachute to settle. The willows snapped in the bitter cold as I yanked on the lines and the parachute with all the strength I had. All I could think about was the wind picking up and dragging me through the snow and trees in a far-northern version of that same ride I had taken in Florida. I balled up my parachute and began crawling on my belly. The parachute felt relatively warm, an insulating barrier between my body and the snow.

I stuffed the chute into my bag. I tried to stand but—*puff!*—sank right to my waist again. I had to go only a hundred yards, but each step, with the combined weight of my parachute and my gear, took serious work, and every footstep sent me straight through the fluffy powder. After half an hour of postholing with the parachute in a duffle bag on my shoulder, in all that heavy winter gear and sub-zero temperatures, I'd soaked my long underwear with sweat. I was lucky a helicopter would be taking me home. Sweat and cold don't mix well in situations like that. A fun romp in the snow can turn disastrous once those chills set in, if you can't get out of the wet clothing and find a source of heat.

The short hike took all my energy in that deep snow, but I got there in one piece. My new glove strategy had worked, and once again I learned the value of landing on the target

On another occasion, I nearly *was* the target, during a water jump in Kachemak Bay, outside of Homer. This area of Alaska may very well be one of the most beautiful spots on earth. Despite the cold water, those jumps were my favorite. The landscape is postcard Alaska. Glaciers. Volcanoes. Whales breaching. It's pure magic to free fall into Kachemak Bay.

In lieu of the RAMZ, my unit started jumping with a Jet Ski of sorts. This was the ARC, an alternative recovery craft. The ARC had a V-shaped hull and could seat four, similar to the Sea-Doo type of vessels you see racing around lakes in the summer. Once in the water, we could attach a broad yellow foam rescue sled behind and scoop people or gear up for transport or rescue.

All the same, the graphic truth about the development of RAMZ and ARC is that, generally speaking, when it comes to aircraft crashes into water, you're more likely to be picking up pieces than survivors. Those pieces aren't going to be concentrated in one little spot. They are spread out all over the ocean by the currents and waves, so the idea is to have the RAMZ act as the little runabout to do the collecting. In the early days, teams would deploy a thirty-man raft and the RAMZ would pick up all the bits and pieces of people and throw them into the big raft. This process evolved into something more efficient, using the ARC as the scooter, because it was a hell of a lot easier to start than the RAMZ. Getting the ARC running was a no-brainer. As long as you could get the craft upright and untangled from the parachute, that machine fired to life every time.

We were doing a series of drills with the ARC, and any time we jumped with the ARC, I couldn't help but feel a little bit like James Bond. I waited below, on our boat, with one of our old-timer PJs. I fiddled with my gear while the C-130 made its approach. I didn't see the craft exit the aircraft, but I looked up when one of the guys in the boat with me yelled, "Oh, God. They messed up."

I looked up. The C-130 flew away, and beyond that was brilliant blue sky. Then I saw the problem. A small, dark object falling through the sky toward us. No parachute. Too big to be a person. Our ARC. Falling. Gaining speed. It wasn't going to drop right on top of us, but it was close. All we could do was watch and wait until it hit the water.

Boom! The craft flattened against the water's surface like an egg hitting a window. Nothing but plastic, cardboard, and a slick of oil remained. Someone had forgotten to hook the vessel up to the static line before they pushed it off the ramp. Whoops. Fortunately, I wasn't involved in that mistake, but I witnessed the devastation of landing in the water without a parachute, and had the joy of helping clean the water for hours afterward.

Alaska has no shortage of water, and Alaska PJs have to be ready to rescue people in a variety of water conditions, from ocean and lakes to rivers with raging white water. One of the alert mission training dives was a scenario involving an emergency call about a man overboard from his fishing boat in one of the small local lakes found throughout the Anchorage bowl. We launched, bringing all of our alert gear. I slipped into my dry suit and pulled on my oxygen supply and a full face mask, which was tethered to the shore with a microphone so we could talk to one another.

I slipped into the lake and began searching through the muck, feeling the cold, icky mud of the bottom. This was a lake I had been to in the summertime as a kid, playing on the beach and splashing around in the water, and there I was, swimming around in the seaweed and the muck looking for a mock drowning victim. I remember thinking I should have brought a probe. Everything was dark, and I couldn't see more than a few inches in front of my mask, if at all. I knew there weren't any sharks and that I wasn't going to find a real body, but then again, you never really know what you're going to find down there.

The voice of one of my buddies on shore came over my earpiece. "Jimmy," he said, "you're breathing kinda heavy. You should try to relax. Try to slow it down."

"Come on, now," I joked. "You know you guys like it."

They were right. I was panting. I inhaled slower the next time and tried to quiet my racing mind and focus on the task at hand.

Swimming in that lake felt like going through the dark tunnels from a horror movie. I pulled myself along, hand over hand, grabbing fistfuls of this slimy vegetative growth as I made a slow sweep through the area, looking for the mock victim. I was careful not to stir up any sediment, because that would ruin what little visibility I had. All the excitement drained out of the training, replaced with the chill at the bottom of the lake. I just hoped I could find the damn thing and end the drill. The other part of me hoped I didn't find anything at all, because I was afraid that, with my luck, if I did find something, it would be something real and scary. Anchorage has no shortage of missing persons and foul play. I knew that, on previous dives, other PJs had found an assortment of objects, ranging from pistols to baby dolls. And if any PJ was going to be the first to find a real body, it would be me. I said to myself, *I don't wanna find anything weird.*

The only thing I found that was not training-related was an old pull-top Coca-Cola can. I don't think any of my education in the pipeline prepared me for those forty minutes of pure tension, frigid water, and suspense, combing through the dark muck searching for a body.

After I waded to shore and removed my gear, I sat on the tailgate of our pickup and caught my breath. The longer I stayed in the game in Alaska, the greater were the odds that I would someday be doing a real search under similar circumstances, not unlike the searches that went on for those who went missing from the Skilak Lake accident that nearly took my grandmother and my mom.

17

. . . .

Saving Barbie

With all the specialized Alaska PJ training completed, I could begin the real rescues. I had sacrificed a lot at that point, in terms of my marriage, precious time away from my son during his first years of life, and the physical damage to my body. Still, I was excited and ready for the payoff. Outside of Clear, Alaska, I would hoist in from the Pave Hawk in the middle of a storm to help an old man with heart issues. I would be credited with a save off Denali, where two climbers fell, one to his death. I'd spend countless hours in the C-130 searching for lost hunters, hikers, and climbers. Each mission, each rescue, and each training only made me love my job more. The position was everything I'd hoped it would be, and more. After my first year, I would receive recognition as Airman of the Year for the 176th. To top that off, I had the honor to parachute with a huge Alaska flag tied to my leg, in front of the cheering crowd at the Reno Air Show. Jeremy Maddamma jumped with the Air National Guard flag and Al Lankford flew the Stars and Stripes.

I hadn't been a PJ very long when an overseas deployment started to look more and more like a reality. After all I had worked for, I had no way of knowing how little time I would have left as a PJ in the Alaskan wilderness. I went into the job to save lives, but that also meant saving lives on the battlefield, and I wasn't naive to that fact. The sorties and trainings I was a part of, from my first to my last, would have to be enough to last a lifetime.

My first mission in my dream job as a PJ came late at night, during the late fall. The call came in from the rescue coordination center, which is located in Anchorage and is staffed twenty-four hours a day to coordinate rescues around the entire state of Alaska within minutes. The call ripped me from sleep, and I was on alert with Chris Robertson, of all people. Chris and I sat alert on the C-130 and the other two PJs had the Pave Hawk.

The call was strange from the outset. We didn't have direct communication with the people on the scene. Instead, we received our information relayed through our dispatch. All the reports seemed to indicate textbook severe head trauma. We were told that the call came from an uninhabited island near Cordova. Some hunters had flown in with ATVs and a bunch of gear. The patient, a female, told dispatchers she had lashed a chain saw on the very top of her gear, on the front of the quad, without a guard on the blade. While driving to the hunting site, she rolled the vehicle. She hadn't been wearing a helmet, and when she flipped, the four-wheeler landed on her, with the super-sharp saw chain between her and the vehicle and solid ground. We were told the blade had cut across her skull, down over her forehead, scalping her. She was stable but needed help. Within minutes we were airborne.

Our flight took more than an hour from Anchorage. We beat the helicopter to the site. This was early November, at night, with a serious winter storm in full effect. I couldn't believe I was out on my first mission, and with Chris Robertson. It was as it should be. With the weather and the impending head trauma, I knew I was about to earn my PJ chops.

We came in low and searched out the sides, watching for an

unmapped airstrip or a possible place to land in our parachutes. The callers signaled up at us from the cabin they were in, and having located them, we could start putting a plan together. We still didn't have direct contact with the people on the ground. We continued to receive intermittent reports that sounded somewhat dire, and that used nearly clinically perfect medical terminology.

We knew where they were, and the pilots searched to find the nearest place to put down the plane, but it was far too stormy. We flew over again, scoping out the situation. I started wondering whether we were going to parachute in.

Chris turned to me and, over the rumble of the plane's engines, said, "Jimmy, get your chute sized up and get ready to jump." On the right side of the airplane, from the belly to the tail, was open ocean. Nothing but snowstorm and whitecaps. On the left side stood a tall, sheer cliff face. On top of the cliff was a narrow patch of flat ground, and then forest running up into the mountains. I knew that trying to land on that small patch of flat ground would be incredibly difficult, even on a good day. To stick that landing in a blizzard? Impossible.

But that's what PJs do, right? I'd heard enough of the stories. I knew the drill. At Chris's command, I began jocking up and prepared to make the jump. What I was thinking? *No way, Jose. No way.*

It would take some sort of parachuting miracle to land there in the squall. My jumping out would only put others at risk. I made this assessment within a few seconds. Nothing good would come of a jump in these conditions. Still, I double-checked my gear and prepared for the orders.

What I didn't double-check was Chris's smirk. I probably should have known he was pulling my leg. I did need to be ready to jump, if the weather broke, but he wasn't sending me out in that shit. If Chris and I parachuted in those conditions, one or both of us would probably die. Not to mention the fact that the aircraft commander would never have let us out the door in the first place.

We orbited around the site, waiting for the chopper. The low ceiling and lack of visibility tested the HH-60 flight crew. They worked their way through the storm and rugged coastal terrain, risking their lives and doing all they could to get to the scene. I did my thing in the back, prepping the C-130 to receive a patient when we landed. The plan that developed was for the PJs in the helicopter to hoist in, stabilize the patient, and then fly her to Yakataga, a small landing strip nearby, for a transfer from the HH-60 to the C-130. We would then deliver the patient to Ted Stevens International in Anchorage, and from there she'd take a short ambulance ride to Providence hospital.

The PJs in the helicopter did what PJs do. They risked everything, dropped in, and collected the patient. I don't recall their exact words, but we immediately had the sense that the situation wasn't as dire as the frantic calls had led us to believe.

At twelve feet in elevation, the Yakataga airstrip isn't much more than a long gravel strip a hundred yards from the ocean, a typical Alaskan bush runway. Tall willows and alders line the landing pad. The surf crashes off to your right as you land, and snow-capped mountains rise up from sea level on your left. The narrow band of crushed gravel comprising the landing strip leads right to the base of single hulking mountain. Our C-130 pilots are as good as they get in Alaska. They can land a Hercules in places most pilots would deem impossible and dangerous. The HH-60 pilots are equally amazing. Both aircraft made the landing without incident, and we prepared for quick transfer of our patient.

The moment we laid eyes on the patient, Chris shot me a look. Something wasn't right. He would later describe her as "Hunting Fun Barbie." Her camouflage bordered on the absurd. Her hat, gloves, pants, and jacket were a matching woodland winter camo print with cute little pink ribbons scattered throughout the pattern.

I clipped her into the stanchions on the litter. She was already stabilized and had an IV. I did my quick assessment, to make sure things were dandy, as we began to taxi down the runway. Hunting

Fun Barbie was conscious, in fresh makeup, stable, and actually in a pretty good mood for a woman who had allegedly just been scalped by a chain saw and crushed by an ATV. She wasn't really bleeding much for a head wound, and I took the bandage off and peeled it back, fully expecting a deep gash with bare, white skull exposed. Not so.

"Is it going to scar?" she asked.

Chris and I stared at the small cut in disbelief. We'd risked life and limb and spent untold amounts of money to rescue a woman with a scratch. A scratch! A glorified cut ran a few inches across her forehead. I don't recall how I responded, but I clearly remember Chris's instructions to me.

Always one to use a good teaching opportunity, and an excellent judge of character, Chris wasn't going to let my first mission go to waste. We had a patient who claimed textbook-like trauma and needed dramatic rescue, and that was what she was going to get. And I would get to practice on her.

"Jimmy," Chris deadpanned. "Get the neck collar."

18

....

The Same Soaking

The chopper had left us in the water, and I knew we couldn't survive much longer. I couldn't be sure whether Roger was testing me or was dead serious about how dire our situation was when he asked that question: "Well, now what, Jimmy?"

It would be like Roger to test the new guy in such a manner. No other PJ went around quoting Yamamoto Tsunetomo's *Hagakure: The Secret Wisdom of the Samurai*. No other PJ I knew had started his career as part of the old-school Marine Corps Force Recon special operations team; Roger had become a Force Recon instructor. I'd never heard of any other PJ having INDOC training interrupted so the cadre could pin a medal on his chest. To me, Roger stood a bit above the rest of us, and not just because of his six-foot-eight frame. It was because of the shit he'd already seen and his approach to life.

I met Roger Sparks during my time as a cone. A tree of a man, lean and strong. He towered over me and ducked as he slipped through doorways. Hair always shaved close, big smile, deep hearty laugh, and dark serious eyes. At first I tried to avoid him, because seasoned PJs like Roger intimidated me. As tall as he was, I avoided him with ease, but I quickly learned that he had a big heart and was a walking encyclopedia. A natural teacher, he took time to teach me knots, climbing, and swimming techniques. I learned from Roger as a cone, and even more as a PJ. He told incredible stories, when it came to training, because he had done it all, as a PJ and in Force Recon. He possessed a powerful and positive perspective on things. He would talk about how our gear was top-of-the-line and would remind us that we were lucky and needed to take care of what we worked with, because he'd seen the other side of the coin during his time in the Marine Corps Forces Special Operations Command (MARSOC). They had to make do with what they had, and oftentimes that involved being creative with substandard military gear in order to survive.

I suspect he also appreciated the fact that our unit worked with him to have the right size of gear when possible. The man is so tall he has to have all his pants and uniforms custom tailored. We all wore thousand-dollar Arc'teryx one-piece Gore-Tex suits for doing work in extreme weather, and Roger had to have his custom made. Same for his sleeping bag.

But neither the best gear in the world nor any amount of Roger's swimming tips and knot knowledge could get us out of the fix we were in that cold winter night in Cook Inlet. We drifted, holding on to each other. Roger encouraged creativity and embraced adversity, but there, in those swift and deadly waters, we had few options. We both knew that each minute of immersion in the cold salt water brought us another breath closer to hypothermia and death.

We had a problem. And we needed to start working that problem. Fast.

We took our bearings. We could see Anchorage—not the city, but the glow of its lights off the clouds—almost over the curve of the horizon from water level. Oil derricks were scattered around the area where we had been dropped. We briefly considered swimming to one of those, but we didn't even know whether we could swim there or, if we reached it, would have the strength to climb a ladder. If there was a ladder, that is.

We didn't know how far we were from shore. At first, all we could do was chill—and were we ever chilling. Dry suits are not completely dry. We were both leaking water at our necks and wrists. Our core temperatures dipped with each passing heartbeat.

We told ourselves they would figure out the issue and be right along to scoop us up. But before long, real concern set in. *Why we were in the water for so long?*

What do we do? Swim for shore? Which way?

We floated there for a while, lost in our own thoughts. Conserving energy. Freezing to death. Listening for an approaching chopper. There was nothing.

"Maybe it's about time we go overt," Roger said.

I reached for the strobe attached to the back of my hoody. The infrared cover is something that you can just pull up, so I flipped it over and pulled that out. I noticed I had little dexterity left in my hands. I cursed myself for not wearing the heaviest gloves possible. Then I remembered something in my dry suit pocket, on my left shoulder. I always carried an emergency light called a buzz saw. I never thought I would have to use one. It's just a piece of string, about three feet long, with a glow stick on the end. Just a regular six-inch glow stick. You crack it, hold the string, and spin it over your head. This creates a glowing disk. The disk increases the chances that you'll catch the eyes of searchers. The easier it is for them to find you, the better, obviously.

I floated there in the water, holding on to Roger with one arm and spinning the buzz saw with the other. Kicking and spinning, kicking and spinning.

I was so in the moment, I didn't have room for reflection or contemplation. The icy grip of death was in my face, and the cold was ever so slowly squeezing the ability to function out of me. It was right at the level of perception but beyond the ability for me to do anything to stop the decline. I felt as if I sat aboard a slow-motion crazy train and could only watch myself out the window. The experience felt similar to running long distances, and it called to mind another mental practice I used to get through during tough times. I visualized my body as a sort of machine, with my mind acting as the pilot inside a head full of control panels, buttons, lights, and gauges. As the pilot, I would think, *Okay! We need to tweak this and adjust that. These lights are lit up. These bones are hurting. This joint is hurting. Let's do this.* That is how I visualized my bodily functions during trying physical moments. But this time, in the cold water, a whole different sort of panic lights lit up.

We were getting to the point where we couldn't function, but we didn't panic. Perhaps we were too cold. We remained calm, kind of at peace with our situation. There was nothing in our vast arsenal of training or life experience that we could use to stop the train or change its direction. We were doing what we could to get help, with our strobes and the buzz saw. All we could do was hope our friends were doing the absolute best they could to get us out before it was too late.

I've got the best gear in the world, but it's leaking. I've got the best training in the world, but I can't use it. I'm swimming next to one of the best guys in the field, but he is no better off than I am. Still, as shitty as the situation was, the cards were stacked in our favor. We held on and kept encouraging each other. Over and over.

"Hang in there, man."

"You okay?"

"Cold, dude."

"Me too."

Any movement of our bodies brought more cold water in through our necks and wrists. We tried to maintain a "heat escape lessening posture," or HELP, but in those icy waters, and given the amount of time we had been exposed, all we could do was hold on to each other.

Then we heard the helicopter. We'd been in the water for an hour or more. Now we were fully hypothermic, but we still had to somehow get on board. Neither Roger nor I remember much of what happened next. They had brought Captain Rick Watson, one of our best chopper pilots, to rescue us.

Roger grabbed the cable and made a motion like he was clipping in, but he didn't have his horse tail, the webbing we clipped in with, in his hand. He handed me the hoist and I fumbled with the clip and somehow got my harness attached. Roger's horse tail had sunk back down, and we were both trying to get a hold of it. His long torso made it impossible for me to reach. Somehow, I managed to snatch it up. I struggled for a moment, then clipped him straight to me.

I faded in and out of consciousness on our way home. I didn't have earplugs and was too cold to ask. I only remember being curled over half of the R2, the helicopter's heater, and shivering. I had never been that cold in my life, and I've never been that cold since.

Roger was as messed up as I was. That poor guy. Unlike me, who had some thermal reserves stockpiled by way of body fat, Roger was a shredded beanpole. We were both spent. Neither of us had anything left. When we landed back at Kulis, a bunch of guys from the team rushed to greet us. The pilot of the helicopter we were originally on came running over and gave us huge hugs. He was on the verge of tears.

"I didn't think I was ever going to see you guys again. I am so sorry," he said.

He felt personally responsible, and you could see it on his face and the way he carried himself. Roger and I were human Popsicles, but we didn't need to add to his obvious guilt about whatever happened. We were alive.

"It's cool," I said. "We've got to go now and get back to the section and wash and pack our stuff. We're still on alert." The guys helped us pull our gear off, there in the hanger. Water poured out.

We went to Denny's after the debrief, around two in the morning. I wasn't ready to go home and be normal and pretend like nothing had happened. I ordered Moons Over My Hammy and laughed at the fact Roger and I were almost dead an hour earlier, and here I was, sitting around a table with my fellow PJs eating a Grand Slam.

New protocols for 212th water work would be put in place from that day forward. A ten-minute hovering limit was established over the men in the water, and on the next attempt, a PJ would be sent in to help his teammates in the water.

A week later, Roger and I were doing water work again, because that is how the section rolls. You've got get right back on that horse. There isn't a "no" unless you want to quit.

From that night we almost died together in the water, I would carry with me Roger's lesson from Yamamoto's *Hagakure*:

There is something to be learned from a rainstorm. When meeting a sudden shower, you try not to get wet and run quickly along the road. But doing such things as passing under the eaves of houses, you still get wet. When you are resolved from the beginning, you will not be perplexed, though you will still get the same soaking. This understanding extends to everything.

19

. . . .

A Bulldog's Bite

Our unit signed on to support Bulldog Bite, an operation in the mountainous Kunar province of northeastern Afghanistan. It has a population of 428,000 crammed into roughly the same area as the municipality of Anchorage, with similar rugged peaks surrounding the city. Operation Bulldog Bite included an army of collaborators preparing to clear out Taliban strongholds in the mountains. A battery of special ops teams moved into the region, including Rangers, members of the 101st Airborne, and air force personnel from such units as Combat Control and Tactical Air Control. It was meant to be a well-orchestrated plan to put a hurt on the insurgency before winter provided them with a break and chance to rearm and resupply. With our high-altitude, vertical-terrain capabilities, our PJ unit would be on alert for rescues. Should anything go wrong.

On the evening of November 11, we prepositioned two helicopters, Pedro 83 and Pedro 84, to Forward Operating Base Joyce and set up shop. Roger stayed behind at Bagram to coordinate and lend support if we needed. Within an hour, our two Pedro crews were mission-ready.

The call sign "Pedro" came about during the Vietnam era. For a short time, the air force flew HH-43 Huskies, a really unique helicopter. It was small, with a lightweight twin rotor, and its call sign was Pedro. This little aircraft had the fastest start-up time available. It was initially designed to be fire response for flight line crashes; the rescue crews could whip this chopper up and dump water quickly.

The PJs took the Pedro and ran with it. The drawback to the Pedro, however, was that it had a range of only seventy miles. To extend missions, they would refuel with a fifty-gallon drum of fuel, in flight, by sticking a hose from the barrel in the aircraft and reaching outside the chopper to manually transfer fuel to the helicopter's tank. These helicopters really gave PJs their notoriety. They could just show up out of nowhere and hoist in and out quickly. Because of the HH-43 Husky, Pedro became one of the well-known call signs associated with pararescue.

Most people understand what search and rescue means. Combat search and rescue, or CSAR, is a whole other beast. CSAR takes the search and rescue element and adds camouflage, boom sticks, and combat tactics. PJs cut their teeth and defined their capabilities during the Vietnam War era. They proved the battlefield value of having medics who could deploy via aircraft and help stabilize trauma patients within what is known as the "golden hour," for maximum survival probability.

The CSAR mission in the Afghanistan theater was divided into two parts. The first call sign was Pedro, the other was Jolly. The Jolly call sign is embraced by the pararescue community; it originated from the CH-3C and the HH-53B/C helicopters, known as a the Jolly Green Giant and the Super Jolly Green Giant, respectively. These were huge green air force rescue helicopters. People got the impression that a giant had walked around in the grass, wherever the two enormous birds landed to rescue soldiers. That's how the PJ green feet came into being, inspiring all sorts of lore and no small amount of tomfoolery, a tradition that started in Vietnam. As the story goes, a group of PJs burning off steam on leave woke up the next morning, hung over, with green feet tattoos.

Call signs helped us to identify teams and their mission. In Afghanistan, Pedro was reserved for rescue in the mountainous northern part of the country, while Jolly designated the south. There were other rescue teams in the theater, such as Dustoff, the closest thing the army has to PJs. Dustoff, too, became well known in Vietnam. They were helicopters with big red crosses on a white square, painted on the sides and the front. Those red crosses were meant to identify the choppers as medical aid units, and by the rules of the Geneva Conventions, the bad guys weren't supposed to be shooting at them. Those same rules keep the helicopters with red crosses from being armed. The personnel on board can carry small personal weapons but no mounted machine guns. Due to the nature of the conflict in Afghanistan, the enemy viewed the red crosses on Dustoff choppers more like targets than medical aid, so Dustoff flight capabilities were more limited than ours. They were active, for sure, but with the steep mountain terrain and the flying Taliban bullets, we were the ones who answered if a casualty evacuation required a direct action response.

The different resources for rescue and response were all coordinated by the rescue coordination center. The RCC was a communications center that operated inside another acronym, the TOC, or tactical operations center.

Once we made the move from Bagram to FOB Joyce, we were deep in enemy territory. Operation Bulldog Bite wasn't expected to bring in too many casualties, but any time you have troops going into the mountains, especially where the enemy has an upper hand in terms of the terrain being in their backyard and in their blood, the situation can quickly degrade.

When we responded, there were a number of big risks. For one, our helicopters had been stripped of armor to fly at those high elevations. This meant the engines, pilots, gunners, flight engineers, and PJs would be vulnerable to small arms fire. The elevation also meant we could carry less of everything, and this included fuel and men. Less fuel meant less hover time. That meant less protection and more chance of being left behind, or leaving someone behind, to refuel. The risks were there, and so was a history of what had already gone wrong.

The summer before I deployed into the Afghanistan theater, a Pedro crew on a mission got shot right out of the sky. It was a horrible crash, with no survivors. A second PJ team went in to pull the heroes out, with a nearby Ranger unit sprinting over a mountain range to set up a ring of fire to support them.

The idea that we, too, could get shot out of the sky was definitely something we thought about. You'd see guys wearing memorial patches on their flight suits in honor of that lost rescue bird. The loss wasn't just about PJs—we're only a small piece of the whole CSAR component. PJs have a big, badass toolbox of capabilities, but our job is only possible because of the people we work with, mainly the helicopter and C-130 crews. The helicopter crews in Afghanistan made miracles happen. Those men withstood direct fire without hesitation. They displayed stone-cold dedication and nerves unlike anything I've seen. I admire and respect those guys, and I would end up owing them my life. It wouldn't take long for us to become close. We knew PJs didn't exist without a gunner, a flight engineer, and a pilot and copilot.

Each PJ team was assigned to a specific bird, with its pilot and support crew. All worked together as a single unit. You learn to build a rapport with your aircrew. It isn't an environment of PJs versus flight crew. You're a team, all working together to save lives. So when one of our own birds gets shot down, the loss is something we all think about. It touches all of us. Even if you didn't know any of the individuals on that bird, the hit to the family and the rescue community is felt. The loss sets a tone.

That morning, as the 9-line came in, we were all keenly aware that what we were doing was dangerous. I was excited, yes, but I had no misconceptions about the danger I'd be facing.

The one thing I didn't know was that my first brush with war could touch me so directly, so early in my new career.

We stood by on five-minute alert. This meant that all of us were jocked up, or half jocked up, close to the helicopters, and ready to be in the air in less than five minutes. We did push-ups and sit-ups. We told jokes. We checked and rechecked our gear. Sitting alert is kind of a funny situation to be in, especially when you know a battle is happening a few ridges over. I think of it as something like being a goalie in a World Cup soccer match. If you're on a team with a solid defense, you want some action, but when the ball comes your direction it means things have gone bad up front. When PJs take the 9-line call, someone is in serious trouble, and it's likely to be the worst day of a soldier's life. You really hope they don't need your skills and services, but at the same time, you're ready to go if they do.

The base of operations for us was the field hospital on FOB Joyce. Joyce was the size of four city blocks. Half was divided into small structures, tents, and things like that; the other half was dedicated to the helicopter pad and refueling tanks. The cinder block hospital included a small medical reception area in a building about twenty by forty feet, maybe a little bigger. A larger portion was divided into a patient reception area with beds, six litter stands on two walls, and a big, wide emergency entrance. One third of the building was split in half, one part for the tactical operations center, the TOC. The other section became the crew rest area, where we could stay close to the action but could rest on a couch and watch TV and movies or pack our gear. In theory, if you could relax a little while on alert, this was the place.

The door led right to the choppers. A hundred-yard dash separated us from the helicopter pad, which was wide enough for two of our sixties to sit side by side. We kept them in the alert ready position, all of our gear staged. I almost always remained half jocked up.

Camo pants. Utility belt. My armor, helmet, and weapon sat on the aircraft, ready to rock and roll. I kept my med-ruck already on board.

We sat all morning. The sun broke over the tall mountains, bathing the area in light and heat. This was the not-so-sexy part of being a PJ: waiting. The topic of lunch arose. We staged outside the door, half in the shade, up against the building—tossing rocks, telling stories, killing time.

The flight engineer came running from inside. "Hey, guys, we're starting to get a nine-line."

That was the warning. Shit was about get real.

We sprinted out to the helicopters. Within minutes we were in our armor and helmets, ready to fly. As the rotors began the spin-up process, Brandon Stuemke and I readied Pedro 84, our bird. Aaron Parcha and Doug did the same on Pedro 83.

Parcha came running over with his camera, for what I will call one of those serendipitous moments. He snapped a quick selfie, though this was before the word *selfie* had come into being. We high-fived each other, and I think we both shared one of those strange eye-lock moments. At least, I did, and I thought, *Oh, shit. Should we have done that? Did we just jinx ourselves?* I had one of those fleeting flashes of the mind: *Will it be one of those infamous "This was the last shot we had together" kind of shot? Fuck. Maybe we shouldn't have taken that picture. What if we did just set ourselves up for something bad?*

Aaron dashed off to Pedro 83. I took my spot on the left side of the aircraft, with my back to the gunner, Technical Sergeant Welles. I held my weapon on my lap, my legs dangling out the side. I would scan the six o'clock to nine o'clock. My partner took the other side. Our pilot was Captain Palmer. Copilot, Captain Brown. The flight engineer was Staff Sergeant Reams.

I could hear the chatter over my helmet. The 9-line was for six individuals. The call, "Three cat Alpha, two cat Charlie, one cat Delta," meant we were flying into some serious carnage. Three category Alpha injuries meant three men had injuries as bad as they get: life, limb, or eyesight. Category Bravo is "stable but needing assistance." Category Charlie is "endangered and needing assistance." And Category Delta was the worst kind of call. A hero. One of our boys killed in action.

Mere seconds from liftoff, Doug, a religious man, stared up into the brilliant blue sky, taking in the combination of sunshine and spinning rotor blades. Perhaps he was saying a prayer for all of us, but he happened to spot a piece of metal falling from the HH-60. A flapper stop had somehow broken free from the aircraft.

Pedro 83 shut down its engines. Doug and Aaron were grounded, saved from what could have been a disaster before they had a chance to save anyone.

The soldiers in the mountains needed help badly, and the aircraft commander requested permission to proceed with the mission in a single-ship formation with support from other air assets. Permission granted. Stuemke and I would insert.

After takeoff, we loitered off set from our objective until command cleared the airspace. As we approached the battle site, we established radio contact with the ground forces. We began to orbit the general location in a counterclockwise direction, with the injured men out my side of the Pedro. We requested that the soldiers pop smoke, then received a reply that purple would be the color of the day. The purple smoke rose in a thin tendril from the side of the mountain. We continued to the insertion point in our wide, sweeping, counterclockwise orbit. I worked to keep an eye on the location of the men and at the same time plot a path up the steep terrain reach them. The smoke began to dissipate, and our attention focused on our intended point of insertion. Our track took us across the valley, over a river, and up to the wall of the valley opposite the insertion point.

Maintaining visual contact with our objective, I noticed a loose collection of square, adobe-colored, single-story mud huts built into the mountain beneath us. In the periphery of my vision, at my seven, several flashes erupted from a darkened doorway. Following the flashes was the unmistakable sound of gunfire. There were more flashes. Repeated sounds of gunfire over the rumble of the choppers and through my foam earplugs. They were shooting, and they were shooting at us. The distance wasn't more than four hundred meters.

I tried to identify the threat to the aircraft, but in the fraction of time it took my brain to process the fact the enemy was engaging us with automatic weapons, I saw a bright flash and heard a loud *thwack!*

I felt myself rising, being lifted and thrown across the aircraft toward my partner.

Darkness. Then searing pain.

I heard myself calling out over the ICS, "Left PJ hit. Left PJ hit."

I couldn't see. I flailed around for Stuemke, half thinking I needed to get his attention and half worried he wasn't there or had also been hit. The blast had relocated me from my initial sitting position to a new position on my right side.

The vision cleared in my right eye, but I feared the worst—that I had lost the ability to see out of my left one. I tore off my sunglasses and the light blinded me for a moment. I blinked hard. I could see. Blood covered my eye protection and poured down into my eyes. *I can see. But what about my skull?* Fire burned inside my helmet.

Stuemke was okay. He helped me strip off my helmet to assess my skull. I reached up to my head, slowly, worried about what I would find. I pressed my fingers against the bone. I didn't know what I would find. Given the intensity of the pain and burning, I expected to find bits of skull fragments, or mush. But my good old hard head still felt solid.

Stuemke was talking to me, saying something, but I don't remember what, just the tone of his voice. He was calm. Assured. He'd made the switch from partner to medic.

My skull was still intact. I didn't know this at the time, but the bullet fragment had traveled over my eye protection and underneath my helmet, slamming into my forehead above my left eye, tracking from left to right under the skin.

Like any good face shot, blood rained from the bleeding wound. I applied direct pressure, and my partner prepared to apply bandages. With the pressure, the pain increased.

"Oh, shit, it hurts, Brandon," I said. "It hurts bad, man."

I could feel myself slipping, but to where exactly, I didn't know. A few weeks later, in the write-up for my Purple Heart report, I would compose a funny line that cracked up my friends and fellow PJs. I wrote, "Focusing on the pain kept me from drifting off into the dark, peaceful bliss that beckoned." It was a bit of overwriting on my part, an attempt to bring humor to a not-so-funny situation, but the reality of the statement was true. I found myself wanting, with all my being, to escape the pain.

The intensity of the discomfort kept me on the verge of passing out, but concentrating on the fire radiating across my skull and answering Stuemke's questions kept me awake. My partner worked hard and kept me continuously mentally engaged. I knew the stabbing pain of heart trauma, knew the crushing sensation of not being able to breathe beneath the water, had endured the intense agony of blowing out my knee, but this felt different. With the pain came uncertainty. I knew enough about brain trauma from my paramedic studies that I was worried. I forced myself to see flashes of images from my life, not because I thought I was dying but because I needed to assure myself they were still there. My son, James, being born. Kissing his forehead the day I deployed. Grandmother. Mother. Brother. The morning sun rising over the mountains of Anchorage.

Stuemke interrupted my thoughts with a hand in my face. "Five minutes out. Hang on, Jimmy!"

As we touched down, I resolved to believe I wasn't going to give in. I wasn't quitting. With the help of my partner and the gunner, I sat up. The shot of pain nearly dropped me back to the floor. With slow, deliberate effort, I staggered off Pedro 84 with my partner on my shoulder, directly into the forward surgical trauma area, the FST, at Asadabad.

I don't know why, but it was important to me that I walk my ass off that chopper. They weren't taking me in on a stretcher. I was walking in on my own.

Once inside the FST, a team of three set to work on me. They stripped me of my weapon, armor, and multicam top. They slipped an 18G IV into my right antecubital vein, just inside my elbow. The medical staff assessed my wound. They wheeled in a mobile X-ray machine and snapped a few photos of my thick skull. The films showed a fragment of the AK-47's seven-millimeter bullet lodged in my forehead. Due to surgical limitations at the FST, the staff elected to leave the fragment in place. They irrigated the wound. After a series of sutures and another twenty minutes of direct pressure, the bleeding stopped.

I took my combat pill pack and two additional 325-milligram Tylenols to ease the pain. After they got the bleeding under control, I was allowed to sit, and eventually to walk. Initially, my legs were a little wobbly, but I soon forgot my woes as the troops we had been sent to pick up began to arrive. I put on gloves and set to work helping the overwhelmed staff assess and treat the wounded soldiers that were stacking up.

As the wave of incoming faded, I was taken to a place to rest and make a phone call home, deep within the SEAL compound. I was lounging on a plush leather couch when Koa found me. He had a helicopter waiting to take us back to FOB Joyce. He looked like he had been working hard all day.

Once back at Joyce, Koa asked how I was doing. He offered me a chance to rotate out of the cauldron of fire coming our way. We had been through some challenging experiences together since I stepped onto the path of pararescue. I thought of him as a brother, and there was no way I was going to leave his side, but I was starting to hurt deep in my neck muscles. I thought of our times as cones, of our buddy carries up Arctic Valley Road, how he had motivated everyone to push themselves. How he had motivated me. I decided to stay, but I asked for a little time to clear my head. I told him I had a bit of a headache and felt a little dazed. He sent me to get checked out by the flight doc. The doc reexamined my injury and approved a temporary break in duty.

In the time since I had left the FST, the endorphins and adrenaline had begun to wear off. Terrible head and neck pain started to overwhelm me. Our flight doctor prescribed an oxycodone in the hope that I might be able to rest. The medication took the edge off the pain, replacing it with a horrible itchiness that covered my entire body. I took fifty milligrams of Benadryl to counteract the side effect of the oxycodone, but to no avail.

After a fitful night of sleep, I decided I would rather deal with the severe headache and neck pain than the unrelenting sensation of a body covered in poison ivy and mosquito bites. I also felt restless and helpless, being sidelined while my teammates were in the middle of an unexpectedly high tempo of missions. Koa and Stuemke ran missions by themselves the next day. The carnage happening in the mountains was horrific, and the Rangers there needed help. I didn't want to just sit by, waiting for my team to bring load after load of wounded back to the base. I wanted to get out there and help. But, at the same time, I was unsure and a bit scared.

I kept the sutures well bandaged and padded. I wore my helmet slightly loose as I walked around the small base, so that the injury would not be further aggravated. I had one doozy of a headache. I felt as if I had the worst hangover ever and had survived a car accident, a heavyweight boxing match, and a bear attack all at once. My head felt as if it weighed fifty pounds, and just holding it upright made my neck hurt. Whenever the bullet fragment received the slightest touch—a brush of my helmet or even a little wind—bolts of electricity would race up my head and into my scalp, creating a sensation of fire and hair pulling.

As night arrived, the fighting slowed. Late that second night, we had a crew debrief. The pilots, the flight engineers, the gunners, the PJs, the maintenance teams, everyone who was part of the team to keep the missions going, plus a third Pedro crew, led by Roger Sparks. About thirty of us crammed into the emergency room of the three-room hospital.

Discussions about how each mission went and the things that were learned kicked off the debriefing. I had been taken out of the fight on that first mission of the day and spent an entire day as a spectator on the sidelines as my friends and teammates worked their asses off fighting two wars at once. One was the fight against the enemy; the other was against the angels of death who feasted on our fallen warriors.

The debriefing was the first time many of us heard the collective story of the operations, from the moment our first 9-line came across the wire. The crazy number of rescues and assists by the Pedro crews on the first and second day of Bulldog Bite, and my near death, made the war very real for all of us.

This was no chill "strip alert," where we would be sitting around watching movies and growing our mustaches. I could feel the shift in mind-set among our team. The war I had watched on TV back in America, sitting on my couch covered in tortilla chip crumbs, suddenly hit home with force. The spectator war was now a participant war, for me and for the others in the room who were new to battle. Instead of hearing about strangers in a strange land fighting a strange fight, the paradigm was entirely reframed. These were people I knew and loved, in a very real place, fighting for our lives. We weren't just in the middle of this war; we were flying into heavy combat, literally sitting ducks as we hovered in the sky. As the enemy took aim, we lowered into the melee.

The room smelled of sweat and blood in a tea of fine Afghanistan dust. Eyes reflected the strain of the day. My neck kept screaming from the whiplash of the frag impact to my head. My left temple erupted into flame at the lightest touch, sending branding irons across my scalp. Each surge briefly paralyzed me with pain. The harsh glare of the fluorescent lighting in the emergency room was like a screwdriver stabbing through my eyes and into my brain. I slid down the hill of adrenaline that flowed during the day, and once that wore off, everything began to ache.

I had been the first in our unit to bleed, but when I looked around the room, I knew I was not the only one suffering the effects of the day. Koa, Brandon, and Doug spoke with a heavy slowness from the trauma they had been exposed to. Matt Kirby, Roger Sparks, Leo Claunen, Ted Sierocinski, and Aaron Parcha listened attentively. We all knew there was a good chance the next day would get crazy, and each part of the debrief was analyzed in the hope that even the slightest bit of information could make the difference between success and failure, life or death.

After the debrief, we went our separate ways. I stepped out into the thin, crisp air and took a moment to look up. The stars stretched across the sky, watching over us. Watching over me. For a brief moment, I stood completely still, thinking. My eyes locked on the constellation Orion. The hunter. The hero. I'd gone out on my first rescue mission at war and, before I could save anyone, took a round to the head. Part of the bullet was still there. Lodged in my skull. Burning, reminding me. *What the hell had happened?* Fractions of an inch of movement. The enemy's barrel. The wind. A twitch in the pilot's hand on the control. Any one variable could have put that bullet in my brain.

Sounds of footsteps on the gravel behind me brought me back. I turned to see a tall figure approaching. It could have been the *Barmanou,* the Afghani version of Sasquatch or the yeti, but it was Roger.

We made small talk as we stood under the stars. I can't remember if I pointed out Orion. I probably didn't need to. Roger had named one of his sons Orion.

Roger understood the precipice on which I stood. He knew war. He'd seen more battle than any of us. He didn't have to tell me what the team needed, or what our soldiers on the ground needed. I knew that. We all needed the same thing. I knew why Roger had come to me. He had come to ask me the same thing I was pondering before he joined me beneath the stars.

What next?

A part of me, a big part of me, wanted to hightail it home. I'd been shot. In the head, no less. And that seemed like great excuse to get out of the fire. But another part of me was screaming the pararescue creed, specifically the line declaring that I "place these duties before personal desires and comforts."

I had chanted the words over and over during all those years of training.

Roger, above all others, knew what I needed. He cleared his throat; I could sense a heaviness in his demeanor. This was no-nonsense Roger. The Roger I'd almost died with in Cook Inlet, back home. This was the *I know what is best for you* Roger speaking.

"Tomorrow morning," he said, "I need you back on alert."

My stomach plummeted to somewhere right above my boots. He knew it was best, and I think I did, too. Roger and I had spent that night freezing in Cook Inlet, and even though it was the last place we wanted to go so soon after nearly dying there, we went back. The best thing to do was to crawl back in the saddle. Plus, if the first two days of Bulldog Bite were any indicator of what was coming, the next morning could be one hell of a rodeo. We were going to need all hands on deck.

I'm sure Roger sensed my reservations, my growing sense of dread and fear. In a way, he was rescuing me from myself. His tall figure hovered over me, his long arm a hoist that offered to bring me up from the depths of fear and what would surely have been a future of doubt and self-loathing.

I had two choices. I could grab the air horn and yell, "I quit!," or I could do my job. For me, it was a matter of embracing a choice I had been making all my life.

20

. . . .

Blessing and Apology

I spent the night fitfully working to find sleep. I tossed and turned until the sun began to creep toward the horizon, replacing the star-swept sky with another brilliant and crisp bluebird mountain morning. Getting up from my rack, I made what must have looked like a drunken stagger to the nearest portable toilet. My head pounded worse than any spring break hangover, and my neck was rigor mortis stiff. Plus, there was a steady throbbing in my temple, where the sharp edges of the bullet fragment sent nasty reminders of the Afghani lead above my brow. I wanted the pain and aching to stop, but that wasn't going to happen there at Joyce.

I had a job to do. I kept telling myself there were people out there in the mountains who, with the rising sun and the resumption of battle, would be hurting much worse than me.

I could barely stomach a light breakfast, but I managed. I sat and waited for the flight doc to come on duty. When he arrived, he took a look at my wound, asked me a couple of questions, and cleared me for duty. Just like that, I headed back into action, stitched, bandaged, and carrying a little scalp souvenir into the next mission.

———

We were all sitting close to the helicopters, waiting. We expected more of the same as the day before, but the 9-line stayed silent most of the morning. We began the rock game, a pastime born of boredom. Basically, it was just guys sitting around the bird, strategically throwing rocks. One guy grabs a baseball-size rock and tosses it underhand out onto the helicopter pad. Then everyone else takes turns throwing little pebbles. The first person to hit the big rock wins, but winning only means you get to throw the big rock. That's pretty much all there was for us, on alert at the chopper—rocks, sand, and dirt.

Our FOB sat in the belly of a broad valley. The valley ran left and right from where we sat, with a small river passing through it. There was only one way in and one way out: two winding roads running parallel to the river. These were rugged country roads by American standards. And there was no shortage of goat trails.

The valley was probably five miles wide at the widest point. In other places it narrowed to a quarter mile. The mountains above stood sharp and jagged, with little in the way of vegetation. The geography reminded me of the mountains of the American Southwest in the summertime. And the higher the sun crept, the higher the temperature.

We sat playing our silly games, trying to pass the time and trying not to think about what we'd be flying into if we were called. Then, in the late afternoon, the 9-line dropped. The first report in to the tactical operations center, with shit already sounding bad. Soldiers injured and one dead.

Roger, Koa, and Ted climbed aboard Pedro 83. Stuemke and I got on Pedro 84.

The HH-60s spun up and lifted off. My stomach was a mess. I was trying to keep my breakfast down as we raced up the valley toward the action. The gunners on each of our birds charged their weapons and ripped a few test rounds off into the mountainside. As we were flying in, the number of injured and casualties started to change. First the radio said three people were category Alpha— the ones who needed the most urgent care. Then, all of a sudden, there was only one of those, but three cat Bs. Urgent, but not right away. Then we had fourteen of them. Then seven.

Clearly something horrible was happening on the ground, and whoever was running the radios was having a rough go of things. The chaos became even more apparent when we got the call to return to Joyce to refuel while the Apaches rained Hellfire missiles on the mountainside in an attempt bring some stability to the situation.

As the ground crew hustled, we could both hear and see the blistering destruction up the valley. Clouds of smoke billowed up and a big low rumble filled the air.

The lead helicopter traditionally provides air support. This was Roger, Koa, and Ted. They would provide the eyes on the ground, placing Koa as the officer above, making the calls on the ground and directing, while Stuemke and I hoisted down to begin the evacuation. From what we were hearing over the radio, the scene on the ground was so confusing that Koa called for a "grinder," in which we rotated positions. The lead helicopter became the first responding bird, while my bird, the trailing helicopter, would provide the air cover. Koa made that judgment call in order to get an officer and some senior enlisted men on the ground to provide leadership and visibility, to figure out what the hell was happening.

As we approached, I heard that the area was "cold" or "safe." This meant no enemy, that the position hadn't been fired upon or shot at for a while. We flew in and the lead chopper made a broad sweep as they searched for the men. Roger told them to pop smoke. A purple cloud erupted from the hillside. I felt my stomach churn. In my mind, I saw a flash of the same scene from the day before.

Pedro 83 slowed in front of us. We maneuvered into a broad arc around them as they began their hover above the men. Roger and Koa prepared to hoist down. I sat with my M4 charged, watching for enemy fire on the outside of the wheel of action. I watched the surrounding mountains and cliffs, faced away from everybody and everything.

Then, over the radio, I heard Koa's voice.

"We're taking fire! Get us on the ground!" he yelled.

I'd been scanning out my door, with my M4 aimed out, and when I swung around, what I saw made me lose my shit.

The terrain reminded me of the Chugach Mountains behind Anchorage and the steep grades in Powerline Pass. Many of the valleys in Afghanistan were like the ones I grew up with, just not as green. Imagine stone buildings, a settlement of maybe a hundred people, with terraced gardens where the people grew their food. Quaint to look at, but those stone buildings happened to be where all the bad guys were hiding. Fire erupted from within the houses and focused in a triangular shape directly on Roger and Koa's helicopter and the area where the army unit was pinned down. This was an intensity of tracers and rocket fireballs unlike anything I'd ever seen or known was possible.

The Pave Hawk hovered in place, rotors beating, with a steep mountain behind. Roger and Koa looked like a single body lowering down on the hoist. In that early evening light, the entire world around them erupted into an orange-and-red fireworks show of tracers and rockets. Every enemy in the entire valley seemed to be shooting at them.

Roger and Koa were getting hammered with heavy machine gun fire and rocket-propelled grenades. I swung my rifle back around; there was no safe way I could shoot through the cabin. I didn't want to accidentally shoot Stuemke or anyone else. All I could do was roll back around to cover my own side. The .50-caliber gun on my partner's side roared to life. Then the one on my side. *Boom. Boom. Boom.*

I never understood the term "hell breaking loose" until the moments that came next. If the earth opened and one could see inside to the fires and boiling pits of hell, then that's what I saw. The hair stood up on my skin, prickling like porcupine quills, and I broke out in an instant cold sweat. My stomach shrank in upon itself. My eyes raced around the valley as I scanned the area with my weapon, looking for a target. All I could see was chaos. Fire seemed to be coming from anywhere. From everywhere. From behind boulders. From stone doorways and rooftops.

I aimed my M4 and began pulling the trigger. The brilliant orange tracers converged from all over the valley on Pedro 83 and the two brave men dropping in to rescue the wounded and dying soldiers below.

I tried to follow the lines of fire to their origin. Men peered out from behind rocks and trees, rifles blazing. *Pop! Pop! Pop!* I focused through my sight, trying to suppress their fire and stop the barrage against my friends in the hoist.

I don't know if I hit anyone, but all of us were doing anything we could do to give Roger and Koa a chance. That moment was one of the only times when I really wished I had spent more time as a marksman. I realized, in those seconds, that, with all my training, I never had the chance to practice my accuracy from inside a moving helicopter.

I've got to credit Captain Marcus Maris, the pilot at the controls of the chopper hoisting Roger and Koa to the ground. He held that hover while taking blazing enemy fire. Bullets chewed up his aircraft, RPGs zipped right past the cockpit, and that pilot and his titanium testicles held that bird stone cold still until Roger, in a full embrace of Koa, stretched his tall body and got his boots on the ground.

As soon as Roger and Koa got unhooked from the hoist, they took a blast from an RPG that knocked them to the ground. I tried to see what was going on and, at the same time, continued to provide cover by shooting anywhere I could see enemy fire on the adjacent mountainside.

Roger's voice came over the radio. *"Holy shit!"*

I looked across the cabin to see what was going on. Ted was

to be next down the hoist, but instead, the cable dangled. The chopper hovered. Roger and Koa had one chance to escape, but instead I saw them scramble away.

"Get out of here!" Koa yelled, over the explosions and gunfire around him.

Pedro 83 lifted away and began a wide orbit.

The hate from the ground became focused on us. The tracers converged on us like a Christmas tree, with the lights streaming down from the star on the top to the bottom. I could hear the bullets ripping past us. Our .50 cal and both our M4s returned our own stream of fire.

"Let us down!" I yelled over the ICS. "Get us in! Get us on the fucking ground!"

"No way. Not a chance," came the response. "I'm not putting you guys down."

Other reports came over our headsets. From Pedro 83 and our flight crew.

"Fuel getting low!"

"Almost out of ammo!"

Both birds were running out of ammo and were dangerously low on fuel. They waved us off. There was no way the aircraft commander was putting us down. The order came to head back to base to refuel and rearm.

No, we can't leave them! I wanted to say. *They are going to fucking die there! We can't just leave them like that. Put Brandon and me in! Set us down somewhere close. Right there! Anywhere! Shit! Shit! Not Roger and Koa!*

Captain Maris's voice came over my headset. It was the toughest thing I'd ever heard. He was addressing Roger and Koa. "God bless you guys," he said. "Sorry."

Hearing that, I unloaded my weapon on the stone houses below in a fit of rage and anguish. *What about "That others may live"?* I couldn't believe what was happening. We were leaving them behind. Our men. Not just any men, but Koa and Roger. Two of our best. Leaving them behind in a torrent of bullets and explosions. Leaving them behind with only a blessing and an apology.

We flew toward Joyce. All of us were silent, trying to make sense of what we'd just witnessed. Trying to understand what the hell had just happened. I needed to vomit, to scream, to cry.

I thought of Roger and Koa, my brothers, alone in hell.

I could see Roger from the night before, standing over me. "I need you on alert," he had said. *I need you.*

I thought back on that frigid night in the inlet. The night we almost froze together. There was Roger again, the thunder of the HH-60 disappearing, his line to safety gone. When the chopper left us, he'd said, "Now what?" And that was exactly what I was thinking at that moment, *Now what? Now what?* Only, this time, I wasn't with him. This time it was I who left Roger behind.

21

. . . .

Beans, Bandages, Bullets

When we hit the ground back at Joyce, I went to work on my gear. Our stuff had been shot to hell and we hadn't even left the chopper. I resupplied my ammunition, reloaded my weapon, and began getting everything ready to get back into the fight. I was doing everything I could to be sure that, when we went back, I was ready. We constantly checked for updates but weren't getting much information about what was happening on the ground. We were out of radio communication with Roger and Koa. We heard and saw Apaches helicopters blasting more Hellfires into the mountain. Then there was nothing for a while. Not a word.

A jet passed overhead. We heard the rumble of two distant and thundering blasts. Explosions like that didn't bring warm, fuzzy feelings. Something bad was going down up there.

Then we got word that, as a last resort, Koa had called in a "danger close" air strike from an F-18. This means that the enemy's location is uncomfortably close to friendlies. This means that calling in an air strike is potentially suicide. You make a danger close call when every other option to survive has evaporated. After confirming Koa's last name, the last four digits of his Social Security number, and authorization, the pilot unloaded two massive five-hundred-pound bombs damn near right on top of them.

Pedro 83 had been shot to shit and was out of operation. Our chopper had taken its own pelting. We couldn't get spun up until repairs were made and the aircraft received flight clearance. There was nothing for us to do but pace, try to stomach a little food, and go over our gear one more time.

Part of me wanted to slip on my running shoes and go light-weight, to run to Roger and Koa. Screw all this waiting and hovering over the radio, stressing out. I could take my weapon, ammo, a stripped down med-ruck, and run to Roger and Koa. The idea was absurd, the distance far, the terrain rugged and crawling with enemies, but anything sounded better than sitting and waiting.

Meanwhile, our gunners bargained hard all over Joyce to get any kind of ammo they could. They wound up scoring a party assortment; they snatched up any kind of .50-caliber round they could lay their hands on.

Sunset and darkness settled across the mountains. The air cooled. The night would be at or below freezing. Orion appeared. An hour passed. Then two. We weren't hearing from Koa and Roger. They were either working hard or something had happened.

Then came the green light. Twenty minutes. I tried to prepare myself mentally for what was coming. We'd be going in tactical black. Night vision, no lights. I imagined a repeat of the scenario we'd survived hours earlier, but with the lights out.

Then came another delay. Our friends were out there dying and we had to wait some more.

Due to the situation on the ground, Koa requested that Stuemke and I carry in what is called a "speedball," a refill of beans, bullets, grenades, and medical supplies. Four men rolled out a cart with a full body bag on it. This thing weighed so much it took all four of them and the two of us to load it aboard. The plan was for me to kick it out my side of the helicopter, which in theory sounded great.

Hundreds of pounds of deadweight in a body bag doesn't move

easily. I'd never seen a speedball deployed before, and this was nothing we had practiced. The PJ rule of thumb is to practice everything until you can execute it nearly blindfolded. I wasn't sure what to do with this speedball idea, but I was rolling with it. How hard could it be?

After the delay, we spun up and lifted off. Finally, with a report from Koa, we knew the area had calmed a bit for the evening, but the situation on the ground in terms of injuries and casualties sounded as bad as it could get. We were prepared for the worst, but American airpower has a distinct advantage in tactical black conditions. We have birds in the sky that the enemy fears, like AC-130 Spectre gunships with capabilities that you can't even imagine. Our night vision isn't perfect, but we've got tactical superiority in the dark because of it. As the saying goes, "Nighttime is the right time." And that night, for us going in, it definitely seemed to be.

Under ideal conditions, we would reach the location and zip right down the hoist to Roger and Koa, but when we arrived, I first had to deploy the damn speedball. The moment I attempted to move that heavy piece of shit myself, I felt instant hate. That body bag of bullets and beans made me furious. More than anything, I needed to get down to Roger and Koa, but first I needed that weight out of my bird. Even with all the strength I could muster, I could not get it out the door. It felt bolted to the floor of the helicopter. I kicked and cussed and kicked more. Finally, the flight engineer, Stuemke, and I, using all our strength, got it to the edge and gave it an angry shove out. The entire sack disappeared into the blackness below. But by then we'd drifted, and the precious speedball that had delayed us twice now landed way off target. I don't think that body bag of goodies was used to help anyone except the bad guys, if they ever found it.

Next we focused on what really mattered: getting down the hoist and to Roger and Koa, in one piece. There were injured, dead, and dying men waiting, and we needed multiple litters and the two of us down on the ground, right now.

Stuemke made the call to attach the litter directly to us. The Stokes litter is a metal cage. Imagine if a colander and a coffin had sex. The Stokes would be the baby. Since Stuemke held rank over me, I wasn't about to question him. It made sense at the time, but we had never practiced an entry like that before. We hooked ourselves to the hoist, clipped the Stokes litter to us, and readied for insertion.

The occasional tracer zipped past us. If they got me again, they got me. I had made my peace with what could happen on that hillside.

The truth was, we never could have readied ourselves for what we would see once we got on the ground, but first we had to get there in one piece.

What goes through the mind of someone crawling out of a helicopter in the middle of the night over enemy territory, under fire, and as vulnerable as humanly possible? Dangling in the air, being lowered on a thin metal wire? A bullet sponge for anyone with even minimal rifle skills?

Everything. Everything, is the answer.

The time it takes to get down a hoist in battle isn't measured in seconds; it is measured in lifetimes. But you can't hesitate at the helicopter door. Those guys flying the chopper are waiting for you to get the hell out, the guys below need medical attention, and every second you hesitate you serve as a magnet for more hate from the enemy. You try to make that move from the door to the dangle as quickly as possible. There can be no hesitation.

I won't lie. I didn't just have butterflies in my stomach; my guts were a writhing ball of water moccasins. I didn't hesitate, but I had enough fear-induced adrenaline rocketing through my veins that, for the second time that day, my head didn't hurt. I didn't hesitate at the door, because I couldn't. Everyone was looking to me to do my job as quickly and as efficiently as possible. Every second I'm in the door, or on the ground, or in that space between the two is a race between life and death for the men above and the men below.

We dropped down on the wire, with the litter, into pure blackness. We're spinning. Spinning in absolute darkness. I couldn't see what we were hoisting into. I knew it was the side of a mountain, class four and five terrain. The kind of steep that is safer with ropes and climbing harnesses. All we could do was hold on and hope for the best.

22

. . . .

Into Hell

Our feet touched the ground, and the next thing I knew, we were falling, tumbling off an embankment, but still attached to the cable. We hit the mountain hard and scrambled to our feet, kicking rocks. Our M4s were banging around; the litter and hoist were a tangled mess in the brush above us. The rotor wash whipped golf ball–size rocks and debris everywhere. We were shouting and cursing and mainlined on pure adrenaline.

With the hoist stuck in the bushes, the helicopter became like an eagle with its talons attached to salmon that is too big. In this position, the aircraft was compromised, and we were attached both to the aircraft and to each other. On any other day, this would have been a comedy of errors. Special operations, with the emphasis on "special."

This was as humbling a position as I had been in, in my entire life. Here we were, coming in to rescue our friends, and we were stuck on the side of a mountain, wrapped up in a bush.

I waited for the enemy to unleash a torrent of bullets and rockets on our sorry asses, but in the rotor wash I couldn't tell the bullets from the flying shit storm of debris. We struggled to get free. I don't know how long it took, but even if we were dangling there all wrapped up in the shrubbery like some high-wire act gone wrong for only thirty seconds, it was way too long.

Between the hurricane of dirt flying from the rotors and the fear that came with being fouled up, I now, in retrospect, completely understood and appreciated the torturous training we endured in the pipeline. We were constantly given impossible scenarios and were tested at every turn. This proved to be one of those tests, but there was no way out if we didn't act fast.

One perfectly placed bullet or rocket from the scattered tracer fire into the helicopter above us would spell the end for us all.

Somehow, we unclipped ourselves and the litter and started working the mess with the hoist cable. The strain of the chopper and our weight had cut into the bark of the tree. I tore at the branches and cable, trying to get the wire free. Finally it pulled loose.

"It's free. Go!" Stuemke radioed up.

The helicopter lifted off us, and we ducked our heads at the final blast of dust, rocks, and branches. Then, all was silence. Our gear lay strewn about the mountainside. We repacked everything and tried to reorient ourselves.

All I wanted to do was get to Roger and Koa, who were somewhere above us. We began working our way up the rugged mountain, our weapons ready. Shots came here and there. An occasional tracer zipped past. We had no way of knowing what we might encounter. We knew it was bad, but we couldn't know how bad until we reached them. And those two guys . . . I wanted to lay eyes on Roger and Koa. I needed to know they were okay.

A lifetime had already passed that night, while we waited for the signal to launch again, then the ridiculous delay with the speedball, and then getting tangled up. Nothing was going right. Nothing.

We climbed to the collection point to find carnage beyond what I'd even known was possible. The entire mountainside appeared to have been chewed up and spat back out. In the green glow of my night vision, I saw men, trees, dirt, rocks, gear, weapons. All shredded and strewn across the ground. The air reeked of cordite and blood. There were shell casings and shells of men. Here was a platoon of the undead and dead all together, huddled in a trench carved into the mountainside by a Hellfire missile. The living were shell-shocked and bloodied. Some had gaping wounds and missing limbs. Several lay faceup, on the verge of death. Many were dead. Moans and crying sounded from all directions.

I'd hoisted into hell.

A voice shot out at us. A direct command to the two delinquent PJs who had spent precious moments snared in a bush. *"Unfuck yourselves!"* Roger roared.

Everything changed, the moment I saw Roger, his lanky body hunched over, M4 in his hand. Every worry evaporated. For him, for Koa. For myself, and for every American still alive on that mountain.

Roger was a beacon of strength and light in the blackest of black Afghanistan nights. I'll never forget his blood- and dirt-splattered face. He didn't need to tell me anything. His face, hewn from a piece of obsidian, said it all. He had survived an apocalypse, endured hours of relentless enemy attack and the agonizing deaths of the men around him, but there he was, calm. Samurai master calm. His eyes radiated intensity. And by looking at those eyes, I knew he had complete control of the situation. Roger Sparks was doing exactly what he had been meant to do that day. He was saving lives.

"Jimmy!" he yelled. With his giant wingspan, he stabbed an arm out and pointed. "Get on this guy here!"

The soldier's skin was glacier blue. He was dying, right there in front of us, lying on his back on the ground. His eyes were closed, his legs straight, arms curled up on themselves. He was rigid, doing what is called "posturing." This is where your brain and your muscles are not working properly, but certain muscles are firing, depending on what part of the brain has been traumatized. This guy's arms were pointed straight down, and his hands were curled inward. I knew that wasn't a good thing. I suspected a brain injury. I went to check his airway, because I'm there to be a medic. That is really what we are, and that's the most important thing. It doesn't matter if you can shoot like a SEAL sniper or jump like a Ranger or do whatever special operations skill. The thing you need to excel at as a PJ is providing top-notch medical care.

My attempt to check his airway got me nowhere. His jaw was locked. The man was in full-on trismus, his jaw clenched shut, tight as a vice. I tried prying, and when that didn't work I rammed my fingers into his mouth and pushed back against his lower molars to muscle his jaw open. It wasn't happening. I tore through my medruck and found an NPA, a nasopharyngeal airway tube, and shoved it up his nose. I did a quick assessment, rolled him onto the litter, and began strapping him down. He wasn't breathing, and I was so in the moment—ignoring the gunfire and hyperfocused solely on my patient—that I didn't hear the helicopters overhead. Truth be told, I was probably trying to block from my mind the horrors around me.

"Jimmy!" Roger yelled at me. "Get this guy going! The bird is coming in!"

The mountain was chaotic. Brandon worked his guy. Roger and Koa had their hands full. I needed to get my guy up and out. His life clock was all but ticked out.

I grabbed the nearest soldier by his jacket and said, "You! Help me grab this litter. You and me. We're walking it down. Now!"

That poor guy. He tried to stand, and he made it to his feet, but when he tried to take one step toward me I recognized the tortured hobble. I'd been there, only the injury to his leg was far worse than mine had been. I looked down and saw the stains of blood and dark bandages around his thigh. He was shot up, too. A tough soldier, willing to do what had to be done. I apologized to him and called for assistance.

I don't remember who helped me down, Roger or Koa. The hoist cable dangled downhill from us. We didn't want the chopper directly over us, because of the rotor wash. The force of those blades would make the whole camp explode, and there had been enough damage done to those men for one day. We moved quickly, struggling, half sliding down the steep terrain.

I reached the pickup point, grabbed the hook, and snapped myself and the litter to the hoist cable. I gave the thumbs-up to the flight engineer and we began our ascent. The whole way up, I was talking to the guy, trying to reassure him that he would be okay, even though I knew he couldn't hear me over the rotors beating the thin mountain air. I didn't think about the danger I was in, and I didn't feel any pain. All I thought about, as I rose into the night sky, was making a smooth transfer and how the hell I was going to get this guy breathing before it was too late.

We reached the top of the hoist and I made the transfer into the helicopter. I was running on pure adrenaline. Nothing had changed for my patient. He still was not breathing. The way I saw it, I had one choice. He needed air and wasn't getting any.

I scrambled around inside the helicopter, on my hands and knees, in the dark. I had night vision goggles on my helmet, but I wasn't using them at the time. I found it almost easier to do the assessments in the darkness of the cockpit than in the goggles' light.

I reached for my cric kit and prepared to perform an emergency surgical cricothyrotomy while hovering over a battlefield. I laid out a mini operating table on the guy's chest. My tools: a scalpel the size of your thumb and a short endotracheal tube. I ran my hand down his jaw to his neck, identifying anatomical reference points. I felt for his Adam's apple. From there, I traced my fingers lower and located the soft tissue of the cricothyroid membrane, the intended point of insertion. There are different schools of thought about making the initial and secondary cuts, but the main thing this guy needed was air. For that, I needed to create an opening in his windpipe, control the opening, and insert the tube. The purpose of the cric is to provide a secure airway, bypassing all the upper issues happening in the head. The chopper jostled and shifted.

I double-checked the location and picked up the scalpel. I pressed the blade to his skin and made the primary slice. The whole time, I'm whispering to him and to myself. "Hang in there buddy," I said. "We got this. We can do this. Air like honey, coming at you any second."

Then the secondary cut. I controlled the opening, just as I'd practiced on the simulation dolls, and slipped the tube in, inflating the bulb to keep fluids from draining into his lungs. There was no time to suture anything closed. I packed gauze pads around the tube and used more medical tape to secure everything in place. I could feel warm, moist air on my cheek. Amazingly, he was breathing on his own.

Even in the dark of the chopper, I could see his color change, the blue turning to pink. He was unconscious, but his chest rose and fell, ever so slightly. "Yeah, brother," I said. "Keep breathing. We're gonna get you out of here."

I reached for an IV and got bumped hard from behind. The hit was unexpected and half scared me. I turned and realized I suddenly had another patient. The conditions in the helicopter were as loud as a rock concert in a hurricane, and I could see this guy's mouth rambling on and on as I pulled him in and got the doors shut. He came in on a Skedco, a heavy plastic litter similar to my childhood plastic roll-up sleds. The Skedco has buckles and straps and can be rolled up and strapped onto or inside a backpack. In an emergency, pull it out and you've got an instant litter to hook up to the hoist cable.

A litter like the Skedco has advantages, but these come at a price. Unlike the solid metal litter, the plastic is not rigid, so the patient becomes engulfed as the plastic folds around him, like a burrito. I moved quickly to free the new arrival from his green plastic cocoon. I unbuckled a few straps and shifted my gear around in a space not much bigger than the floor of a small minivan.

The scene on the ground was still beyond any level of chaos I had ever seen. Communication with the PJs on the ground was very limited. But, without talking to Roger or Koa, I had no idea what the hell was going on with this guy, so I needed to perform my own quick assessment. The man was fully conscious and talking.

On my headset, I heard the pilots ask how the PJ was doing. They glanced back, I gave the thumbs-up, and we were out of there. We didn't lift off; we were already too high. Instead, they tilted the whole chopper and we rocketed down the valley in a dive, with everything sliding and falling forward, until we reached the valley floor.

I was one medic working two critically injured men. I knew that if these were the first two guys Roger had sent out, they were the most critical, and their lives were in my hands alone. I turned from the unconscious guy to the new guy. He was fully aware of the situation.

"What's your name? What's going on?" I yelled over the roar of noise inside the cabin. To be heard, I had to yell directly into his ear, and he into mine. We sprayed spittle into each other's ears every time we spoke.

Before I could finish my initial assessment, he belted out, over the chopper clamor, "Don't fuck with me, mate! Take care of him. Take care of him!"

The guy was thick, a big bear of a man, with dark hair, a black goatee, and a British accent. Not regular military; clearly an operator of some sort. If he was good enough to understand that the man behind me clearly needed my help, and to swear and call me a mate at the same time, I would do what he said.

I pivoted on my knee pad, back to the first guy. The spins back and forth got easier as blood lubricated the floor. I redirected my focus, pouring all I had into my patient with the cric. I hooked him up with oxygen and established an IV line. His clothes looked as if he'd been dragged through a bloody mud bath. Since he could finally breathe, I focused on the rest of his body and discovered the source of the blood making the helicopter floor slick. He'd been shot in the shoulder. I finished packing and dressing that wound, then spun back around and yelled to the big guy, "What's your name? What is wrong with you?"

"Karl!" he yelled back. "And don't worry about me! Take care of him, mate!"

My patient with the airway really started to pink up and come around. He responded to his name and nodded when I asked him where he was from. Once I knew he would make it, I rotated again to Karl.

"Don't worry about him," I said. "What is wrong with you?"

I began my assessment, despite Karl's protests to focus on the soldier. I unbuckled the Skedco and started feeling down to his waist. Everything was soaked. I lifted up his shirt and froze. Hiding beneath Karl's shirt was a massive open gut wound. Later, I would learn it was a miracle Karl was even alive. He had been shot through the hips with a .50 cal. The soldier helping him, John Snow, died from an AK-47 round to the back of his head. Snow fell on top of Karl, covering him, so that the enemy thought Karl was dead. Then the Hellfire missiles rained down out of the sky. A blast from a rocket blew Karl up into a tree, with his intestines hanging out. Roger and Koa picked him out of the branches and stuffed his intestines back in, then tucked the shirt back in to hold them in place. Of course, I knew none of this at the time, but I received one hell of a surprise when I pulled his shirt up to find Karl's guts spilling out.

Oh shit! What the hell do I do about his guts?

The answer came over my headset. I could hear the aircrew counting down from five as we settled into a landing. I could do nothing. I tucked his blood-soaked shirt right back in as the wheels touched down with a jolt. I didn't even have time to get an IV started.

The litter bearers came running and I crawled out of the helicopter, half paralyzed, unfolding myself from being hunched over the men. My back and hips felt crushed from the weight of body armor and gear in that position. My M4 was still strapped to me, along with my night vision goggles, medic kit, and full battle rattle. The litter bearers had Shanghai carts, a wheelbarrow contraption with two wheels, which the litter rides on. One at a time, we lifted the litters from the helicopter, set them on the Shanghai carts, and they were off, running to the surgical team. I trotted alongside them with my back muscles in spasm. I was running on pins and needles. The sweat in my clothes chilled my skin in the cold night air.

There was a only a moment of transition in which I gave the doctors a five-second briefing. They didn't have any more time. They needed only the basics. I was as no-nonsense as I could be.

"This guy here," I said, "he has a gunshot wound to the left shoulder, he's been unconscious for the last fifteen minutes. I cric'ed him on the way in and he's breathing on his own now. And this guy's guts are a mess. They're not inside his belly. He's alert, responsive, and aware. He's been conscious the whole way, telling me to take care of the other guy."

Their response was even shorter. "Good. Got it."

As I left, Karl reached up and gave me a big high five.

The next helicopter was already descending with its patients. While my helicopter refueled, I ran over to the medical supply closet. Having seen the bloodletting on the mountainside, I knew I needed to restock my med kit and the helicopter. We would need more IVs, more bandages, and more body bags.

They finished refueling, and as we hosed the blood and grime off the floor of the helicopter, we received word that Roger, Koa, the last of the wounded, and the heroes were on their way out. I dropped my med-ruck on the floor of the helicopter and leaned against the aircraft. I turned my eyes toward the stars in the night sky and let out a long, deep sigh of relief.

23

. . . .

War Is the Realm of Uncertainty

I'd like to say there was one of those climactic moments when we returned to get Roger and the last of the soldiers, alive and dead. One of those perfect Hollywood-style endings, where I race back to the battle on the mountainside to help in the final rescue, perhaps with my M4 blazing as I hoist in, because Roger insists on being the last man out. We send the last wounded soldier up, we high-five, we look around, surveying the damage, and then we ride up together. Back on base, we'd be welcomed to cheers from a crowd, including the men we rescued. That sort of shit.

The truth is, Roger did insist on being one of the last to hoist out, with the remaining injured and heroes. With the floor space occupied by wounded and dead, Roger and the other PJs had to do the unthinkable. They rode home on top of the heroes. On the way back to the FST, Roger insisted that the heroes be placed in body bags. They had no room to sit, let alone to maneuver the bodies into the black bags, but they did it. He knew the men from the quick reaction force would be hovering around burn barrels, trying to stay warm. They would be waiting, but not to celebrate the arrival of the chopper. Roger didn't want them to see their brothers coming off the helo in bloody pieces.

When the HH-60 landed at Joyce, they parked with the left door away from the burn barrels and the FST. Another request from Roger. He insisted the pilot land with the door away so they could finish the job of matching limbs to bodies, doing their best to treat the heroes with the respect they deserved.

The truth here evaporates for me into the fog of war. I had of course heard the term before, but now I have an intimate knowledge of exactly what it means. A Prussian military analyst, Carl von Clausewitz, in 1832, described my recollection of these events perfectly: "War is the realm of uncertainty; three quarters of the factors on which action in war is based are wrapped in a fog of greater or lesser uncertainty. A sensitive and discriminating judgment is called for; a skilled intelligence to scent out the truth."

Perhaps I am not intelligent or discriminating enough to scent out the truth about everything that happened after that. My memory goes foggy, from the moment I crawled into the back of the helicopter with the floor still smeared with blood to nearly a week later, when we arrived back at Bagram, survivors of a series of rescues longer than any Hell Night or training scenario we ever could have imagined.

Another 9-line dropped thirty minutes after Roger and Koa returned, and only moments after I finally had a chance to talk to Roger. Gore covered his uniform. He was war incarnate: rage, grief, love, loss, guilt, adrenaline, all at once. I had no idea the hell he had been through, but I wanted to share with him something good. "Rog," I said. "I cric'ed that guy in the bird. He's alive!"

Then we received the coordinates of the new 9-line. I watched the recognition spread across Roger's face.

"Shit. That's the same spot," Roger said.

The remaining men had been all shot up. I hoisted in to a rooftop on one of the stone houses. There was one hero. Another guy was shot through the neck and bleeding everywhere. Two others were injured. I sent them up on a horse collar. The flight engineer helped guide me into the cabin with the Stokes litter loaded with the nonambulatory patient. I scooted in and, as fast as I could, unhooked the hoist cable from the litter. I spun around to check on the two guys I had sent up earlier. I looked each in the face and gave a thumbs-up/thumbs-down sign to see how they were feeling. I did a quick blood sweep on each of them. Then I moved back over to the guy in the litter to see if he was doing okay. In that instant I realized that, somewhere in the mix, we had acquired a hero, and in the urgent hustle, I placed the litter right on the corpse. My heart, having managed to keep beating through all I'd been through, took a measurable pause. I felt like shit for doing that, but we had to do what we had to do. I rode out like my brothers on their last run from the same site, no room in the helo. One wounded soldier in a Stokes, resting directly on top of a hero, and two soldiers sitting against the back wall, bleeding all over.

The rest of that night and the days and hours that followed are little more than a blur and a collection of images, all cobbled together. The memories of my time in the teeth of battle are disconnected, like a pile of snapshots that capture moments of sight, smell, sound, and emotion. There is no linear, logical flow. I could lay the blame squarely on my head injury, the lack of sleep from the bullet fragment still jostling around beneath my scalp, the intensity of the nonstop rescues, or that fog of war.

Some of what I remember through that fog is vivid, though. It will no doubt be the scaffolding for nightmares and guilt for years to come. Silver tape patches covering our helicopter. Stuemke and I trying to clean the pieces of human body mixed with blood, shit, piss, and dirt coating the floor of the helicopter. Men in agony, broken, bruised. Battle weary.

At one point, I stood next to the aircraft, catching my breath and attempting to process events. This was a time for a pinch of chewing tobacco. I dug a can out and opened it without looking. When I went to grab a pinch, I noticed that my fingernails were rimmed with maroon. Specks of blood and dirt covered my hands. Every-thing had soaked right through my gloves.

"Fuck it," I said, and took a dip anyway.

On each return to the base, the litter bearers came running. I would slide open the minivan-style door of the helo, and evidence of my medical handiwork would form a blizzard in the rotor wash. Pack-aging for bandages, IVs, and paper bits whirled about the cabin.

And sometimes in the darkness of war there could be comedy, of sorts. At one point during the blur of rescue, on a night mission, I didn't see the blood pooled on the chopper floor. As I spun on my knee pad to reach the supplies hanging behind the two wounded guys leaning against the aft wall, the helicopter lurched and I started to slip. I couldn't stop the slide. I crashed right onto the leg of a soldier, recently shot in that very same limb. He screamed. I jumped back, skidded, and fell right back onto him again. He shot me a look that could kill. I dove to work on an IV with painkillers, stat, and soon he was almost smiling. Almost.

Alongside my brothers, I grew accustomed to the smells that accompany war and death. That rich copper smell of blood. Smeared shit. Piss-soaked pants. Sweat, bile, filth, and fear. The intimacy of gore in my first few days of seeing combat permeated my uniform, my flesh, and dug itself deep into my being.

There also would be moments that no injury or exhaustion or fog of war could erase. A day or so later, on another rescue, I en-dured another first for me as a PJ. As the helicopter raced and bounced toward Asadabad or Jalalabad, I took a safety pin and pushed it through the corners of a thick black body bag, securing the American flag to it. His wounded teammates watched me as I performed this sacred rite. I tilted my head and said a silent prayer over the fallen hero. Then I pushed all personal thoughts and feelings aside and set to work on the two living soldiers in my he-licopter. This was no time to quit. This was so that others may live.

Epilogue

NEVER QUIT

It felt like a lifetime later that our team arrived back at Bagram. We were credited with pulling out sixty soldiers during the mission, forty-nine of them wounded. Instead of a warriors' welcome, we walked into the lights and cameras of an NBC News crew. Friends and family back home learned of my injury while eating dinner and watching the evening news.

First shot by an AK-47, and then by cameras. They filmed me lying on my back on the gravel, pointing out to Lester Holt the bullet hole in the bottom of the HH-60. Beside it, in thick black marker, I'd written "—Almost Got Me.—Jimmy 11/12/10."

The surgeons removed the bullet fragment and gave it to me as souvenir, to go with the raging migraine headaches, constant hot-lava burning sensation across my scalp, and nightmares.

After we left the NBC crew behind, we ran into another film crew, this one led by world-famous filmmaker Casey Neistat. Neistat was shooting a documentary with David Kuhn about another world-famous artist, Scott Campbell, renowned for his tattoo work. They asked if we wanted to get some of Campbell's ink laid on us.

And just like that, the rescuers themselves were rescued. Campbell worked for days on our team. We told our stories to Neistat while Campbell turned our pain and trauma into art.

Campbell inked the coordinates of the mountain on Roger's arm.

Me? The Cheshire Cat, smoking a hand-rolled cigarette, wearing a maroon beret.

We would see even more action before finally returning home to Alaska in late December. In my short stint at war, I logged 277 hours of combat search and rescue. They credit me with saving thirty-eight lives and assisting in saving twenty-eight others in combat. There were medals and awards for our team. Roger received a Silver Star, Koa a Bronze Star, Aaron a Bronze Star. Roger's miracle jacket, riddled with eight shrapnel holes and a piece of the hoist cable, which was struck three or four times, was placed on display at the National Archives. I collected an Air Medal with Valor to go with my Purple Heart. But, because of my injury, I faced an uncertain and tenuous future in the field as a PJ.

I thought I'd walked away from that bullet unscathed, with only the headaches and the horrible burning sensation from the nerve damage in my scalp, but I wouldn't be so lucky. Apparently my skull wasn't as thick as I had always joked. There were lapses in my memory, beyond just the fog of war. I couldn't recall some events. Sleep became nightmarish. I struggled to remember the faces of old friends. And one of the most devastating effects: my injured brain couldn't seem to contain all the information I needed to be a PJ. I fought against my memory to remember dosages of this or steps for certain medical procedures. I couldn't put the lives of others, or my fellow PJs, at risk with bad medicine or delayed reactions in situations that had no room for anything but instant reaction.

I had to hang up my beret.

War had taken away all that I had worked so hard for.

I suffered through some dark times as a wounded warrior, but unbeknownst to me, Chris Robertson, the guy who inspired me to become a PJ in the first place, led the charge to get me a full medical retirement. Chris and my unit came through again, but this time the rescue came not in the form of a Pave Hawk and a hoist but as full retirement benefits and a hope for a new future. I can see the line through the trees again, and with the same intensity and heart I used when I jumped into the pararescue pipeline, I'm diving into college again. I'm happily married, and I'm trying to be the dad I always wanted to have. I have a future now that I would never have had without the pararescue community, and I have one hell of a story to tell my children.

War wreaks havoc on the human heart and mind, and on the memory. There are events and people you don't want to ever forget, and those you wish you'd never remember. For me, the lost memories, good or bad, the rescue counts, the medals—they don't matter. That isn't how my mom or my grandmother raised me. What mattered to me then, and what matters to me to this day, are the fine men and women I worked with, the PJs who stood up for me, who fought beside me, and who rescued me from a life of regret, a life of never knowing what my true potential was or what I could become. The men like Roger, who knew enough to tell me "We need you," because he knew the best thing for me in that dark hour was to get back on the horse. Without them, without men like Chris Robertson, Koa Bailey, Major Adrian, Roger, and so many others, I wouldn't be able to share this one life lesson that has been my own guardian angel: never quit.